BODIES AND SOULS

ALSO BY ISABEL VINCENT

Hitler's Silent Partners:
Swiss Banks, Nazi Gold, and the Pursuit of Justice

See No Evil: The Strange Case
of Christine Lamont and David Spencer

BODIES AND SOULS

The Tragic Plight of
Three Jewish Women Forced into
Prostitution in the Americas

ISABEL VINCENT

RANDOM HOUSE CANADA

www.randomhouse.ca

FIRST EDITION

Designed by Mia Risberg

Printed on acid-free paper

Library and Archives Canada Cataloguing in Publication

Vincent, Isabel, 1965–
   Bodies and souls : the tragic plight of three Jewish women forced into prostitution in the Americas / Isabel Vincent.

Includes bibliographical references.
ISBN-13: 978-0-679-31162-1
ISBN-10: 0-679-31162-9

1. Jewish women—Brazil—Rio de Janeiro—Social conditions.   2. Jewish women—Argentina—Buenos Aires—Social conditions.   3. Prostitution—Brazil—Rio de Janeiro. 4. Prostitution—Argentina—Buenos Aires.   5. Jewish women—New York (State)—New York—Social conditions.   6. Prostitution—New York (State)—New York.   I. Title.

F2646.9.J4V56 2005   306.74'2'08992408   C2005-903763

Printed and bound in the USA

10   9   8   7   6   5   4   3   2   1

For Nélida Piñón,
who introduced me to "the other America."
And for my mothers,
Irene Vicente and Nada Hodzic.

CONTENTS

ACKNOWLEDGMENTS

This book took nearly five years to research, largely because it was so difficult to convince people to speak openly about the *polacas,* the prostitutes from Eastern Europe. By the time I began my research in South America, I found that hospital and police archives had been destroyed long ago, some by unscrupulous "historians" and public administrators who no doubt wanted to make sure that the story of these women would stay buried forever.

But while many saw the saga of the Jewish prostitutes only as a source of shame, others clearly saw it for what it really is—a story of strength. And I am grateful to them, above all, for sharing that story with me. Alberto da Costa, the faithful accountant and caretaker of the Society of Truth, demonstrated great courage by speaking to me about the nearly two decades that he served the prostitutes, and about his relationship with Rebecca Freedman. Seu Alberto, as he was known to them, is their final witness. And in telling their story honestly and straightforwardly, he has honored the memory of the women he respectfully called "the Superior Sisters." Throughout it all, he remained a consummate professional, and extremely loyal to the women who were so loyal to him and his family.

In New York, I want to thank Claire Wachtel, my editor at William Morrow, for her determination and courage in standing by this project when few others believed that this story could or should be told.

In Brazil, I am grateful to Zevi Ghivelder, for sharing his research on Rebecca Freedman and the Society of Truth. He also made important introductions for me in the Jewish community. The writer Ester Largman was another great source of information and inspiration. I will never forget her generosity in handing me her copy—seemingly the only available copy in the entire country—of Francisco Ferreira da Rosa's *The Brothel,* written in the 1890s, which informs the research in the early part of this book. I am also extremely grateful to the historian Beatriz Kushnir, for generously handing me many of the files from her master's thesis on the prostitutes. Thanks are also due to Luís Krausz in São Paulo who helped me to contact one of the surviving *polacas* in the city.

In Rio de Janeiro, Katia Borges doggedly pursued what must have been some of the most obscure historical references of her career as a researcher. I am grateful that she refused to give up, believing as much as I did in the importance of this footnote in history about marginalized women. Daniel Rodrigues, custodian of the Inhaúma Jewish cemetery, went out on a limb to help me. I will always be grateful to him for opening those gates whenever I showed up.

I am deeply indebted to my friend Francis Pauly for his hospitality in Rio de Janeiro. I am also grateful to the journalist Rosa

Cass for her insights into Rio's Jewish community. There are numerous others in both Argentina and Brazil whom I want to thank, but they have chosen to remain anonymous. I am also very grateful to the staff at both the municipal and national archives in Rio de Janeiro for never so much as blinking whenever I walked in with what seemed an impossible search request. The same is true of the staff at the London School of Jewish Studies Library, who helped me do serious work on this controversial subject. Professor Nora Glickman's research on Rachel Liberman was also very helpful in bringing to life this courageous woman.

In Toronto, where I wrote the book, I am very grateful to David Kilgour, my longtime editor and friend. David was immediately fascinated by this story and helped me through the entire process. Selfishly, I believe that my friends Caroline Bongrand and Martin Brossollet temporarily left their home in Paris to help me reshape the book in the final editing stages. During their Toronto sojourn, they generously offered their expertise as screenwriters and helped me bring out the human stories in this book. Caroline especially was merciless in her critique of my work. For that kind of honesty I will always be grateful.

Dorian Karchmar, my agent in New York, was also tremendously helpful in the final stages of this book.

I also want to thank Kelly Connelly, at the Baycrest Centre for Geriatric Care in Toronto, for introducing me to elderly former shtetl dwellers. Interviews with Baycrest residents, especially with the incomparable Tamara Wolman, helped me to bring the first part of this book alive. I also want to thank Shoshana Yaakobi, a social worker at Baycrest, who so generously offered to translate these interviews from the Yiddish. Adam Fuerstenberg, director of Toronto's Holocaust Centre, was also extremely helpful with Yiddish translations.

Both Anne Collins at Random House in Canada and Helen Heller were also early supporters of this story, and I am grateful to them for their work on my behalf. Also in Toronto I want to thank Kenneth Whyte, who allowed me to report from South America so that I could complete my research. In London, my good friend Jean McNeil also offered a great deal of support through the entire process.

Finally, I want to thank Zoran Milich, who has my greatest debt.

Introduction

They stopped coming to the cemetery at Inhaúma, a run-down suburb of Rio de Janeiro, when the last one died in the mid-1980s. That's when the wild manioc and the hearty weeds the locals call jackknife grass began their steady, silent approach—at first peeking through the cracks in the older headstones and then, bolstered by a relentless equatorial sun and steamy afternoon downpours, choking the tombs in a labyrinth of dense vegetation.

A banana plant sprouted outside the small mud-and-stucco building where the women used to wash the bodies and prepare them for burial at the edge of the cemetery, near the plot of land that had been reserved for the children's graves. Inside, the roots burst through the elaborate mosaic floor, shattering the cobalt blue and red Moroccan tiles that are barely visible now, hidden beneath a thick blanket of dirt and rodent droppings.

For years, after the last one died, nobody bothered to maintain the cemetery, which became a paradise for snakes and the drug traffickers from the Wet Rat favela, a nearby shantytown of rubbish-strewn dirt roads and half-finished red-brick houses with corrugated tin roofs. For the small-time drug lords, dressed in long surfer shorts and rubber flip-flops, the abandoned cemetery became the perfect hiding place. They could easily scale its low, crumbling mud walls. They pried open the largest tombs with crowbars, unearthing their grizzly contents—bits of polished, yellowing bones—in order to stash their supplies of cocaine and automatic weapons. The drug dealers rarely worried about leaving their valuable commodities unattended in the graves, which they tagged with graffiti. They knew the authorities would never follow them there.

But after a while even the drug traffickers stopped coming. Perhaps they were spooked by the stories people started to tell about the place. There's a witch buried in the cemetery, they said. Those who could read—although just barely—told the illiterate ones that they had seen her name, inscribed in block letters, on one of the headstones: BRUCHA. In fact, the headstone belongs to a Polish woman named Brucha Blanck. For the drug dealers, many of whom have little more than a primary school education, *Brucha* looks and sounds like *bruxa,* the Portuguese word for "witch."

Still, people say the cemetery is cursed. Some cross the street to avoid passing too near. The more superstitious locals refuse to leave the clay bowls of sweets and manioc flour that are the ritual offerings to the Afro-Brazilian *orixás* or gods in *Candomblé* ceremonies outside the cemetery's imposing iron gates, adorned with a large Star of David, painted with a thick coat of gray enamel. The offerings, which are made alternately to seek blessings or curses from the gods, are regularly left at crossroads throughout Brazil. But there is an unspoken understanding about the corner of Piragibe and José dos Reis Streets, where the cemetery's gate stands. It's strictly off limits, to both mortals and gods.

But it wasn't always the case. As recently as twenty years ago, on the Jewish holy days, small groups of elderly women in floral-print cotton dresses and bright red lipstick left their comfortable middle-class neighborhoods in Rio and boarded crowded buses for the hourlong journey to the cemetery in Inhaúma, a bleak industrial suburb whose name means "black bird" in the language of the Tupi Indians, the original inhabitants of Rio.

The last regular visitor to the cemetery was a woman everyone knew only as Rebecca. She was thin and frail, her face dominated by thick, black-rimmed spectacles in her final years. She arrived once a week in a blue-and-yellow Rio taxi, tipping the local children with sweets in exchange for help removing her walker from the trunk. Rebecca, who was well into her nineties, puttered around the cemetery with some authority, pulling up weeds with trembling hands and ordering the cemetery's custodian, a mechanic named Daniel Rodrigues, to sweep the stone walkways between the graves and rebuild the mud walls to keep out intruders.

But the other mourners never lingered by the graves of the women they called their "sisters"—most of them sturdy, Eastern European matrons who fixed the mourners with steady, even gazes captured forever in the fading enameled daguerreotypes that are prominently displayed on some of their graves.

In contrast, the mourners arrived with their heads bowed to avoid the stares of the locals. Some hid their faces behind the umbrellas they carried to shield them from a blistering midday sun. They came in silence, and when they returned to their homes in the more fashionable parts of the city, few of them ever told their friends or their families (if they had any left) where they had been.

— 3 —

"Piranhas," some of the locals whispered among themselves whenever they saw the elderly mourners enter through the gates of the cemetery. In Portuguese as in English, piranha is the name of a ferocious Amazonian fish. But in Brazil it is also slang for prostitute.

"YOU WANT TO KNOW who's buried here?"

The question startled me as I made my way through the rows of crumbling gravestones. It was an unseasonably hot morning in July, the beginning of winter in the southern hemisphere. In the sparse shade afforded by a crumbling child's headstone, a dog had just given birth to three puppies. The tiny, hairless beasts, still wet from their mother's womb, were bleating mournfully as they struggled to open their eyes.

"You want to know who these people are?"

I turned my attention from the puppies and looked at Daniel Rodrigues, a middle-aged, sunburned man in long camouflage shorts, his white T-shirt tied around his waist, a diamond stud in one ear. His eyes were bloodshot, and the white hairs on his chest and prominent belly glistened with tiny beads of sweat. Daniel told me he was in charge of the cemetery. For years he has pulled the weeds around the graves, swept the walkways, and fixed the broken headstones. He recently built new mud-and-stucco walls, so high that even the drug dealers can't scale them, he assured me. Still, it's hard work, and he says he can't devote too much time to the cemetery's upkeep. Daniel owns the taxi-repair shop next-door. When the Sociedade Cemitério Comunal Israelita, the organization that oversees Jewish cemeteries in Rio, discovered that he was encroaching on the cemetery's land, they struck a deal with him. Daniel is allowed to use the land for free, provided that he cleans up the cemetery on a regular basis and keeps the iron gates firmly locked. However, nobody from the Jewish Communal Cemetery Society ever makes the journey to Inhaúma to check that Daniel is doing a good job.

"I'm not supposed to let anyone in," said Daniel apologetically the first time I knocked on the gates of the cemetery. "It's off limits here."

But there was something in his voice—a slight quaver of uncertainty, guilt, perhaps—that told me he wasn't serious. As Daniel would confess to me much later, he rarely enforced the cemetery society's rules at Inhaúma. He seemed to let just about anyone in. Not that there are many people coming to pay their respects to the "piranhas, pimps, and gigolos," as Daniel calls them, laughing heartily. In fact, he is hard-pressed to remember any visitors in the last decade.

Which may be why he is so eager to show me around. There are 797 graves in the Inhaúma cemetery, which was founded in 1916 and abuts a municipal cemetery, located on the other side of the high, whitewashed wall. In contrast to the prostitutes' cemetery, the municipal burial ground is well maintained, tended on a regular basis by work crews from the city. Daniel can't remember the dates he read on the large stone-and-marble memorial plaques that are now covered in spiderwebs and debris in the small, decaying building that used to serve as the cemetery's office. He reckons the last burial here occurred in the 1970s, although he can't say for sure. The cemetery's registry book disappeared several years ago, which is why it is almost impossible to trace many of Inhaúma's dead, most of them prostitutes but some, surprisingly, their pimps and exploiters.

Today much of what is known about them is written in Hebrew and Portuguese on the headstones themselves. But as it turns out, even some of the families seemed to know little about their deceased relatives. One grave, for a man named Lazard Klein, mentions that he was born in France. Below his dates of birth and death is a dedication phrased as a question: "Respects from his children and wife?"

Many died before their fortieth birthdays. Their names are strange amalgams of the Old World and the New: Zirel Leizerovitch Moreira, Bebe Fridman, Manoel Winogrado, Marcos Israel. They were born in places that Daniel has difficulty pronouncing, much less imagining. He reads aloud from a few of the headstones the names of what to him must seem like strange and exotic places: Odessa, Lodz, Kraków, Kiev, Bessarabia.

The handful of children's graves, in a far corner of the cemetery, are surrounded by rubbish, and the first time I visited there I saw the bloated remains of a dead dog, baking in the sun. Most of the miniature headstones are so old that it's difficult to read the inscriptions. A little girl whose name I could barely read is buried there. Is it Rivka Markenzon? The letters are faded, but I can make out part of the inscription: "Here lies the innocent Rivka, daughter of Adolpho Markenzon and Anna Markenzon." She was born on October 19, 1916, and died less than three years later. Perhaps, like tens of thousands of others, she died in one of the many yellow-fever epidemics that ravaged the city at the time, just as public-health officials struggled to develop a vaccine. The vaccine started being administered only in 1937, too late to save the first immigrants.

"Some of these people were so rich, they were buried covered in gold," said Daniel.

But how did they end up here, forgotten, in an overgrown tropical graveyard? What drove them to leave their families and friends in Europe and sail to this corner of the world so long ago?

Daniel shrugged. He said he didn't know.

I FIRST READ ABOUT the prostitutes buried at the Inhaúma cemetery in an article in a small Jewish newspaper in London, although I had heard passing references to them in popular songs and literature when I was living in Rio de Janeiro as a foreign correspondent in the 1990s.

Brazilian novelist Moacyr Scliar wrote about them in *The Cycle of the Waters,* and in the 1950s the legendary samba composer Moreira da Silva composed a samba for a woman named Estera Gladkowicer, one of the Eastern European prostitutes, who was his lover. Like so many of the women who came to work as prostitutes in South America, she killed herself, and is buried in a special section of Inhaúma reserved for suicides.

Today Estera Gladkowicer and the other Eastern European prostitutes are part of the local folklore in Brazil. Moreira da Silva's samba includes the lyrics *"Ich bin meshugene fur dir,"* which is Yiddish for "I am crazy for you." Moreover, the Brazilian slang for "trouble," *encrenca*, is derived from the Yiddish *ein krenk,* "a sick one," which was whispered among the prostitutes about clients who were suspected of being infected with venereal disease.

Stefan Zweig, a Jewish Austrian writer who went to Brazil to escape the Nazi regime before committing suicide there in 1942, became fascinated with the women he noticed working in Rio de Janeiro's red-light district, a down-at-heels neighborhood of shabby colonial row houses near the port. "Jewish women from

Eastern Europe promise the most exciting perversities," he wrote in his memoirs of that time. "What fate made these women end up here, selling themselves for the equivalent of three francs?"

Five years ago, when I set out to find the answer, I had no idea that this would be the most difficult investigative work of my career. There is a code of silence—some have used the word *omerta,* borrowing a term usually reserved for the Italian mobster code—surrounding the lives of the women buried at Inhaúma and at cemeteries in São Paulo and Buenos Aires.

I received little more than alarmed, quizzical looks from some historians when I brought up the subject. I did so gingerly, faintly aware of the stigma that still surrounded the subject in South America, always referring to the prostitutes as "those women." Immediately, people knew what I meant, but few agreed to speak to me.

A young Rio historian told me that after she had finished her master's thesis on the *polacas,* she received numerous threats from anonymous callers who denounced her for writing about them. Every time I tracked down a name on a death certificate that might be a relative or friend of one of the prostitutes, I was politely but firmly told to leave. In one instance, a woman whose name was listed as the next of kin and main beneficiary of Rebecca Freedman—Dona Becca, the last of the *polacas,* who died in 1984—claimed to have no recollection of the deceased.

"But your name is listed here on this official document," I said to the woman as we stood outside her high-rise apartment in the beachfront Leblon neighborhood of Rio.

"Yes, isn't that interesting," said the elderly woman, who was preparing to take her granddaughter to the beach.

When I consulted police archives and municipal records, I found that many of the historical documents were missing. This is not in itself an unusual occurrence in a place like Brazil, where public institutions are often riddled with corruption and mismanagement. At Rio's National Library, for instance, there are sleek state-of-the-art computers for scholars and students to conduct catalog research. The problem is that most of the library's collection has yet to be entered into the database.

I was pretty much confounded at every turn, and I began to believe the rumors I had heard about the history of the *polacas*: Most of the documentation had simply been destroyed by well-meaning "historians" who wanted to erase what they considered a black mark on the past.

By the time I visited the Jewish Communal Cemetery Society office in a shabby high-rise on President Vargas Avenue, in the heart of Rio's business district, I was prepared for what I would hear. Since the organization oversees Jewish cemeteries in Rio de Janeiro, the cemetery at Inhaúma is technically under its control.

But there are no documents relating to Inhaúma to be found, said Chaim Szwerszarf, the society's director, when I first visited. He was a thin, elderly man with tobacco-stained fingers and a razor-sharp mind. On his calling card, which he handed to me later, he wrote in English that his surname means "sharp sword." "Why are you so interested in that particular cemetery?" he asked me more than once. When I finally told him that I knew about the prostitutes, he seemed almost relieved, although he regretted to inform me, he said, fixing me with a steely gaze, that it was impossible to visit Inhaúma because the cemetery was so run-down. I returned his gaze, but I did not tell him I had already been there twice.

"I would like to write to the families who have gravestones falling apart at Inhaúma, so they could help pay for the upkeep, but there is no one to write to," admitted an exasperated Szwerszarf, drinking sugary coffee from the kind of tiny plastic cup that is usually reserved for serving mouthwash in dentists' offices. "You must understand that people are embarrassed. They don't want to be reminded of the past."

Slowly, I began to reconstruct that hidden past from archival documents, academic studies, and interviews. When official sources wouldn't speak, I went to underworld sources. I became a frequent visitor to Vila Mimosa, Rio's red-light district, where crack-addled prostitutes, their stomachs hanging over skimpy bikinis, walk in stiletto heels through open sewers that spill out onto the main street. At every corner, vendors ignore the sewage as they barbecue skewers of meat and cheese at their lean-to stalls.

One of my greatest champions became a woman I will identify only as Claudia. She was a feisty former prostitute who was trying to go straight. In the mornings Claudia studied for a social work degree at a local university. She spent her afternoons volunteering at the prostitutes' local association at Vila Mimosa, handing out free condoms and publicizing government-sponsored HIV awareness workshops. At Vila Mimosa Claudia introduced me to some of the older madams and prostitutes. I met one prostitute who was seventy-one years old and had once worked with the *polacas*.

What finally began to emerge from the interviews and documents is one of the darkest chapters in the history of the Americas. From the end of the 1860s until the beginnning of the Second World War in 1939, thousands of young, impoverished women, most of them from the hardscrabble shtetls of Eastern Europe, were literally sold into slavery by a notorious criminal gang made up entirely of Jewish mobsters. In its heyday, the Zwi Migdal criminal enterprise controlled brothels in places as diverse as Johannesburg, Bombay, and Shanghai. But the centers of their criminal activities were Rio de Janeiro, Buenos Aires, and, to some extent, New York City, all of which became the focus of my research.

South America was by far the Zwi Migdal's most lucrative domain, and by the turn of the last century they had established their headquarters in Buenos Aires. For young women caught up in the trafficking, the rapidly growing Argentine capital was often their first stop in the region, although they arrived by many, often purposely circuitous, routes, in order to evade international authorities. From Buenos Aires they were clandestinely shipped to brothels in the interior of the country, or to Rio de Janeiro or São Paulo. There are no firm estimates of how many women the Zwi Migdal sent to the New World, but they were enough to establish its most prominent members among the criminal elite.

As with everything else about this story, documentation has been either lost or destroyed. The most complete set of archives relating to the Zwi Migdal was destroyed in the 1994 Islamist terrorist attack on the Asociación Mutual Israelita Argentina (AMIA), a Jewish community center in Buenos Aires. Still, some statistics survive. In Argentina the Zwi Migdal operated some three thousand brothels, most of them in Buenos Aires. In Rio de Janeiro many of the 431 brothels operating in the city in 1913 were controlled by Jews associated with the Zwi Migdal.

Of course, Jewish criminals did not have anything like a monopoly on the white-slave trade. At the time, other criminal gangs trafficked in women from all over Europe and parts of Asia. According to historians, the Japanese and Chinese played the biggest role in what became euphemistically known as "the Traffic" in women worldwide.

But what made the Zwi Migdal unique, and so successful, was its focus on impoverished Jewish women and girls who were easily duped into religious marriages. When they sailed from European ports, many of the young women who found themselves working as prostitutes in places like Rio de Janeiro, Buenos Aires, and New York thought they were going to join their husbands in America. Many of them never overcame the shock of realizing that their "husbands" were pimps, who had "married" several other young women for the same purpose. However, the record also shows that many of the women knew what fate awaited them in America. Some would even become successful brothel owners and recruiters for the Zwi Migdal.

Once they realized the scope of the problem, numerous anti-slavery organizations tried to stop the Traffic. They informed the American authorities and posted their representatives at ports warning young women of the perils of white slavery. Trafficking in women was considered such a grave offense that the delegates who met in Paris to sign the Treaty of Versailles after the First World War declared it an international crime and, under Article 282 of the treaty, urged all member states to severely punish those involved.

But these lofty efforts by the international community were largely in vain. The Traffic was driven by the crushing poverty that pervaded Eastern European Jewish communities at the turn of the last century. Many of the Jewish girls recruited for prostitution hailed from teeming urban ghettoes or desperately poor rural shtetls where Jews were also the target of numerous pogroms.

THE PROSTITUTES AND WHITE SLAVERS in Latin America were completely banned by the respectable Jewish community. As one rabbi noted, they could not be served in Jewish restaurants or sit on the governing boards of Jewish institutions. "If [they] would come to a Jewish theater, all Jewish persons seated within fifteen feet of [them] would find seats elsewhere, or leave the theater. Any Jewish hostess inviting to her home any member of a family tied up with the Traffic, would find she had no other guests at that gathering, nor at any other gathering in the future."

Forced into sexual slavery far from home, and shunned by the very community that might have come to their aid, the Jewish prostitutes in Rio de Janeiro formed an extraordinary religious and charitable organization that has no historical precedent anywhere in the world.

The organization began as a burial society to ensure that its members would receive a proper Jewish burial. By 1916, its members had acquired the plot of land at Inhaúma for their cemetery, and by the 1940s they had bought a building in downtown Rio that they converted into a synagogue and administrative offices. Although its official name, translated from Portuguese, was the Jewish Benevolent and Burial Association, most of its members called it by its Hebrew name, Chesed Shel Ermess, or the Society of Truth. Members referred to one another as "sisters," and board officials became known as "the Superior Sisters."

Similar charitable and religious organizations existed in São Paulo, Buenos Aires, and New York, but they were largely run by the pimps. In New York the most important white slavers, who owned and operated the brothels where Eastern European prostitutes worked on the Lower East Side, formed the Independent Benevolent Association in 1896. The organization was set up as a trade and burial society, which in its heyday was clearing more than a million dollars in profits from the white-slave trade in New York alone. Today the mostly Russian Jewish mourners at the Washington Park Cemetery, a bleak graveyard under an elevated-train platform in Brooklyn, might be surprised to learn that those buried under the stone arches carved with the name of the rather innocuous-sounding Independent Benevolent Association were once among New York's most feared white slavers and prostitutes.

Throughout the Americas, Jewish white slavers set up mutual-aid organizations in order to ensure continued prosperity and as a way of gaining the prestige they would never be granted in communities of respectable Jews. But the women's organization in Rio de Janeiro was unique because it was founded not by the oppressors but by the oppressed—the prostitutes who found themselves without any support mechanisms in a new and what must have seemed to them a very alien world. "What's extraordinary about this story is that nowhere in the world did prostitutes, especially Jewish prostitutes, get together and form their own religious association," said Zevi Ghivelder, who was one of the first journalists to investigate the *polacas* in Brazil. And they kept it going for more than half a century.

Ghivelder, himself a Jew, stumbled onto the story nearly three decades ago when one of his friends, a Brazilian general he will not identify, called him early one Sunday morning at his home in Rio. The general, who had grown up as a Catholic, was distraught because his mother had died the night before. "She was one of those," confessed the general in hushed tones over the telephone. Ghivelder knew immediately what he meant and offered to help bury the general's mother in a Jewish cemetery.

Intrigued, he pursued the story. He interviewed Rebecca Freedman, the last president of the Society of Truth, on her deathbed. Rebecca was extremely religious and an early supporter of the state of Israel. According to Ghivelder, she had two photographs above her bed—one in sepia of her family in Poland and the other of Chaim Weizmann, Israel's first president.

But just as Ghivelder was about to break the story, his father, a prominent Jewish community leader in Rio de Janeiro, abruptly asked him to stop his research. He offered little in the way of explanation. For Ghivelder, who knew of the terrible shame surrounding the *polacas* in the Jewish community in Brazil, none was necessary. "He told me that as long as he was alive, he didn't want me to pursue the story," said Ghivelder the first time I met him. "I honored my father's wish."

RETURNING TO INHAÚMA after a long absence, I noticed that the cemetery was in much better condition than on my first visit. I asked Daniel Rodrigues if there was any special reason, other than his arrangement with the Jewish Communal Cemetery Society, for what seemed like his newfound devotion to the cemetery.

Rodrigues himself looked a lot more respectable at our second meeting than he had at the first. The camouflage shorts that had made him look a bit like a crazed jungle commando were gone. He was wearing a white, neatly pressed polo shirt, jeans, and sandy-colored, suede oxfords. "I don't know," he said. "When you left I got to thinking about these people, and how they've been forgotten by the rest of the world."

I began to suspect that Daniel had some kind of attachment to these women that he wasn't telling me about. He must have read my mind because he immediately blurted out that his mother, who had died two years earlier, was a Protestant. He said this twice, and looked me in the eye to make sure that I understood him.

For a long time we stood under an intense midmorning sun, watching the black vultures that the Brazilians call *urubus* swooping silently down on what must have been a pile of rubbish or a dead animal on the other side of the cemetery's walls.

"The longer I'm here, the closer I feel to them," he said, pointing to the graves in front of him. "I just don't know what it is about these people."

CHAPTER ONE

Gentlemen from America

Isaac Boorosky hated the shtetls. He hated the mud, which always formed a hard crust around his patent-leather shoes and splattered his finely tailored trousers. He hated the stench—the slightly sweet smell of moldy hay mixed with human excrement and wood smoke—that assaulted his nostrils and seeped into his clothes. He might have learned early on from his business associates to soak a silk handkerchief in rose water and hold it to his nose as he squelched through the mud, past the mangy dogs and the packs of filthy children dressed in rags, snot streaming from their noses. But the handkerchief trick worked only for a few minutes. Nothing could block out the odors of poverty. They lingered on, invading his pores, thrusting him into the past.

Had he really grown up in such a place?

Sometimes it may have seemed difficult to believe that he, Isaac Boorosky, man of the world, had spent his childhood in such a backwater, surrounded by Jewish peasants in their coarsely woven garments and their wooden clogs, their looks forlorn.

These were his people, to be sure, but he was—what was the phrase they liked to use about him now?—an *American* gentleman. Isaac was Russian by birth, but how convenient that his impressive array of travel documents—all of them forged by a colleague in South America—identified him variously as a Brazilian jeweler and an Argentine rancher. It's true he had "interests" in Brazil and Argentina, and even in South Africa. But the source of his lucrative business was still in Russia and Poland—in the miserable shtetls that he so despised.

Still, he never corrected the Jewish peasants when they referred to him as "that gentleman from America" and treated him with the same reverence they would bestow on a nobleman or even a rabbi. His sudden wealth had taught him quickly to play the part of the elegant gentleman. He smoked cigars and drank champagne from crystal goblets, and his hands were always beautifully manicured. In Rio de Janeiro—how far away it must have seemed to him now!—his Spanish tailor sewed him beautiful silk-lined suits, which he was fond of wearing with a black silk top hat.

In what would become his last official portrait—a sketch made by a Rio police officer shortly after his arrest in 1896—Isaac, a solidly built man with fleshy cheeks and almond eyes, is beautifully dressed in a frock coat, matching vest, starched collar, and silk cravat. His hair is jet black and oiled, his mustache perfectly trimmed.

Sophia Chamys had never met a man like Isaac, and years later in Brazil, when she told her story to the police, she could still recall the smell of the lavender oil that he used on his hair and the feel of his silk handkerchiefs against her skin. But most of all she remembered his hands—so refined and smooth, like a child's. In the shtetl on the outskirts of Warsaw where Sophia shared a one-room thatch-roofed house with her parents and younger sister, people had working hands—misshapen, permanently chapped, sunburned, and covered in hardened blisters.

Sophia's father had such hands, from years of working the fields, eking out a living by collecting hay that he sold to local farmers. Already at thirteen, Sophia had hands that were rough and calloused from helping her parents. Perhaps she instinctively hid them behind her back when she felt Isaac's gaze upon her for the first time.

They met in Warsaw, at Castle Square, under the bronze statue of King Sigismund III, who stood defiantly clutching a large cross on a tall majestic column, overlooking stately row houses and the fifteenth-century royal castle. The Chamys family gazed up at the legendary king, who spent much of his long reign on a war footing, trying to reconquer his native Sweden. He was, on rare occasions, good to the Jews, introducing legislation that made it possible for them to do business, to work the land. It's unlikely that the Chamys family was familiar with seventeenth-century Polish history, but something about the noble figure of this handsome, wild-eyed king seemed to inspire reverence, even nearly two and a half centuries after his death. Congregating at the statue had become something of a tradition for the Chamys family on these fruitless trips to Warsaw. Perhaps they considered this rendezvous beneath the king a pilgrimage to hope: Things would be different on the next trip to the city; bad luck could not last a lifetime.

Sophia and her family had walked the twenty-five miles from their shtetl to Warsaw, where her father had been promised work. But as was so often the case in the unhappy history of the Chamys family, the job never materialized. Standing with their oily cloth bundles under Sigismund III, the family was preparing for the long walk home when the elegant stranger loomed over them.

Isaac Boorosky approached the bedraggled family, introducing himself to Sophia's father as a successful businessman and a Jew. He told them he was looking for a maid to work in his widowed mother's kitchen in Lodz, which was just a six-hour journey over dirt roads from Warsaw. He nodded toward Sophia. *How old is she?*

Isaac didn't waste any time. After years of training, he knew how to spot a lucrative prospect. He knew to look beyond the ragged, loose garments and the filthy clogs worn by the peasant girls. He quickly saw Sophia's attributes—the milky skin, the outline of budding breasts, the full red lips, the wisps of raven hair peeking out of the dark kerchief. What luck to discover such a specimen in the center of Warsaw! How fortunate that his expensive new shoes and trousers would be spared the shtetl mud. "Eight rubles," said Isaac, barely containing his excitement and removing the money from his pocket. The amount was an advance on Sophia's first six months of service, and Isaac pressed the coins into her father's rough, sunburned hands.

Sophia's father hesitated, even though the money must have seemed a huge amount—the equivalent of a year's wages for the family.

Later Sophia recalled the stab of anger she felt as her father refused the handful of coins. For even at thirteen, Sophia must have been aware that there were few prospects for young women from the shtetls, particularly those on the teeming outskirts of Warsaw. One foreign visitor had described them as manure-carpeted encampments—"the eternal dwelling place of poverty."

Sophia knew that girls from the shtetl ended up exactly like their mothers and grandmothers. They seemed to spend a lifetime covered in soot as they cooked over a woodstove. They left their homes at sunrise to work in the fields, returning at dusk to prepare the evening meal, which many days was nothing more than a thin potato soup or cucumbers and onions in brine mixed with buttermilk—if there was any buttermilk to be had.

Even elderly women worked continuously to survive. One grandmother, who single-handedly supported nine children in a shtetl near Minsk, worked the fields all day. Between Purim and Passover, she took an extra job working in a matzo bakery, kneading dough until past midnight. One of her grandsons recalled years later how she returned home two days before Passover, "her hands as puffed as the dough she had kneaded, her back so twisted she could hardly straighten up without cracking her bones. . . . The first night of Passover, Grandmother's groans mingled with Grandfather's sad chanting of the Passover Haggadah at the seder."

Although little is known about Sophia's life in the shtetl, she must have been surrounded by such long-suffering women. What was the Yiddish rhyme—"Helf Ikh Mamen" (Helping mother)— that the girls learned to sing about their mothers?

> *Every Monday Mother washes,*
> *I help her with the washing.*
> *This-a-way and that-a-way*
> *I help her with the washing.*
> *Every Tuesday Mother irons,*
> *I help her with the ironing.*
> *This-a-way and that-a-way*
> *I help her with the ironing.*

The rhyme enumerated a different chore for each day of the week. The drudgery ended for only a short time—on Saturday—when Mother was finally allowed to rest.

For a girl like Sophia, there was no escape from the same kind of drudgery. Her parents were poor, even by shtetl standards, and could do little to improve their lot in life. They could not afford to send their daughters to school. In the nineteenth and early twentieth centuries, there was little in the way of education for girls, even among wealthier Jews. Some of the luckier ones were educated at home schools known as *chedarim*, where they were taught basic arithmetic, some writing, and so-called women's prayers in Yiddish. But formal educaton was reserved for boys, who studied Hebrew so they could read religious texts. After the 1860s, increasing numbers of Jewish women did begin to study at modern schools, but this occurred only in the major cities and only for the girls of well-to-do families.

The luckier shtetl girls, those from families of merchants or tailors, could apprentice as seamstresses or shopkeepers. But in the end most young women in the shtetl simply repeated the cycle of drudgery experienced by their grandmothers and mothers. Usually, in their late teens, they ended up marrying one of the impoverished young men they glimpsed on the other side of the curtain in the *shtibl*, "the little room" where religious services were held in many of the more backward shtetls. With its clay floors, mildewed walls covered in spiderwebs, and thatch roofs, the *shtibl* took the place of the synagogue in small towns where a rabbi was considered a luxury.

Every important event in the life of shtetl Jews—weddings, bar mitzvahs, and High Holidays—were celebrated in this damp, dimly lit little room. On Fridays, when the mouthwatering smell of baking challah filled the small communities, the men headed for evening prayers at the *shtibl,* always located in the richest man's house. In the shtetl, wealth was a relative term, often measured by the number of rooms a man had in his home, or the number of times he could afford to buy a chicken for the Sabbath meal. Most people could rarely afford such a delicacy and had only one room, heated by a wood-burning stove. The room served as the kitchen and the bedroom, even for families with several children. A man who had more than one room (usually a merchant or a tailor) was considered rich by his neighbors.

Under such circumstances, people worked to survive, rarely to prosper. For although some shtetls were surrounded by plentiful crops and herds of cattle and sheep, shtetl dwellers were rarely able to keep any of the profits of their labor. Most of the crops and livestock were earmarked for the landlords, the royal court, and the police, who often took much more than their share of "taxes."

"I may have to beg to feed my daughters," Sophia recalled her father telling the handsome stranger in Warsaw. "But I will never be separated from them."

Isaac refused to give up. He was solicitous and charming, assuring Sophia's father that he would watch over Sophia as if she were his own daughter.

Like my own daughter.

The words might have sounded vaguely ominous to Sophia's father, but he chose to keep his fears to himself. Perhaps sensing the man's suspicions, Isaac handed him a card with his mother's address in Lodz. It was an open invitation for the family to visit Sophia whenever they found themselves in the city. No doubt, Isaac knew the amount of sacrifice involved for the Chamyses in traveling even the shortest distance. He had been poor once too. He knew what it was like to have no shoes, to live in filth, to scrounge for discarded objects in open sewers.

No, he would be safe from their scrutiny in Lodz. It was un-likely the Chamys family would ever make the journey. They were so poor they couldn't afford to take the train or travel by cart. They would have to walk if they wanted to see Sophia, and the trip would surely take them several days.

Finally, through heart-wrenching sobs, Sophia's father nodded his acquiescence. Of course, he had misgivings—the kind that lodged themselves at the pit of his stomach and made him feel queasy. He knew it was wrong to hand his daughter over like this, even to this obviously refined, worldly man.

Had he heard the rumors of Jewish girls being taken into white slavery by fellow Jews? Young, beautiful girls like Sophia never heard from again? Was it the stuff of urban legend, crafted by wary peasants like himself who had an innate fear of the big city? Or was it another tall tale invented by the anti-Semitic authorities to dredge up hatred against the Jews—another pretext for a bloody pogrom? Did Jewish strangers really prey on the daughters of the poor, and sell them into bondage? It was hard to believe.

Yet in the early 1890s, when Isaac Boorosky first encountered the Chamys family in the center of Warsaw, details had begun to emerge of a large Jewish white-slavery ring. The traffickers and their victims were based in Galicia, then one of the most impover-ished provinces of the Austro-Hungarian Empire, where Jews lived in subhuman conditions and faced epic famine. From 1880 to 1914 some five thousand Jews in Galicia starved to death every year.

In 1892 the province became well known as a global center of white slavery. Twenty-seven Jewish traffickers were convicted at a two-week trial in the Galician capital, Lemberg. The traffickers had organized the sale of mostly Jewish girls to brothels in Constantinople. Fourteen-year-old Feige Aufscher, an orphan, was one of the victims and a star witness. She testified that she had been kidnapped by a Jewish pimp named Mendel Goldenberg. He had promised to marry her and obtain work for her as a house-keeper. Instead, she and others ended up in a series of brothels in Constantinople, forced to service dozens of clients a day. When foreign consular officials tried to search the brothels for the kid-napped women, the traffickers hid them in nearby caves. Some-how Aufscher had managed to get a message to the authorities, who were able to liberate her and the others. The trial was front-page news in all the Polish newspapers. But it's unlikely that Sophia's father followed the news reports. While he read Yiddish and Hebrew with some difficulty, he could barely communicate in Polish. In the shtetl, people spoke Yiddish. Polish was considered the language of the elite.

In the end, Sophia's father agreed to take the elegant stranger's money. He might have tried to shrug off his suspicions. Surely this was the lucky break the Chamys family had wished for—to find work for their eldest daughter in a proper gentleman's home in the big city. Perhaps he believed Isaac's repeated promises to look after Sophia. *Like my own daughter.*

But at last, with that reluctant nod from Sophia's father, the deal was done. Sophia was sold to a stranger in a public square in broad daylight in the civilized center of Europe. Deep in his heart, Sophia's father must have known that he was indeed selling his daughter. Perhaps it was the dark realization that led to his wrenching sobs during the negotiations. Sophia's father must have known that some shtetl parents sold the services of their daughters to men and women from the city, that some even bargained for the highest price they could get for the girls. "They buy girls from their parents, by *contract,*" observed one reporter of the "business-men" who preyed on impoverished young girls. "A contract bit-terly discussed, properly signed, and handsomely embossed."

But with respect to Sophia there was no contract; the gentle-man's word seemed enough. *Like my own daughter.*

After the reluctant nod, everything seemed to happen in a hurry, like a scene from a melodrama, a silent film. Isaac took his leave, and he whisked Sophia away. At that moment Sophia must have realized that her life was going to change forever. What went through her mind as she prepared to leave her family? Was this stranger, with the beautiful almond-shaped eyes, her savior? Was this the Messiah?

Or was he a devil?

But there was little time to think and even less time for tearful good-byes. The man was clearly in a hurry as he guided thirteen-year-old Sophia Chamys through the crowds of pedestrians in Castle Square.

AT THE TURN OF THE LAST CENTURY, men like Isaac Boorosky belonged to a cadre of well-organized Jewish pimps who scoured the impoverished shtetls and urban ghettoes of Eastern Europe looking for girls and women to sell into prostitution around the world.

Over the years, these men became such regular fixtures in the lives of Eastern European Jews that they were immortalized in early twentieth-century Yiddish literature. In his short story "The Man from Buenos Aires," Sholem Aleichem describes a meeting on a train traveling through the region. The unnamed narrator finds himself sitting beside Motek, a salesman who lives in Buenos Aires but is returning for the first time to the small town where he was born, partly to show off his newfound wealth, but mostly for business reasons.

"His face was smooth and round, and heavily tanned, without a sign of a beard or mustache," the narrator says of the sophisticated-looking but rather dubious character he meets in his third-class compartment. "He had small, unctuous, laughing eyes. . . . He had on a snow-white elegant new suit made of real English broadcloth, and a pair of smartly shined shoes. On his finger, he wore a heavy gold ring with a diamond that blinked with a thousand facets of the sun."

But what sort of merchandise did he sell, this businessman from Buenos Aires? When the narrator puts the question to Motek, his answer is characteristically enigmatic: " 'I supply the world with merchandise, something that everyone knows and nobody speaks of. What do I deal in?' (He burst out laughing.) 'Not in prayer books, my friend, not in prayer books.' "

In real life, such characters preyed on poverty. They arrived in the most miserable backwaters, armed with gifts of coffee, chocolate, or cheaply made garments—luxuries that were unattainable for most Eastern European Jews. Like Isaac Boorosky and Sholem Aleichem's salesman, they were impeccably dressed and spoke vaguely of their business holdings abroad. Some said they were ranchers, others that they owned jewelry stores or garment factories. They told the shtetl elders that they were looking for young girls to work in their factories, or, as in Isaac's case, that they needed another person on their domestic staff.

But most often the elegant strangers said they had returned to their own roots in the shtetls to search for suitable brides. Of course, it was an outright lie, but it was calculated to allay the fears of ignorant and suspicious peasants who knew little of the world outside their isolated communities.

The introductions probably occurred following Friday prayers at the *shtibl,* where the trafficker would confess his predicament to the men of the community. Women in America, a catchall description for both North and South America, were simply not as beautiful or as virtuous as the Jewish girls from my shtetl, the trafficker might say to the approving nods of the men, as they wrapped up their *tefillin* and prepared to walk back to their homes for the Sabbath meal. Perhaps some of the shtetl men even invited the respectful strangers to join them for dinner. Maybe they even happily introduced them to their teenaged daughters, who might have blushed at the sight of a handsome stranger in their midst. Did their hearts beat faster as they lit the Sabbath candles and passed the steaming challah?

"A respectable Jewish girl," says Motek in Sholem Aleichem's story. "I don't care how poor she is. I will make her rich. I will shower her parents with gold, make her whole family wealthy."

The prospect must have appealed to many shtetl families. For men like Isaac Boorosky were smooth talkers, who sold a vision of paradise. For many Jews, especially those in small, isolated shtetls where they lived in constant fear of starvation or of being massacred in a pogrom, these men who came offering Jewish girls what seemed like decent jobs or proposals of marriage must have seemed like modern-day saviors. "Believe me, those poor souls are waiting for me as though I were the Messiah," confesses Motek, the man from Buenos Aires.

In some instances even the most deeply religious Jewish families found themselves consenting to a hastily arranged marriage for their daughters to one of these hucksters, who said they couldn't afford to spend too much time away from their businesses in America and needed to return in a hurry.

Of course, Jews were not alone in preying on impoverished

young women. Around the world criminal gangs of various religions and nationalities had been doing the same for decades. But before the nineteenth century, women were procured for brothels that were fairly close to home. Young women and girls recruited into prostitution from the shtetls of Poland and Russia usually ended up like the orphaned teenager Feige Aufscher in brothels in Constantinople or other large cities in Europe, or in the Middle East.

But by the late nineteenth century, the vice circuit had become truly global in scope, as pimps began trafficking in women from Asia and Europe and sending them to new markets farther afield. Gangs of organized criminals took advantage of improvements in travel and communications to traffic in women to service the mostly male immigrants making their way to America and the Far East, where there was a chronic shortage of women.

Procurers in Japan bought up poor girls from their families in the countryside and shipped them to brothels in Australia, India, and Singapore. Thousands of Chinese girls were kidnapped from their parents' homes and shipped to brothels in California, where they were forced to service the Chinese laborers working in the gold camps and on the railway in the western United States.

In Paris, one pimp explained his methods for procuring poor women for his overseas brothels. Watching a young woman outside the Café Napolitain, his favorite haunt, he approached her and offered her a meal. When she complained that she was sick, the pimp took her to the doctor, bought her some dresses, stockings, and new shoes. "I gave her something to eat in the middle of the day and in the evening," he said, obviously impressed by his own cunning. "You can imagine how pleased she was. Then one day I told her I was going away. You should have seen her cry."

But unlike most of their counterparts in the white-slave trade, the Jewish traffickers went to the greatest trouble to procure their recruits, and confined their dealings to the Jewish community. While Japanese pimps kidnapped their victims and French pimps recruited prostitutes off the streets of the country's largest cities, the Jewish pimps always worked within the strict confines of the traditional family circle. They regularly visited the shtetls looking for suitable girls, or hired local matchmakers to do their reconnaissance work.

Traveling through Poland in the early part of the twentieth century, a French newspaperman described how the village matchmaker sometimes worked with the traffickers, cynically giving them advice on which women to target in small towns: "Such and such a house is no good: the girls are sickly. Avoid such and such a family: the father and mother mean to ask a high price. There's only a grandmother in that house and she won't last long. Take the child, she's the best bargain in the district. I've watched her for you like a peach on a wall. You need only pick it!"

One such matchmaker was a woman named Guinda Wainrouse, who was convicted in Odessa for luring two girls, Malka Altman and Rivka Rubin, into white slavery. At her suggestion the girls met two traffickers posing as would-be suitors and boarded a ship to Constantinople, where they were locked up in brothels. After several months Malka, pregnant and recovering from injuries in a local hospital, managed to contact her family. Thanks to Malka's testimony at the Odessa trial, Wainrouse was convicted and sentenced to ten years of hard labor in Siberia.

The practice of recruiting young women for prostitution through promises of marriage became so commonplace that after the First World War, the League of Nations began to issue warnings. In one of its reports, the world body recounted the offenses of an unidentified Polish trafficker, arrested in Poland following the war, who had "married" thirty girls, all of whom ended up in brothels in South America. The trafficker had found them through a marriage broker in Warsaw, who regularly put ads in the Yiddish newspapers.

After the Lemberg trial in 1892, white slavery took on sinister proportions. Although Jews never achieved a monopoly on the trade, they were singled out for their participation by anti-Semitic authorities. In Romania and Poland there were stories "about a [Jewish] slave-ship plying between Black Sea ports from which girls were thrown overboard after they were ruined." In South America, police officials blamed "the degenerate Jew for shaming the human race" by setting up brothels, even though most of the brothels in the region were controlled by French traffickers.

By 1912, two years after it was first published, *The House of Bondage,* an American novel about the evil specter of white slavery, was already in its fourteenth printing. In the book, written by Reginald Wright Kauffman, Max Grossman is a pimp and described as "a member of a persistent race; . . . his gray glance had a penetrating calculation about it that made the girl instinctively draw her coat together and button it." Max drugs the young protagonist, Mary, and forces her to work in a brothel as soon as she arrives in New York from her hometown in Pennsylvania.

In the shtetls of Eastern Europe, no drugs were necessary.

"Sometimes the men arrived in the Jewish quarter just to pick up photographs of suitable girls," said Laya Rosenberg, who is eighty years old and spent her early childhood in Radom, a large town sixty miles south of Warsaw. "They promised them everything. They promised them jobs, they promised them marriage. And many of those poor, ignorant girls would practically line up to be chosen."

But did people in the shtetls have any idea that these girls were really being recruited for prostitution? Perhaps in the early days of the Traffic, people were completely ignorant of their intentions. But thirty years later, in the 1920s, Jews in the shtetls and the larger towns and cities began to have their suspicions about these traveling salesmen.

Some young women may have willingly sought out the elegant strangers in order to escape their wretched lives. The notion that impoverished Jewish girls would actively seek out prostitution as a way to escape the drudgery of their lives in the shtetls was simply too uncomfortable to contemplate.

"Do you not know that numbers of these girls are ruined on account of silk stockings?" noted a Jewish feminist at the beginning of the twentieth century. "Silk stockings are a great danger to morality." The same might be said of poverty.

"Everyone knew the business of those beautiful strangers: They bought and sold *kurves*," said Laya Rosenberg, using the Yiddish term for "prostitute."

DID SOPHIA'S FATHER suspect Isaac Boorosky of being a pimp?

There must have been something sinister about the man, something he didn't trust. A week after their emotional good-bye in Warsaw, Sophia's father decided to visit his daughter in Lodz. He was determined to return the eight rubles to Boorosky and take Sophia back to the shtetl where she belonged.

But Sophia did not want to leave with her father. For seven days, she had worked hard for Boorosky's mother, who lived in a large, well-appointed apartment in the center of Lodz. Sophia had never known such luxury and couldn't believe her luck. Perhaps she was enjoying the luxurious sensation of sleeping on cotton sheets in her own bed. Had she tasted chocolate for the first time? Perhaps she had taken a bath in a real porcelain tub filled with hot water. In any case, Sophia must have imagined that she was turning into a proper lady. Isaac had bought her a beautiful taffeta dress and even petticoats made of silk!

Yes, everything is fine, Isaac told Sophia's father. Sophia is a hard worker, and well liked. Besides, confided Isaac to Sophia's father, if she continues to do such excellent work, perhaps she would even make a good wife.

Was this a marriage proposal? Did Isaac Boorosky mean to marry his daughter?

The promise must have done much to allay the old man's fears of bondage and white slavery, if such thoughts had actually crossed his mind. Now that he was convinced that Isaac Boorosky's intentions were noble, Sophia's father could return to the shtetl confident that she would be properly treated. His daughter would marry a gentleman, and perhaps now the family's life would change completely.

In fact, the day after Sophia's father returned to the shtetl, Sophia's life did change radically. Isaac told her she would no longer be working in his mother's kitchen. He asked her to put on the silk petticoats and taffeta dress. Sophia learned that she was to accompany Isaac to another one of his apartments, on the outskirts of Lodz. When they arrived, Sophia and Isaac ate what seemed to Sophia a sumptuous feast. Later, she would recall little of what they ate, and only remembered that Isaac filled and refilled her glass with beer, which tasted bitter and made her feel light-headed and sleepy.

Sophia later told police that she had no memory of what happened next. But when she woke up the following morning, she was deeply embarrassed to find herself lying in bed naked. Worst of all, Isaac was lying in bed beside her. "Now you are my wife," he said simply.

Did he pull her body close to his, caressing her breasts with his soft hands? Or did he feel even slightly guilty or remorseful for raping a thirteen-year-old girl? Probably not, because by the time Isaac met Sophia Chamys in the early 1890s, he was well accustomed to deflowering young virgins. For Isaac and his business associates, rape was a tool of their trade, a kind of initiation into the brothels they operated in Poland and in America. They didn't do it all the time, of course, only when they met a particularly desirable prospect, like Sophia Chamys. Beautiful girls like Sophia could fetch high prices, even in Poland. But why not try her out first, before handing her over to the paying customers? She was so young, so innocent-looking, that it would still be relatively easy to pass her off as a virgin. The virgins always fetched the highest prices.

There is no record of what went through Sophia's mind as she lay on the white sheets, now streaked with blood. It's a measure of her utter naïveté and lack of experience that she did not know she had been raped. She believed and trusted Isaac Boorosky the way a child might trust a beloved teacher. When he said he loved her, when he told her that he would marry her, she believed him.

But she had seen other young women in the Lodz apartment where she had worked for Isaac's mother, and had thought that one of them must surely be his wife. Wasn't he already married?

"It's a lie," said Isaac, seemingly stung by her question.

For the first time in her life, Sophia felt secure. This man had chosen her to be his wife, and now she and her family would be protected. Perhaps she could arrange for them to leave the shtetl, to settle in the Lodz apartment with Isaac's mother. She would ask him to find a doctor for her younger sister, who suffered from consumption. Over the years, the coughing fits had gotten progressively worse. In recent months, her sister could barely breathe when the fits started. But now that Sophia was going to be a wealthy lady, things would be different. They could only get better. "I thought he was my husband," said Sophia in her testimony to police.

Brought up in a society where women rarely questioned men, least of all their husbands, Sophia believed everything Isaac told her. On the morning following the rape, when he deposited her in a house full of women—a place that Sophia mistook for a hotel—she didn't think to ask him why.

The prostitutes soon set her straight. Isaac Boorosky was a ruffian, they said. He bought and sold women, and he had bought her, Sophia Chamys, who was now the newest addition to his brothel. Sophia never talked about what she felt when she found herself in a brothel for the first time. She would only say that there must have been some kind of mistake; she refused to believe the prostitutes, and naïvely walked back to Isaac's mother's home in the city to sort things out.

Isaac greeted her warmly, but he made no mention of the brothel. How sorry he was that things had gotten out of hand. Yes, they would be together again soon, he reassured her, but first she must do him a favor. Perhaps he told her he needed to pay back a loan and would have to hire her out to a business associate in Konin. She would work as a scullery maid for a few months, until his debt was paid, and then they would be reunited in Lodz. On some level, Isaac must have made it clear that as his wife, Sophia would need to help him as much as she could, obey him without question.

Sophia wanted to help the man she considered her husband,

but she was reluctant to leave him. Isaac, who understood the mentality of ignorant young girls extremely well, seemed to know how to persuade her. Shtetl girls are like children, he was fond of telling his associates. They are easily manipulated, and happiest when you give them a new toy.

Years later, Sophia readily admitted to police that the reason she decided to go to Konin was because Isaac had promised to send her by train. How many times had she and her sister heard the trains rattling to Warsaw! No one in the shtetl could afford to ride on a train—not the tailor, the storekeeper, or the cantor. She would do anything to ride on a train, and believed Isaac when he said they would be separated for only a few months.

When she arrived in Konin, Sophia knew instantly she was destined for another brothel; this time she understood the brutal reality of what her young life had become: Isaac had sold her to a pimp named Libet, who ran a decrepit brothel on the outskirts of town. For more than a month Sophia worked as a prostitute for well-oiled and mustachioed gentlemen like Isaac, the man she still stubbornly considered her husband.

It's not clear how Sophia managed to escape the brothel. She told police that after she found out she was pregnant, she decided to return to the shtetl. She would have to tell her parents she was pregnant with her husband's child. There was no shame in that. But she could never, ever, tell them that she had been working in a common house, as a prostitute.

Sophia might have been uneducated and naïve, but she grew up in a community that put a high value on sexual purity. For Jews, prostitution is the most reviled of the professions. Jewish prostitutes have certainly existed throughout history, but they were never seen as a necessary evil, or even tolerated, as they were among people of other faiths. They are hated figures in the Old

Testament. Although Sophia would not have beer
miliar with Jewish religious texts, she would
knowledge of the shame attached to prostitutic
Jews. After the destruction of Jerusalem's Great Temple
B.C.E., the prophet Ezekiel described the sins of the Jews in terms
of prostitution: "She did not give up her harlotry which she had
practiced since her days in Egypt." Following the destruction of
the second temple, Roman conquerors found that the most effective form of humiliation of the Jews was to force Jewish women to
become prostitutes; most of these women ended up committing
suicide.

Although Jewish prostitutes did exist in the major Eastern European cities, they were virtually unheard of in the shtetls.
Throughout history, rabbis and other Jewish authorities vigor-
ously suppressed brothels wherever and whenever they appeared.
Between the sixteenth and eighteenth centuries, Jewish leaders in
countries such as Poland, Russia, Lithuania, and Hungary began
to implement strict moral codes of behavior over what were then
the tightly knit communities they controlled. At the end of the
eighteenth century, the vast majority of Poland's Jews lived like
the Chamys family, in rural shtetls, where strong family and religious ties formed the backbone of the community. Sexual trans-
gressions were brought before boards of morals, and community
members were encouraged to report their neighbors' various
moral breaches.

In fact, years after Boorosky's arrest in Brazil, Jews in Warsaw
went on a rampage against the Jewish pimps who controlled many
of the city's brothels. In May 1905, with Poland in a state of political upheaval, Jewish workers looted and destroyed brothels
throughout the city, beating and killing prostitutes and pimps.
Forty brothels were torched, eight people were killed, and more

nan one hundred were injured in the uprising. A reporter for the Reuters news agency said that the honorable, working-class Jews in Warsaw had become tired "of hearing themselves called keepers of disorderly houses, thieves, userers and other opprobrious epithets, and resolved, as the police were receiving bribes from these classes and protecting them, to take the matter into their own hands and resort to drastic measures."

In the end, Sophia could say nothing about her ordeal to her family. The news would cause unbearable shame. But as she approached her old house in the shtetl, her parents and sister embraced her, and all began to speak at once. They touched her hair, felt her new taffeta frock, admired her shoes. Look at Sophia! they exclaimed with great joy. She's fat and so beautiful!

But where is your new husband?

At that moment Sophia learned that Isaac had promised her father that he would marry her when the old man showed up in Lodz to take her back to the shtetl. So it was true, Isaac's intentions were good. But why did he want her to work in a brothel?

Three days after she was reunited with her family, Isaac appeared at their door. He told Sophia's parents that he had urgent business in America and could not possibly leave without his new bride.

Isaac must have recoiled in horror when he entered the tiny, damp hovel where the Chamys family lived. Had he been chased by packs of starving dogs when he entered the shtetl? Were his shoes caked in mud? Did the soot from the Chamys stove fall on his exquisitely tailored overcoat?

Sophia's family received him with great warmth and countless apologies. Sophia, they said, is young and inexperienced. She knows nothing of life, they said. She's innocent. She's only thirteen. Isaac waved away their concerns, and to show his good faith he promised to make their union official. There was no time for a proper wedding, he said. Could the Chamys family round up two witnesses, and could they meet in the *shtibl* for the ceremony?

Even though the wedding was organized in such haste, and would not be officiated by a religious leader, the Chamys family would not have thought anything amiss. In the nineteenth and early twentieth centuries, such ritual weddings were common in the smaller, poorer shtetls where rabbis were rarely present. The ceremony required only the presence of one Jewish witness, and was commonly referred to in Yiddish as a *stille chuppah* or "silent wedding."

In the presence of the witness, which in Sophia's case could have been the local cobbler or the tailor, Isaac would make her an offer of a ring or money, and the witness would pronounce the couple officially married. It's not clear what Isaac presented to Sophia as a token of his affection, but it became clear to police years later that this was not the first time that he had entered into such a union.

The ritual marriages had absolutely no validity under civil law, so women entering into these compromising situations had no legal protection. The practice had even been outlawed in some parts of Eastern Europe but continued in the more backward regions well into the twentieth century.

Of course, this was very convenient for pimps like Isaac Boorosky, for whom the *stille chuppah* became a very important tool, allowing them to entrap ignorant women and rob them of their civil rights. It is not known how many impoverished young women Isaac married in these "silent weddings." It is clear that pimps working in America would typically return to Eastern Europe and travel from shtetl to shtetl acquiring multiple wives in *stille chuppah* ceremonies.

Sometimes the multiple marriages got out of hand, and traffickers would find themselves juggling too many women. The authorities who arrested Boorosky in Brazil said that it was not uncommon for him to return to South America from his frequent business trips to Eastern Europe with more than one wife. On one trip he "married" a Russian girl, took her to Austria, and hid her in a hotel while he used the same means to secure a local girl. He told the Russian wife that he needed to stop in Austria to buy up properties and to hire a housekeeper for his home in America. Like Sophia, the Russian woman would not think to question the man she took to be her new husband. A few days after his marriage to the new woman in Austria, Isaac confessed to the Russian woman that in order to arrange the Austrian's documents, he had to marry her as well. The police records do not reveal how Isaac managed to travel to Brazil accompanied by both wives. Perhaps they posed as sisters, using false passports crafted by Boorosky's many underworld friends in Poland and South America.

"It often turns out later on that the man has been through such a marriage in every town through which he has passed," noted an Eastern European Jewish community leader concerned about the frequency of the *stille chuppah* ceremonies in the outlying regions. "And every woman he has married has been twice deceived; first, she believed the tall tales the man told her, and secondly, she was absolutely convinced that the *stille chuppah* was a legal marriage. Our experience has taught us that the *stille chuppah* is nothing more or less than a veiled form of traffic on a smaller scale."

The *stille chuppah* had other implications, beyond white slavery. In many cases it allowed husbands to abandon their wives without suffering any legal consequences. At the first meeting of the Council for the Amelioration of the Legal Position of the Jewess in London, in 1922, a group of middle-class liberal Jewish

women decried the use of *stille chuppah* among the more Orthodox Jews. They presented lists of women who had been abandoned by their husbands, who in turn refused to grant them a
Jewish divorce or *get,* forcing the women into a legal straitjacket.
On the one hand, they couldn't complain legally because their
marriages were not recognized under civil law; on the other hand,
they could not remarry within their communities because many of
their husbands refused to divorce them.

Why did women put such blind trust in men like Isaac? The
answer is easily summed up in one word: America.

"IN AMERICA, people eat an orange every day."

How many times had Sophia and her sister heard their neighbors say that? In the shtetl, oranges were rare, and reserved for
very special occasions. Sometimes, if a family could scrape together a few extra coins, they could buy an orange, and carefully
divide it into sections for every member of the family. But in
America everyone was rich and oranges were plentiful. People in
America also ate chicken every day, and had clothes made of silk.
In letters home to their families in Poland, young men who had set
off on their own to America often enumerated the riches that they
found waiting for them in their new land. "Before my arrival, they
had already prepared for me clothes made of silk," wrote a man
named Yaacov Ferber to his wife in Warsaw. "Silk on the outside
and silk in the lining. It would cost a fortune in Poland."

In Sophia's shtetl, people were fond of telling one another that
in America people were so wealthy that they capped their teeth
with gold and brushed them with solid gold brushes. Such exag-
gerations fed the shtetl-dwellers' imagination of what life was like
in both North and South America. People rarely distinguished be-

tween the two landmasses, in their ignorance pronouncing them as equally rich and splendid. In the shtetl, America was paradise, "its glories shamelessly exaggerated in Yiddish and Hebrew brochures that tempted Jews with stories of riches and freedom." Many of these brochures were published by Jewish philanthropic agencies based in Europe, such as the Jewish Colonization Association, which sponsored Jewish immigrants to settle in South America.

Jews from the shtetl who had immigrated to America often returned with tall tales of easy wealth. Even though many of them found themselves living in poverty in the tenements of New York or the *conventillos* of Buenos Aires, they returned to the shtetl much as Isaac Boorosky did—posing as the moneyed artistocrat, wearing fine clothes and distributing little gifts—razor blades, pen holders, a music box—to their neighbors.

In addition to the fabled riches, America offered Jews the opportunity to live peaceful lives, to practice their religious beliefs without fear of violence and anti-Semitism. In Eastern Europe, Jews were the eternal scapegoats, blamed for everything from the Black Plague in the 1300s to Poland's economic downfall after its disastrous wars with Russia and Sweden in the seventeenth century. In Poland and other parts of Eastern Europe, Jews had worked as the middlemen between the nobility and the peasants, collecting taxes and running business enterprises. They were deeply resented for these activities, especially by the peasantry. In the first wave of widespread violence against the Jews of Poland, in 1648, the peasants rebelled, attacking Jews and razing their communities. They were led by an army officer named Bogdan Chmielnicki, who had the support of his fellow Greek Orthodox Cossacks. The revolt targeted not only Jews but also the Catholic Polish landowners who employed them. Between 100,000 and

500,000 Jews were killed in the chaos following the so-called Chmielnicki revolt, in scenes of horrific violence. In one of the most chilling reports, Cossacks slit open Jewish women and sewed live cats into their bellies. Following the Chmielnicki rebellion, invasions by Sweden and Russia plunged Poland into war for three decades.

More pogroms followed. In Russia, following the first revolution in 1905, a wave of attacks against Jews left some one thousand dead and eight thousand injured in the course of one week. In addition to subversion and revolution, Jews were blamed for everything from natural disasters to the kidnapping of young Christian children—and, later, white slavery. They were accused of practicing witchcraft in the Grand Duchy of Lithuania, of using charms to cause "natural disasters (particularly epidemics), cattle plagues and even Tatar invasions." It was widely believed that Jews abducted Christian children and used their blood in the baking of Passover matzo and in order to improve their eyesight. One of the many local superstitions about Jews was that they were born blind "and could only see after rubbing their eyes with this blood."

Although Jews fleeing persecution in other parts of Europe had been encouraged to settle in the region centuries earlier, they became objects of hatred toward the end of the nineteenth century. The massive social and economic upheavals of industrialization, urbanization, and a host of anti-Semitic laws throughout Eastern Europe all but destroyed many small, traditional Jewish communities.

Anti-Semitic legislation, which severely restricted Jews in everything from travel to employment, made their lives a misery, forcing them out of traditional communities and contributing to the breakdown of the strict social controls that they had established. In 1882, with the introduction of the so-called May Laws,

Jews were forced out of the rural areas in the Pale of Settlement, a zone created by Catherine II of Russia, who forced Jews to live there after the first partition of Poland in 1772. The laws restricted their right to travel and prevented them from conducting any form of trade. Unable to make a living, many simply left. Between 1881 and the beginning of the First World War, one third of Eastern European Jews left their homes in the biggest single exodus since the Inquisition. Most went to America. Those who remained endured wretched poverty and the enmity of their neighbors.

"Filthy Jew!" How many times had Sophia and her sister heard those words on their trips to Warsaw? How many times had they found the doors locked to them at the cheap pensions where they tried to find a room for the night? How often had they been roughed up and spat on when they were forced to sleep on the streets?

A teenager growing up at the beginning of the twentieth century in Rawa, a town on the outskirts of Warsaw, recalled the taunts she and her younger brother endured from the non-Jewish schoolchildren: "One day as my brother and I returned to school, we were chased by gangs of children, shouting 'Grab the Jew! Kill the Jew!'"

Did the shtetl children dream of escaping their narrow world? Did they ever dream, as some of the adults did, of going to America? In Sophia's world, only the luckiest girls ended up in America. For most it was a forbidden dream, like the land in "Di Toyb" (the dove), a game children played in the shtetl.

> *The dove flew*
> *Over all the world*
> *And saw a lovely land*
> *But the land was locked*

And the key was broken
One, two, three
Out you go

There is only one surviving portrait that shows Sophia and Isaac together. Is it the wedding portrait? If it is, the couple do not appear very happy. Their posture is stiff, their gaze far off. Perhaps they were caught off guard, understandably unaccustomed to portraiture, the novelty of standing in front of a photographer in a studio. Are they looking forward to a long journey, to a future in a new land? Both look equipped for travel. As usual, Isaac is dressed in a light-colored frock coat and trousers, stiff collar, bow tie, and impeccably polished black leather shoes. In his left hand he is holding an umbrella, and an overcoat is draped over his forearm—the posture of the nineteenth-century businessman in a hurry to catch a train. His other hand is stiffly extended toward Sophia, who stands next to him wearing a dark frock with puffed sleeves. Is it the taffeta dress he first gave her, or is this some other present for her devotion? Her dark hair is discreetly pulled back, making her look older, like an earnest schoolteacher. She appears plump and healthy, perhaps due to her pregnancy. She is trying to reach Isaac's outstretched hand. In her other hand, she is holding a carpetbag.

Following the ceremony in the shtetl, Sophia returned to Lodz with Isaac, who told her she would sail with one of his business associates—a man he only identified as Chumpaisk—to Buenos Aires, a city on the other side of the world. The journey would take exactly twenty-two days by sea, he told her.

Buenos Aires?

Yes, America, you're going to America, my dear, he might have told her, kissing her cheek and reassuring her that he would make the trip shortly, after he attended to some urgent business matters in Lodz. Chumpaisk was a good sort; he would certainly look after her on the trip, Isaac must have assured her.

It's unclear why Sophia would allow herself to be duped again by this man. Did he need to remind her that as his wife it was her duty to obey him? He probably said none of that. For Sophia, the promise of America was enough. She would finally journey to the "locked land" from the skipping rhyme. Isaac had given her the key. Surely he would open the way.

CHAPTER TWO

The End of the World

The Jewish prostitutes and their pimps loitered at the port, congregating behind the green metal gate of the immigrants' hotel, a holding center where new arrivals to Argentina in the 1890s were lodged while undergoing the requisite customs inspections and medical tests that would allow them to enter the country.

The *polacas,* as they were known to the Argentine border guards, were clearly a nuisance—easily recognizable by their flamboyant outfits, their heavily rouged cheeks, their utter contempt for order. "Accompanied by fat-bellied men in top hats," they made a racket, singing out in Yiddish to get people's attention, banging on the metal gate, and pressing pieces of chocolate and candy through the railings whenever they saw the bedraggled immigrant children go by. They were friendly, solicitous even. Perhaps many new arrivals even mistook them for homesick landsmen, desperate for news from the shtetls of Russia and Poland. But while they may have taken the opportunity to learn the latest gossip from home and speak their Spanish-accented Yiddish to their compatriots, the pimps and prostitutes at the port were there on business. They went to pick up their latest recruits from the shtetls and to prey on the other innocents who had the misfortune of traveling by themselves to join their new "husbands" in America. Everytime a transatlantic ship docked in Buenos Aires, a group of eager prostitutes and pimps seemed to rush to the port to gawk at the new arrivals.

Do you need a job, miss?

Are you looking for your relatives in the city, little girl?

Do you need help, young lady?

They always shouted the questions in Yiddish, directing them to the tired, slightly dazed young women who disembarked alone, most of them carrying a worn carpetbag containing everything they owned. But in many cases it didn't matter whether the girls were alone or with family. The prostitutes and pimps were shameless, greeting entire stunned families with gifts of sweets, cigarettes, and even small toys for their children. "After a short period of friendly association the girls would be subtly induced to cooperate, submitting themselves to living in a brothel."

Was it really that easy to recruit? Did the girls go so willingly? Were they so quick to put such blind trust in these colorful strangers?

The stern-faced policemen who patroled the Buenos Aires port and the immigrants' hotel must have known the answer. Maybe that's why they were so vigilant, shooing away the *polacas* and the pimps. On occasion they could be persuaded to look the other way, and a few pesos discreetly dropped into the right pockets could ensure access, for these rowdy welcomers refused to give up. "One by one they approached the guard with muttered requests," wrote a Jewish immigrant who arrived in Buenos Aires in 1891. "He kept

shaking his head and waving 'no' with his hands. Under no circumstances was he about to let them in."

The guards repeatedly warned new arrivals to stay away from
the ruffians and their women. So did the representatives of the
Jewish Colonization Association, known as the ICA in Yiddish,
the philanthropic agency that sponsored most of the first Jewish
immigrants to the country. "Don't let your wives and daughters
take to the street!" warned one ICA representative speaking at a
crowded orientation session for recent arrivals at the immigrants'
hotel, which smelled of disinfectant and sweat. Shortly after a
shipload of new immigrants arrived, the hotel dormitories were
quickly transformed into a gypsy encampment. Tin cups and
utensils were set out on coarse blankets on the whitewashed floors,
while ragged laundry was spread like miniature tents between the
metal, hospital-issue beds. "There are hardly any decent Jews
here," continued the ICA representative, speaking to a large group
of weary men from Russia and Poland. "Just those impure souls,
the dregs of humanity."

Hearing this, a new Jewish immigrant might have wondered
why he had decided to leave his home in Eastern Europe. What
kind of a promised land was this, where Jews already hated one
another? But for those first Jewish immigrants who arrived in the
1890s under the auspices of the ICA, Argentina was their last resort, a bold experiment in global resettlement that had to succeed
if their bleak lives were ever to improve. There was no going back
to their miserable lives in the shtetls now. Argentina had to be
their salvation.

That was the idea, anyway, the one hatched by Baron Moritz
von Hirsch, the spectacularly wealthy railway entrepreneur and
philanthropist who founded the ICA. Baron von Hirsch, who
came to the Bavarian court from a family dynasty of bankers, felt

that the only way to help Europe's Jews escape poverty and violent discrimination was to settle them in a new land. The ICA's Yiddish-language brochures pronounced Argentina "a great, free and fertile land" and the best place on earth "to establish a home for our oppressed brethren."

It was partly true. In those days, Argentina was a sparsely populated, resource-rich country at the other end of the world, and a magnet for new immigrants. In order to feed a huge industrial boom, the country's industrialists pressured the government to recruit unskilled laborers from Eastern Europe, promising them free lodging for a week and subsidizing their travel costs to Argentina. Not only would they be a good source of cheap labor but they would be more likely to work as strike-breakers and subvert the new country's fledgling unions, which were beginning to wield political power. For the baron, these factors combined made Argentina a rich land of opportunity, and in 1891 he endowed the ICA with some fifty million dollars and bought up more than 200,000 hectares of land in the Argentine countryside.

In its first few years, the ICA settled thousands of Jews from Russia and Poland, helping them found farming cooperatives and set up religious institutions. But life on the bleak, windswept pampa was not easy—not even for hearty peasants from the hardscrabble shtetls of Eastern Europe. In a land more suited to gauchos than to settlers, the Jewish agricultural pioneers arrived ill prepared for survival—with little more than the clothes on their backs, only a cursory knowledge of the local customs, and not a word of Spanish.

In the early days, at least, the resettlement plan proved a disaster as some three hundred Jewish children perished from hunger and cold in the new agricultural colonies. Many surviving family members demanded to be repatriated and returned to Buenos

Aires on foot. Those who stayed suffered "unspeakable deprivation." Destitute, many of their wives and daughters might have remembered the elegant strangers at the port of Buenos Aires with
their promises to find them jobs. In the end, most of them ended
up in the brothels.

Seeing these women on a trip to Buenos Aires in November
1892, a British visitor was moved to write an emotional letter to
the editor of London's *Jewish Chronicle*. "A vile traffic has been
long the curse of the city, and many a poor Jewess has been invei-
gled here by these beasts in human form," he wrote. "The pity is
one cannot write in a newspaper of these horrible doings."

SOPHIA CHAMYS KNEW LITTLE of "these horrible doings." But
by the time her ship docked at the port of Buenos Aires, she probably had a vague idea of what kinds of things awaited her in this
new land. Still, it's impossible to know what went through her
mind as the ship made its way to the mouth of the Río de la Plata
and finally sailed into the "locked land" of the shtetl rhyme. Had
she, Sophia Chamys, really arrived in this unbelievably rich country from the fairy tale—the place called America? If she noticed
the pimps and prostitutes who regularly congregated at the port,
she might have innocently and even excitedly asked them in Yiddish if their teeth were lined with gold, if they brushed them with
gold brushes. Did they eat oranges every day? Was everyone really
rich?

But Sophia might not have been in the mood for questions. She
was unsteady on her feet when she disembarked, the result of an
unknown illness aboard ship or perhaps complications arising
from her pregnancy. The police reports never made it clear. What
was clear was that she left the ship on the arm of the man to whom

her new husband had entrusted her, the man she only ever knew as Chumpaisk.

We don't know if Chumpaisk was as well dressed as her husband, his hair oiled with lavender, his mustache impeccably trimmed. But Chumpaisk almost certainly posed as her husband or her father when the Argentine federal police official greeted him in Spanish, asking to see their travel documents, pointing to the young, obviously pregnant girl on his arm.

Sophia could neither read nor write, and she could understand nothing of the strange language that Chumpaisk seemed to speak with such ease to the authorities. He had obviously done this before, and while Sophia might have seemed nervous when confronted with the Argentine port officials, Chumpaisk would have been in his element.

Like Isaac Boorosky, Chumpaisk was by now skilled at—what did the French pimps call it at the Café Parisien?—*negotiation*. At this the pimps were terribly skilled, especially when it came to the South American authorities. How different they were from those Prussian-trained border guards in the old country! Always playing by the rules, never giving an inch. In South America a few francs always did the trick; silk stockings, cigarettes, and champagne proved even more effective currency. Government officials in South America had wives, and many also had mistresses— women who knew the value of Austrian or Frenchmade silk stockings. Men such as Chumpaisk and Boorosky always came prepared with these more imaginative negotiating tools. There was no situation they couldn't handle. In South America they knew how to get what they wanted.

Later, when the white-slave traffic was in full swing, bribes proved essential as gangs of well-dressed pimps headed to the port expressly to pick up their "baggage"—the young women from the shtetls who had been promised jobs as seamstresses or shop attendants or who were the new "wives" of their associates in the country. Sometimes ten to twelve such women would arrive on each of the ships that pulled into the Buenos Aires harbor.

French reporter Albert Londres became the only independent observer to document how the European pimps smuggled young women like Sophia into Argentina. In fact, in some ways Sophia may have been one of the lucky ones. In order to evade the authorities, she probably traveled first-class with Chumpaisk. The authorities rarely detained the well-heeled, first-class passengers, preoccupying themselves with the bedraggled masses who traveled in steerage. These were the problematic arrivals, the ones to be locked immediately behind the green metal gates of the immigrants' hotel. Did they have lice? What kind of diseases were they bringing into Argentina? Did they have any money? A job? Any friends or family in the country? How did they intend to survive?

Few of the women traveling to Argentina for the purposes of prostitution ever ended up at the immigrants' hotel. If they had, perhaps they would have been saved from a life of slavery in the dilapidated brothels that lined the port at La Boca, literally the mouth of the Río de la Plata.

In the early days, many of the women who did end up at Boca brothels sailed to Argentina as stowaways, posing as laundresses when they boarded at European ports. Perhaps they lacked travel documents and were underage. No doubt most of these girls thought they were going to South America to work as seamstresses or shopgirls. Few knew what fate awaited them when they boarded the transatlantic ships in Europe. "She has no hat, and carries a bundle of men's shirts," wrote Londres of the young women he saw on his trip from Le Havre to Buenos Aires. "If she is stopped, she says: 'I'm taking this washing to my father.'" Such women were hidden by corrupt crew members belowdecks for the entire journey. "The sailors look round carefully before taking them any food. It will mean twenty-one, twenty-five, twenty-eight days in prison, in accordance with the boat."

During inspections, the pimps' accomplices on the ship would "hide them in empty boilers, ventilators, bunkers among the engines or in the funnels." Once the boat stopped at Buenos Aires, the pimps would often wait a few days to get them off the ship. "The boat stops there a week," noted Londres. "There is plenty of time to get them off. When the girls are discovered, if they are not agreeable to the eye, the South American authorities re-embark them."

Pimps used other ruses to get past the authorities, both in Europe and in South America. One procurer, dressed in a monk's habit, was arrested with six young women in tow. Other pimps dressed girls as boys. In 1904, a woman identified only as Golda "left Odessa with two innocent girls and managed to beg her way across to Buenos Aires, having the party pose as victims of the Kishinev massacre and touching Jewish benevolent societies for passage."

But while it was relatively easy to bribe the border guards in Argentina, it was unwise to take any chances, especially when trying to get the younger girls across the border. Chumpaisk would have to be careful with Sophia, who was pregnant and visibly underage. In order to evade police officials in Argentina, Chumpaisk might have decided to leave the ship at Montevideo, the capital of Uruguay and the last port of call before Buenos Aires. In Montevideo, a short distance upriver from Buenos Aires, the authorities seemed much more amenable to negotiation, and by the 1890s, the pimps had turned the city into an alternate arrival port.

But even Montevideo posed problems. You never knew when you were going to meet a crusading immigration official, someone who looked too closely at the Eastern European couples disembarking from the transatlantic ships. Why did these well-fed businessmen have such beautiful, young wives? Why did the young women always appear so forlorn, skittish even?

The Jewish pimps became spooked when authorities at Montevideo alerted their counterparts in Buenos Aires to be on the lookout for a young girl from Poland traveling with a much older man. Like Sophia, Jancka Kostoska was an impoverished Jewish girl who had made the long trip from Lodz to South America. Eighteen-year-old Jancka was accompanied by a Jewish pimp named Moses Lachman, who had acquired false travel documents for her. The documents stated that Jancka was twenty-one, the legal age of majority in Argentina. But there must have been something about this couple that aroused suspicion. Perhaps Jancka looked particularly unhappy traveling on the arm of a much older man. Or the customs officers noticed her bruises—the ones she had received on the ship when she vehemently refused to work as a prostitute upon her arrival in Buenos Aires.

Jancka and Lachman disembarked at Montevideo, boarded a train, and took a circuitous route to Buenos Aires. But although they managed to evade the Argentine border checks, arriving without incident in the Argentine capital, they were eventually caught. Jancka, petrified and sobbing, was freed from a Buenos Aires brothel, and Lachman was arrested.

Later the Montevideo-Salto-Concordia-Buenos Aires train route that Lachman took with Jancka would become so popular among pimps that authorities at the League of Nations charged with investigating the white-slave traffic demanded immediate action on the part of Argentine and Uruguayan police. But the continuous stream of champagne and silk stockings must have ensured that no such action was taken.

Other women destined for the brothels of Buenos Aires would make the short trip from Montevideo on river steamers, which were "illuminated like casinos." Few of the *Mihanovich* boats, named after their Polish owner, were subject to searches by the border authorities, most of whom were on the pimps' payroll in the early 1900s.

But Sophia could remember nothing of travel by train or steamer. She had only vague recollections of her arrival in America, as she called it. Perhaps her experience onboard the ship had been similar to Jancka's. Maybe it had been so disagreeable that she simply blocked the entire journey out of her mind, or at least refused to speak about it publicly.

Did Chumpaisk rape her on the ship? Did he beat her so hard that she could now walk only with great difficulty?

It was a common occurrence among pimps who sailed with their young "wives" to South America. Aboard the ship, the men would at first calmly explain that once they docked in Buenos Aires, their "wives" would be expected to begin working as prostitutes. If a woman resisted, she was often raped and beaten into submission aboard the ship. The pimp, according to one police report, "undertook a system of planned demoralization on board ship, where he completely changed his language and manner." Young women who found themselves in these situations were entirely helpless. Whom would they complain to on a voyage at sea? Would they denounce the men who were officially identified in their identity documents as their husbands? Who would take pity on them now? For girls like Sophia, who could only speak Yiddish, communication with any of the ship officials proved impossible. Like Sophia, most girls must have resigned themselves to their fate, enduring as best they could their nightmare at sea.

Sometimes the "planned demoralization" of the women at sea took on much more subtle forms, as in the case that Albert Londres witnessed on his journey to Buenos Aires aboard the *Malta*. In Bilbao, the ship's first port of call, Londres befriended a French pimp named Lucien Carlet and his beautifully dressed "wife," Blanche Tuman. During the journey Londres learned that Carlet had found Blanche starving and dressed in rags on a Paris street corner. As Carlet later confessed to Londres, he thought she would make an excellent prostitute in Buenos Aires. "The man was about thirty-five and the girl about nineteen," wrote Londres of his traveling companions. "He was dark, with handsome, innocent blue eyes. I would have gladly exchanged his gray suit for mine. He looked a pleasant fellow." The girl, who had "little freckles on her little nose—a straight little nose in a neat little face," was nicknamed Galina (Latin for "hen") because, a child herself, she entertained herself by playing with the children on board the *Malta*. At first Blanche seemed thrilled at the prospect of sailing to Buenos Aires, even though she confessed that she had absolutely no idea where she was going.

Typically, both were traveling on false passports. Carlet's passport identified him as a merchant; Blanche's stated that she was a dressmaker. To their fellow passengers, Blanche and Carlet must have seemed like the perfect couple. At every port of call Carlet showered Blanche with little gifts and took her out sightseeing. But at Rio de Janeiro, Blanche's mood changed completely. She locked herself in her cabin and cried for the rest of the journey.

"Did you beat her yesterday?" Londres asked Carlet over drinks in the third-class lounge. "She was crying."

Carlet, who was already married to another French prostitute he had installed in a brothel in Buenos Aires, simply shrugged. It was always this way with the girls, before they got used to the idea that they were going to work in a brothel, he said matter-of-factly. "I just told her all about it," said Carlet, sipping his champagne. "We were due at Montevideo in two days, and she would get off the boat there. It was time to talk to her."

Blanche may not have been happy about heading to a Buenos Aires brothel, but according to Carlet, who bumped into the journalist in Buenos Aires a month later, she was doing surprisingly well. Although little is known about Blanche's previous life in Paris, Londres hinted that she might have already dabbled in prostitution before arriving in Buenos Aires. Perhaps her past on the streets of Paris was good preparation for her life on the streets of Rosario and Buenos Aires. Following her bout of crying on the ship, Blanche seemed to accept her fate.

It's not clear when Sophia found out that Isaac Boorosky, her "husband," had sold her to Chumpaisk in Lodz. Did Chumpaisk tell her on the ship, during the beatings and her frequent crying fits? Or did he tell her when they arrived in America?

It didn't matter, in the end. By the time they cleared immigration formalities in Buenos Aires, Sophia probably already knew she was Chumpaisk's slave and would have to do his bidding. The situation seemed to make her sick to her stomach, or maybe it was just the physical transformations of pregnancy, or the smell of rotten fish that pervaded the narrow hallways of the tenement building where Chumpaisk left her in the care of a woman known to her only as Madame Nathalia.

Madame Nathalia operated a brothel out of her one-room flat in a *conventillo*, one of the crowded tenements that were jokingly referred to as "little convents" in working-class districts of the inner city. Most new immigrants to the city found themselves crowded into these filthy *conventillos;* in one such building, more than fifty Jewish families shared two bathrooms.

Sophia's new accommodations must have reminded her of the shtetl in some ways. After all, entire families, some with five or more children, were crowded into a narrow, filthy space, which they shared with rats, fleas, and all manner of vermin. They ate potatoes and hard black bread at most of their meals, just as they had in the shtetl. They also took turns cooking over a woodstove in a corner of the courtyard, their bodies covered in soot and ashes after every meal. When a prominent rabbi visited a *conventillo* in the working-class Once district of Buenos Aires, he was shocked by the "the filth and promiscuity we found in the rooms of over fifty Jewish families (some 450 persons) living around the same yard."

Another Sophia—Sofia Markovich—an immigrant girl from Russia, lived in a *conventillo* where she shared a bed with her mother, Masha, and her two sisters. Her four brothers slept on the floor. Two doors away lived a Polish prostitute, who "served as a warning for Sofia and her two sisters of the example that they should not follow." For how could a woman who wore so much makeup be honest? asked Masha. "It's not enough to be honest," Masha told her daughters; "you also had to look it." Like many immigrant mothers, Masha sought to protect her daughters from the pimps, who often prowled the *coventillos* looking for new recruits.

Many of these upright mothers may have shuddered at the sight of Sophia Chamys, a girl they would take to be a pregnant prostitute, limping around the *conventillo* in her taffeta finery. Did they spit at her, call her *kurve?* Perhaps it was the stares of those worthy mothers that finally broke her spirit. Perhaps she imagined her own mother's shame and repudiation in their eyes. For when Madame Nathalia explained to her that she would have to walk up and down the dark alleys outside the *conventillo* in search of customers, Sophia broke down sobbing, saying that she could never work as a prostitute again. Pregnant and sick, she refused to go out into the dark streets prowling for men. She demanded that Madame Nathalia take her to her husband.

Clearly annoyed, Madame Nathalia warned her to stop carrying on. There were *consequences* for girls who misbehaved so badly, who disobeyed their own husbands, she told her.

It's not clear how Sophia ended up in the waiting room of the local police station, sitting upright in a hard-backed wooden chair as Madame Nathalia spoke to an officer in rapid-fire Spanish, both of them gesturing to Sophia. Although Sophia had no idea what was being said about her, she believed Madame Nathalia when she told her in Yiddish that if she didn't submit to being a prostitute, the police would throw her in jail.

This is America, Sophia. Their customs are very different from ours.

Of course, Madame Nathalia and the others who exploited her played on Sophia's ignorance. Madame Nathalia might have gone on to explain that prostitution was legal in Argentina, and might have added for good measure that if a husband wanted his wife to work as a whore, well then, she had no choice but to obey him.

For Sophia, the concept of civil rights must have been as foreign as the country she found herself in. She was trapped. She was married, but her husband was nowhere to be found. Divorce would not have occurred to her because in her shtetl it was never initiated by women. And now the police had told her in no uncertain terms that they would throw her in jail unless she obeyed her husband. "Girls knowing that in Russia there was neither civil marriage nor civil divorce were convinced that in Argentina the same law prevailed, and thus were drawn into a miserable existence of almost slavery."

But slavery was good for business. In order to make sure that the women remained helpless and ignorant of their rights, the pimps bribed everyone from ship stewards to politicians, government bureaucrats, and even police chiefs. The police officer who informed Sophia of her rights was no doubt on the payroll of Isaac Boorosky or the man known as Chumpaisk.

In addition to police informers, pimps such as Boorosky maintained spies in many of the nongovernmental antislavery organizations that were trying to shut down their trade. One of the most notorious Jewish pimps among them, Jose Solomon Korn, had so many high-level connections that when he was put in jail in 1930, he managed to strike a deal with the prison guards to let him out for regular weekly visits to his dentist. Another pimp, Simon Rubinstein, was said to be so well connected in Argentine society that he stored furniture for a judge at one of his brothels.

Sophia could never have imagined such a complicated network in which pimps paid the authorities to traffic freely in women. But what kind of place was this where women were thrown into jail if they refused to work as prostitutes?

This is America, Sophia.

Maybe, in order to make her feel better about her situation, Madame Nathalia told Sophia that she was one of the lucky girls. Lucky because most girls who arrived in America were treated like cattle. As soon as they cleared customs, the pimps took them to be auctioned off. In the early days, women were stripped and put on the auction block, located in the back rooms of some of the legitimate business enterprises run by the pimps. Zacarias Zitnitsky's restaurant regularly functioned as a makeshift auction house, as did the back rooms of Brutkevich's beauty parlor. One of the most popular venues was the back room of the Café Parisien, in the upscale Recoleta neighborhood, where the viewing was by invitation only. The posh café was a favorite meeting place of the Eastern European and French pimps, who sat every day at the outdoor tables sipping peppermint water and champagne. According to one eyewitness at an auction at the Parisien, the pimps "came to see them, examine them, touch them minutely, because one decayed tooth or one feature deformed by an accident diminished more or less considerably the intrinsic value of the object."

It was not uncommon for local authorities, such as high-ranking politicians or judges who were on the payroll of the pimps, to make the rounds of the auctions, in order to get an advance preview of the new "merchandise" from Europe. Usually, the auctioneer spoke in a loud voice while women were paraded nude through the room—"these unhappy girls, like Phryne, exposed before this areopagus of vile people." In this "stockmarket of women," as one local newspaper called it, the male viewers were encouraged to "approach the slaves in order to feel their forms or examine parts of their anatomy in order to assess their value for the brothels." Some buyers behaved as if they were at a livestock auction, grabbing the women's breasts, sticking their fingers in their mouths to examine their teeth, and pulling their hair.

Virgins fetched the highest prices, usually between three hundred and four hundred pounds sterling, a significant sum in fin de siècle Argentina. Of course, the high prices were justified. A plump, good-looking, virginal "specimen" was worth her weight in gold and could earn more than triple her purchase price within her first few months on the job.

Sophia was probably spared the public humiliation of the auction because she was sick and pregnant. None of the pimps wanted the burden of buying a woman who was going to have a baby. There would be hospital bills or abortion fees. Of course these could easily be subtracted, like all other expenses, from the prostitutes' earnings, but in the end a pregnant woman was simply not good merchandise. Not like a virgin, who no matter what she looked like could fetch a high price.

What had Madame Nathalia said? Lucky. Sophia was lucky because she was not stripped nude and auctioned off like livestock. She was in America, and she was free.

Still, it may have been difficult for her thirteen-year-old brain to grasp this new concept of freedom. What was freedom to a shtetl girl, anyway? Maybe she thought about this as she walked the dark streets in her stiff taffeta dress, her torn silk petticoats dragging through puddles.

Like the other pimps, Isaac Boorosky may have attended the auctions, but he really had no need to purchase women in this fashion. The shtetls of Eastern Europe were his greatest market—a huge open-air auction block where every girl could be had for a handful of rubles, a box of chocolates. Still, he must have frequented the Café Parisien. A shrewd businessman, he would surely have made a point of finding out what his competitors were doing, what kind of girls were fetching the highest prices. Besides, it was a good excuse—as if any were needed—to drop by the Parisien, where the vitrines were filled with chocolate éclairs, madeleines, and the delectable, sweet croissants that the locals quaintly called *media lunas,* or half-moons. At the Parisien, waiters wore gloves to serve afternoon tea to the smartly dressed wives of government ministers. Perhaps on sunny weekend mornings Isaac sat on the terrace with a peppermint water and a newspaper from the old country. Or maybe he ordered a glass of champagne in the afternoons and watched the elegant couples promenade through Recoleta, with its grand mansions and pristine public parks.

And after the café, did he wander through the Recoleta cemetery, admiring the family crypts that looked like miniature versions of the neighborhood's Beaux Arts mansions? All the aristocratic families were buried at Recoleta. What would the peasants in his shtetl make of such a place? Isaac knew that to be buried at Recoleta meant something. It required prestige, power, nobility. Surely, it was every respectable businessman's last wish, to be buried among the greatest entrepreneurs and statesmen in this cemetery!

For while Isaac and the other pimps made their living buying and selling women, they thought of themselves as moneyed gentlemen, aristocrats in the making. They may have behaved like common criminals in the brothels, but in their homes they were perfect gentlemen. "They no longer even considered themselves criminal because they were friends with Mr. So and So, traveled in official cars and even had opinions about the changes in public administration." They sent their children to elite schools in Vienna and Paris. One pimp boasted to his friends in Argentina that his son was studying at a medical school in Switzerland.

They had conservative tastes, and many were averse to risk. "In politics, they like solid, secure governments that are good for trade ... [and] their tastes are frankly middle class," noted Londres. "They grew enthusiastic over quiet evenings at home, card parties, shooting and fishing. Their dream is of a country house on the shore of a placid lake."

Like Isaac, they were deeply concerned with their appearances, wearing enormous diamonds, dark, tailored suits, silk shirts, and gold tie pins. They carried walking sticks and attended the theater or the opera daily; "they felt comfortable in the Jewish neighborhood, knowing many of the tailors, shopkeepers, and jewelers depended on them as clients." They also frequented the barbershop, generously tipping the Italian barbers who carefully trimmed their mustaches and applied fragrant oil to their hair. They paid particular attention to their nails, which were always beautifully manicured and sometimes glistened with the slightest hint of clear polish. You could always tell the elite by their hands, how well they took care of their nails, the older pimps liked to say. Only peasants had dirt under their fingernails. A businessman needed to take care of his hands.

The pimps carried themselves well, and few people questioned what line of business they were in. What mattered was money, of course. At the elegant restaurants off the Calle Florida, the best cuts of meat were reserved for them by the sycophantic waiters who seemed to indulge their every whim. They smoked expensive cigars. The wealthiest ones even conducted legitimate businesses, mostly as jewelers, tobacconists, and clothing vendors. But these businesses were mainly used as fronts for their illicit trade. They spoke Spanish, accented with Yiddish or French, and some even had a flair for the dramatic, discarding their difficult-to-pronounce Eastern European and French names for more grandiose titles: Victor the Conquerer, Vacabana, alias the Moor; the Bear; El Zeze.

Most of them hated the term "pimp." It sounded cheap and amateurish and may have reminded some of them of their early days in the Warsaw underworld, when they were still unschooled, unrefined. They may have been breaking the law in Argentina, but they were entrepreneurs and visionaries and in many cases part of the elite. How else to explain their ability to recognize early on the enormous market for young European women in Argentina, a country that in the 1890s was bursting at the seams with single men?

In contrast to immigrants to the United States, where entire families often made the difficult journey to escape the horrors of poverty and persecution in the Old World, immigrants to Argentina before the First World War were largely economically motivated and almost entirely single men. They came from Italy, Spain, Poland, Russia, Germany, and the Middle East. Many left their wives and families in the Old World for years at a time, until they could make enough money to support them in Argentina.

It is not known why or how Isaac Boorosky first made his way to Argentina, but as he wandered the wide, leafy boulevards of Buenos Aires for the first time he must have been struck by the numbers of single men he saw, many of them forming long queues outside brothels and smoking on the patios of the *conventillos*, waiting for prostitutes to become available. The shortage of women seemed so dire that in Buenos Aires men actually resorted to dancing with men.

At first men like Isaac thought it was little more than a strange local custom, brought to Argentina by the Spaniards or the Italians. Eastern European Jews looked down on anyone from southern Europe. Everyone knew they were lazy, disorganized, wouldn't amount to much. In Argentina, the southern European men worked all day at their backbreaking construction jobs and then drank and chain-smoked cigarettes in the courtyards of the *conventillos* until the small hours. Instead of saving their money, investing it wisely, they spent it on women. Isaac couldn't really fault them for that, could he? These were his customers, after all. But how they carried on! They danced the tango outside the brothels and on the patios while they waited their turn with a prostitute. You really couldn't call it dancing. It was more like fighting than dancing as each man tried to outdo his partner. Sometimes this sexually charged display of strength and machismo was simply too embarrassing to watch.

"The city swarmed with males," wrote Londres during his visit to Argentina. "The women were mostly at home in their husbands' or their parents' houses. All these men went without women, drank without women, ate without women." Respectable single women would rarely venture outside unaccompanied by a male chaperone, so charged was the sexual climate "lowering over the city like a thundercloud."

It didn't take long for men like Isaac to figure out that there was money to be made in such a place. Yes, this was definitely the land of opportunity, where gold was just waiting to be picked up on every street corner. Even an ugly hag from the shtetl could strike it rich here. But you had to *know* how to capitalize on this opportunity, you had to *know* how to exploit it. It wasn't for everyone. You had to have skills to succeed in the business of buying and selling women. You had to be seductive, charismatic, shrewd, and an excellent manager. Pimping was a demanding profession.

"Do you think we have only to pocket our money?" the older pimps were fond of telling the younger, greener men who wanted to enter the profession. "The profession of pimp is nothing for an ordinary man to undertake," they said. "We must be administrators, instructors, comforters and experts in hygiene. We need self-possession, a knowledge of character, insights, kindness, firmness and self-denial; and, above all things, perseverance." There were also important moral codes. Gentlemen must behave correctly everywhere, "in the worst joints as well as the drawing room." A gentleman needed to know how to "help those in trouble" and denounce a woman to her "husband" if she made advances to you.

To any observer, the traffickers' code of conduct and business acumen were indeed impressive. Even the Argentine police were impressed by the way the Jewish pimps did business. Following an exhaustive investigation of their financial dealings, one Argentine police commissioner noted that their organization was "set up like a commercial enterprise based on mathematical calculations and financial forecasts. These people are incredibly disciplined; they think of everything and pay a great deal of attention to the tiniest details." Men like Isaac realized in the early days of the white-slave enterprise that the business of buying and selling women needed to function like, well, a business. A successful businessman never acted alone. After all, there were expenses that needed to be paid up front in order to ensure that the business ran smoothly. It was difficult and costly for one man to single-handedly bribe immigration officials and the police every month. What if one of the shtetl women became ill or pregnant and couldn't bring in steady earnings? What would happen if their cash flow was interrupted? What would they do if they needed a loan? These were pressing business concerns, all of them no doubt hotly debated by the gentlemen traffickers over peppermint water and champagne at the Café Parisien.

In the 1890s, when the white-slave traffic was beginning to gain momentum, these Jewish gentlemen traffickers—all of them independent suppliers—decided to form a trade association that would ensure that their businesses prospered. The Warsaw Jewish Mutual Aid Society functioned very much like a coalition of independent businessmen, spread throughout the country.

At the height of its power, following the First World War, the association in Buenos Aires became an "octopus, achieving an almost unassailable position." The organization had four hundred members in Argentina alone, with branch offices in Brazil, South Africa, India, China, and Poland. They controlled thousands of women in Argentina and at the turn of the last century were making combined annual profits of more than fifty million dollars.

The Warsaw Society was a tightly controlled corporation. Shareholders could vote on changes to the bylaws and elect a board of directors, but the board's decisions were often final. "They live under a servile discipline which they all accept," noted Albert Londres about the shareholders. "They have a Chief. He is a kind of Pope, whose decisions may not be disputed. . . . There is also a Deputy—a sort of Secretary of State. Each province— Rosario, Santa Fé, Mendoza—has its club. The club has its president and vice-president. And all this under the authority of the Pontiff aforementioned."

Every month the president of the organization "fixes the sum every one has to subscribe for the benefit of the police," municipal authorities, and, in some cases, high court justices. Monthly dues were directed to an insurance fund, which compensated shareholders for their losses in the event that one of their prostitutes escaped or died of venereal disease. The board regularly fronted members up to twenty-five hundred pesos so that they could travel back to the shtetls to find replacement women.

Members who were late with their dues were subject to fines imposed by the board. This strict commitment to discipline and organization ensured that shareholders had unlimited credit with one another. "They lend each other, without the slightest written acknowledgment, sums which seemed to me, and still seem, enormous," noted Londres. "It is all based on order, discipline and honesty."

These were not *common* criminals, by any means. It's a measure of their success in Argentina that, in the early days at least, they were able to influence decisions at the highest levels. They had a stable of lawyers who were "organized into another mafia even more dangerous than the pimps. These men jumped through laws, ordinances and regulations without ever revealing the mysterious power that gave them so much clout."

This "mysterious power" was quite useful, especially when dealing with their women—the ones who didn't know their place. Such as Lola Goskin, the prostitute who thought she could work on her own account when her pimp, Felipe Lopachin, disappeared. Lola was warned: If she wanted to continue working peacefully, then she would have to split her profits with the trade association. When she refused, the traffickers knew how to put her in her place. They simply bribed a few police officers, who beat her and then claimed she had violated a city ordinance. In the end the pimps had the authorities do their dirty work. They shut down her brothel and put her out of business.

Even respectable members of society had no influence with the pimps. When members of standing in the Jewish community in Buenos Aires sought out high-level government intervention to shut down the Warsaw Society because it was "exclusively made up of people who lived a dishonest life, delinquents, white slavers and prostitutes," they met with failure even after they sent Argentine authorities a list of brothels operated by the Jewish mobsters. The respectable Jews even enlisted the help of the Polish ambassador in Argentina, who resented the fact that a trade organization of pimps had been named after his country's capital.

Pressured by the Jewish community to act, the Argentine authorities duly dispatched a government functionary named Martin Perez Estrada to investigate the Warsaw Society. Unknown to the irate Jewish protestors was the fact that Perez Estrada had been on the pimps' payroll for years, and perhaps it was not at all surprising that he concluded his so-called investigation in less than a week. "The society considers all of its members to be of irreproachable conduct," noted Perez Estrada in his final report. The Argentine government shelved the report. It was only when the Polish authorities threatened to lodge an official complaint with the Argentine foreign ministry that the pimps decided to change the name of the Warsaw Society.

At a board meeting urgently called to deal with what could have turned into a nasty diplomatic row, Zacarias Zitnitsky told his fellow traffickers that they needed to come up with a new name. After much debate, one of the pimps suggested naming the society after Luís Migdal, an elegant man who was one of the organization's earliest benefactors and acted as a kind of godfather to its younger members. The resolution was unanimously adopted on the spot, and the Warsaw Society was officially renamed Zwi Migdal, which, coincidentally, also means "the great power" in Yiddish.

Some of the pimps grumbled about the name change. Surely with all their *connections,* they could have fought to keep their old name. But under the circumstances, it was the best thing to do. After all, the organization didn't want another battle with the respectable Jews. In many ways, it was one of their biggest weaknesses: the battle for respectability. The pimps had money and influence, but respect among their fellow Jews was elusive. In fact, even in the early days, when the Jewish community in Buenos Aires comprised just fifteen hundred souls, the respectable Jews hated the traffickers. What had the ICA representative called them? *Impure souls. The dregs of humanity.*

As one prominent Jewish colonel noted in 1893, "In Buenos Aires there are Jews who are a disgrace to Judaism, and when I think of them, I am an anti-Semite of the most bigoted description."

But the traffickers refused to give up; they were determined to be respected Jews at any cost. At the turn of the last century, they bought their own cemetery in the outlying suburbs of Avellaneda. They also donated a portion of their profits to purchase a property where they maintained an office and a synagogue. When they established their headquarters on an upscale stretch of Córdoba Street in Buenos Aires, most of the members were tapped for donations. The donor list was found years later by investigating authorities, who noted with interest that most of the donations were objects used to outfit their synagogue. According to the list, Simon Briel donated a chandelier for the party room; Herman Drayman a chandelier for the women's bathroom. M. A. Rosmarin donated a velvet sheath embroidered with gold for the Torah, while Selij Rubinach gave a set of Bibles. David Brostein donated an oak altar.

Their bourgeois sensibilities extended to charitable causes. Men like Isaac clearly wanted to be remembered after they died. In Sholem Aleichem's "The Man from Buenos Aires," the pimp Motek enumerates a dizzying array of his pressing social responsibilities: "There isn't a thing in the world that doesn't cost me money—synagogues, hospitals, emigrant funds, concerts. Not so long ago I received a letter from a yeshiva in Jerusalem. A handsome letter with a Star of David on top, with seals and signatures of rabbis. The letter was addressed to me personally in very impressive language: 'To our Master, the Renowned and Wealthy Reb Mordecai.'"

Isaac seemed to be accorded the same respect in the shtetls. People knew he was rich, and they treated him with deference. Didn't everyone want something when you were rich? Even the ancient, tubercular rabbi, who always had crumbs in his straggly beard—didn't he look up to him too? Did he ask Isaac for a contribution? A new Torah for the shul? Pencils for the children? Strange the old man didn't seem to remember the dirty street urchin, the way-ward Talmudic scholar who could barely read his Hebrew, the one everyone had given up on when he took off for the slums of Warsaw as a boy.

Despite their line of business, men like Isaac respected their re-ligion and tried as best they could to fulfill its commandments, to live as pious Jews. They were known to be ruthless and nasty in business, but that was strictly business. Everyone was ruthless when he had a business to protect. The traffickers thought noth-ing of selling and reselling human beings, of raping and brutaliz-ing women to force them to submit in the brothels. The women they took from the shtetls must have seemed to them subhuman, nothing more than commodities.

Take Raquel Spertzein, Natalio Zisman's woman. It was only natural that after Zisman died, leaving no assets for Zwi Migdal, Raquel should pay his medical costs and funeral expenses. She was his property, after all, the girl he had taken from a life of hardship and drudgery in the shtetl and set up as a "lady" in Buenos Aires. Raquel would, of course, agree to pay for Zisman's tombstone and the cost of his burial. They were married, after all. Raquel reluc-tantly paid Zisman's expenses, and when she was flat broke, the pimps decided they would resell her to Max Zisman, Natalio's brother and fellow Buenos Aires pimp.

Of course, the same thing happened with poor old Samuel Feder's last woman. On a ship to Buenos Aires after marrying his latest prospect, Esther Jadzikoba, in Odessa in 1906, poor old Feder died quite suddenly in Montevideo as he was preparing to usher Esther through customs. Luckily, there were always other shareholders—the flamboyantly dressed pimps and prostitutes would always help out in an emergency—who would take a young, helpless girl like Esther under their wing. The shareholders sought out Ema the Millionaire, one of the few madams they entrusted with the trafficking business. Ema, who earned her moniker working as a loan shark, set Esther up at a brothel in the provincial town of Rosario. Ema must have taught her well, for after about five years of working in the trenches, Esther opened her own house in Ensenada. She proved so loyal that the shareholders admitted her into the organization.

The pimps often used Esther as a shining example of how women could succeed, take charge of their lives, even in the brothels. If they worked diligently, they could be almost as successful as the men, they said.

It was the other women whom they refused to talk about—the ones they forced to work at La Boca, next to the port of Buenos Aires. These were the "unlucky" girls, the ones who were too unsophisticated or worn down to ever own brothels, or who had tried to defy their pimps when they arrived in Argentina. La Boca may be Spanish for "the mouth," but for the women who worked there it was "the end of the world"—the mouth of hell.

Perhaps the pimps never mentioned these girls because they knew that their suffering gave their men a bad name. In the fashionable parts of the city, they could pose as respectable gentlemen who dined with cabinet ministers and cabaret artists. But anyone visiting La Boca knew that men who forced women to work like this for profit were really rotten to the core. At La Boca, the Jewish women worked in dilapidated clapboard brothels, servicing dozens of men a day. "To see the poor creatures about midnight, when the houses have already been open a considerable time, is a sight never to be forgotten in its sadness and its horror," noted one British visitor.

Similarly, Albert Londres never forgot what he saw at La Boca, and after weeks of living among the pimps and interviewing prostitutes in Buenos Aires, it was the Jewish women, shuttered away in La Boca's filthy brothels, known as *casitas,* who had the most profound effect on him. Each *casita* had an attendant, in most cases "a very old Chinese woman who sits mumbling in a sort of derelict hutch, with a chicken bone and a banana skin on her knees." Her job was to make sure the men lined up outside the little house did not swarm the brothel as they often threatened to do.

"The women who prostitute themselves there burden the air with sadness," wrote Londres, who likened the brothels to factories where a single woman could find herself servicing seventy men a day. At some of the *casitas,* dozens of men, most of them immigrants from all over Europe and the Middle East, waited their turn, "humble, patient, resigned, like a queue of poor people waiting outside a relief office in winter."

LA BOCA MADE THE SHTETL look like paradise, which may explain why Sophia made the fateful decision to leave America.

She begged Madame Nathalia to send her back to Poland. How could she possibly live in a place that was worse than the shtetl? She would not survive here alone, pregnant, working as a prostitute. "I don't have the strength," she protested, sobbing. "I don't have the strength."

To her utter amazement, Madame Nathalia seemed to take pity on her. Chumpaisk even fronted the money to buy her two new undershirts, a new skirt, and three pairs of silk stockings for the journey. Now, clutching her carpetbag, Sophia knew she lacked nothing. On her way to the port of Buenos Aires she caressed the strange gold coin that Madame Nathalia had thrust into her hand as she left the *conventillo.*

Maybe it was for luck.

Perhaps there was the usual rowdy group of prostitutes at the port this time around. Perhaps not. They seemed to function only as a welcoming committee for stray or wayward young women. They were rarely around to wish anyone bon voyage.

Sophia, who was by now seven months pregnant, settled herself as best she could aboard the transatlantic ship. When one of the ship stewards asked to see her ticket, she gladly obliged. She now understood enough Spanish to get by.

"Rio de Janeiro," said the steward, laughing. "You'd better watch out for yellow fever."

She must have given him such a blank stare that he repeated the joke.

"Yellow fever," he said. "The plague. Everyone is dying there."

Surely this was a mistake. Yes, Chumpaisk had said something about a place called Rio de Janeiro. A colleague of his would board the ship at Rio and take the sealed envelope that Chumpaisk had given her. But after the meeting, he had promised her that the boat would sail on to Europe. "No Rio de Janeiro," said Sophia in broken Spanish and Yiddish. "Europa. I'm going to Europa."

"I'm sorry, miss," said the steward, no longer in a joking mood when he noticed how upset he had made his young pregnant passenger. "Your ticket is for Rio de Janeiro."

Sophia nearly fainted from despair, but then she remembered the gold coin—the one that Madame Nathalia had given her. For luck. She needed it now, and somehow through her tears and mustering every Spanish word she could remember, Sophia handed the steward the gold coin and made him understand that she would pay the difference.

Europa. I want to go to Europa.

By now, a group of passengers who had been watching the pathetic scene broke into peals of hysterical laughter. The steward

looked stunned, and perhaps he gently pressed the gold coin back
into Sophia's hand. It was just a twenty-franc piece, he said.
Enough to buy a ticket on a tram in downtown Buenos Aires, not
a ship's passage to a European port. "I'm sorry, miss," said the
steward again. "Your ticket is for Rio de Janeiro."

America?

The steward nodded, and the heavily pregnant young passenger sank wearily back into her seat.

CHAPTER THREE

The Streets
of the Women

The man the pimps called Professor Kneizer was described by police as tall and thin, with "a tubercular aspect." He sported a mustache and goatee, wore gold-rimmed spectacles, and spoke bad Portuguese, heavily accented with Yiddish. But in the underworld of Jewish pimps in Rio de Janeiro, the professor had an important job. How else to explain why he was the constant companion of men like Isaac Boorosky and Sigmund Richer, an Austrian Jew who owned a jewelry store but was best known to police as the kingpin of the Jewish traffickers in the city?

The professor was not a pimp, although he seemed to spend a lot of time with such men. On most days he could be seen at the more fashionable downtown cafés hunched over little cups of sugary coffee, gesturing wildly with his lit cigarette, obviously imparting important counsel to Boorosky and Richer, who seemed to hang on his every word. For the pimps rarely made a move without their professors.

In addition to brothels in Buenos Aires, both Boorosky and Richer also controlled important "holdings" in Rio de Janeiro and traveled frequently between the two cities. Perhaps a leading cartoonist of the day had them in mind when, in an editorial cartoon in a Rio daily, he likened the white-slave trade to a tennis match between Argentina and Brazil.

But this, after all, was the very nature of their global empire; their assets were not confined to one location. They were spread out around the world. For this reason, the professors proved indispensable. They were important underworld consultants—the misery secretaries, who tallied up the earnings of the trade, oversaw the brothels, and arranged for false travel documents, especially for the underaged shtetl girls.

Professor Kneizer also wrote the letters—the ones the girls sent to their families in Russia and Poland, giving them details of a fairy-tale life in Brazil, constructing what for many became their "official" histories. For decades, the professors successfully suppressed the truth, reassuring nervous parents in Eastern Europe and keeping the reputation of the deeply religious shtetl girls officially intact. The pimps also encouraged the writing of fictitious letters because it provided a front for their illicit operations in America.

Professor Kneizer was one of the most prolific writers, although there were others who could do the job just as well. But there was something about Kneizer—the way he put together a sentence, his choice of words. Even the illiterate prostitutes who sought out his services sensed he had a passion for writing when he read aloud from the letters he wrote their parents. On paper, he could transform their wretched lives in the brothels into brilliant success stories. To long-suffering parents in the shtetls of Eastern Europe, he wrote page after page in florid script, detailing the lives of their happily married daughters in America. He constructed scenes of lavish feasts during Rosh Hashanah, made up journeys to the beach, and enumerated the wonders of a tropical paradise, complete with chattering parrots, tamarind monkeys swinging from trees, and smoky mists shrouding the mountain the locals called Corcovado, or "the hunchback."

It didn't matter that in most cases the truth was something quite different, that the happily married women were really working as prostitutes. In fact, many of the victims might be forgiven for not quite understanding how they came to be prostitutes in the first place. This crafty duplicity was the hallmark of men like Isaac Boorosky. How many times had Isaac lied to his victims, telling them that while he was away in Poland, his business partner sold his fashion business and disappeared? Now he owed a huge sum of money that he couldn't possibly pay. What was he to do if he didn't come up with the money? Why, he would surely go to jail, unless, of course, his new wife could be persuaded to make some "sacrifices."

If this kind of gentle persuasion didn't work, Isaac knew of other ways to convince his women. There were the cigarette burns to the skin, the punches and well-aimed kicks. There was rape. But acts of violence could ruin fine silk or Egyptian cotton. Bloodstains were impossible to remove.

Of course, Kneizer's letters contained none of these details. Even in the letters he wrote for the so-called single girls—those who told their parents they were working as seamstresses or chambermaids or shop attendants—he conveyed a sense of comfortable lives in a new country. Most of the letters were accompanied by small packets of money. For the loyal shtetl girls, they were small gestures to help alleviate the poverty of their families in Europe, as well as a concrete demonstration of just how well they were doing in America.

From what was left of their earnings, the prostitutes paid a small fee to Kneizer and the other professors to write their letters, then another fee for them to read the letters that they received from home.

In the tightly managed universe of the brothel, everything had a price, and the prostitutes paid for everything. They were responsible for their food, clothing, and medical expenses. The pimps trapped them in debt, in most cases forcing the women to hand over most of their initial earnings to reimburse them for the cost of their trip to America.

In Rio de Janeiro, the network of brothels operated by the Eastern European pimps was extremely well organized. In addition to the professors, pimps like Isaac Boorosky and Sigmund Richer pooled their resources to employ an army of cooks, madams, lawyers, and others whose sole purpose was to ensure that their brothels operated without mishap.

The first station in this assembly line of commercial vice was the "house of instruction" for newly arrived women and girls to learn the trade. These were operated by madams who were often married to high-ranking underworld figures, and were scattered throughout the down-at-heels red-light district in downtown Rio. Once a new recruit arrived in the city she would remain in a house of instruction for up to two weeks. However, there was often little in the way of "instruction" involved. Women were usually beaten and raped until they seemed to consent to work as prostitutes. Later they were taken to "work at the window," a euphemism for soliciting men. After the afternoon heat, the women leaned out the windows of brothels, "a rose in their hair, another in their hand, smiling at the young men who passed by."

Klara Hohn, a nineteen-year-old Jewish girl from Austria, was sent to one of these "houses of instruction" in the 1880s. On the ship to Rio de Janeiro, Klara had been promised a job by Anna Scheler, a madam, who told her she owned a boutique in the city. Klara was on her way to Brazil with a friend in order to seek what she later told police was "honest work." Her father, who had heard rumors that there was fabulous wealth to be made in Brazil, had bought his daughter a passage on a boat to South America, where he sent her to seek her fortune. Klara must have thought that the meeting with Scheler was part of that good fortune. But once she arrived in the city, Scheler confessed that there were no openings at the boutique, and that Klara would have to do another kind of work. Scheler bought her "a cheap pink dress, six slips, six pairs of stockings and a pair of cheap coral earrings" and told her to stand at an upstairs window to "receive" the men. After a few days, Klara was saved when a sailor she had befriended on the ship made his way to the red-light district, recognized her at the window of the dingy, run-down brothel, and immediately told police.

From the streets, the brothels smelled of lavender or rose water, even though most were miserable affairs in decaying clapboard row houses near the port. Inside, the houses, once respectable single family dwellings, had been converted into "a labyrinth of rooms" made out of cheap, flimsy wood. One reporter described them as "a mess of primitive construction."

The "food houses" that catered to the brothel workers were just as shabby. In Rio in the 1890s there were three such clandestine kitchens, set up like army mess halls, where the prostitutes took their meals, or where meals were prepared and then delivered to their respective brothels. In one of these "food houses," tucked into the dark rooms of a colonial row house, the dining table was little more than "a huge, dirty pine board suspended on two stands." The rest of the room was given over to two large shelves "covered in dust, bits of left-over bread, dead flies and greasy plates." The cook, an aging black man, would stuff the food into small tin containers that would be delivered to the women.

The elaborate infrastructure ensured that the women trafficked from Eastern Europe could function as important cogs in what were highly efficient enterprises of exploitation. Women who refused to comply or dared to denounce their pimps to the police were often the victims of savage treatment. Some were physically abused. Others were killed.

Rosa Schwarz, a well-known Jewish prostitute known as "Lili of the Jewels," was found dead in 1910. She was beautiful, spoke several languages, and was particularly fond of jewelry. Her delicate neck always seemed to be swathed in long strands of pearls and gold, and at first police thought robbery was the motive for her murder. Later, a Rio newspaper reported that she was the victim of a ring of pimps whom she had threatened to denounce.

But for many Eastern European prostitutes there seemed to exist a fate worse than physical abuse and death, and it was readily administered by the professors when women dared to challenge the pimps. For although Professor Kneizer wrote sunny letters about life in Rio de Janeiro, he displayed his greatest talents when he penned his darker missives—the ones about wayward girls who had lost their virtue in the tropics. Nothing was worse for a shtetl family than to receive a letter denouncing their daughter as a whore. Young Jewish women, for whom sexual purity was so important, knew that such a denunciation would bring terrible shame to their families and would isolate them forever in their religious communities.

Klara Adam, who denounced Sigmund Richer, the king of the underworld, quickly learned about this kind of retribution. The letter that was sent to her family in Poland was signed by Richer, a man the family thought to be a wealthy factory owner who had given their daughter a job as a seamstress in Brazil. "Your daughter lived quite respectably in my house, working honorably and honestly for her money," the letter began. "But she quickly lost her head, and fell in love with a Negro, and fled with him."

Of course the truth was much more complicated. Klara had met Richer and his wife, Leonor Jacobowitz, in Poland, and the couple had promised her a job as a seamstress in Brazil. Richer raped Klara on the journey to Rio de Janeiro, then forced her to work as a prostitute in the city. According to Klara's testimony to police, he rotated her through several brothels and stole all of her earnings. "One night after I could no longer work, he abused me so much that I decided to flee," said Klara in her testimony to police. "And that's how I left, at four in the morning, wearing a slip and wrapped in a sheet because the wretch used to keep my clothes locked up at night to prevent me from fleeing the brothel."

Although Richer had repeatedly warned Klara that he could land her in jail for the rest of her life if she tried to complain about him to police, she decided to go to the authorities anyway. She told the police what they probably already knew—that Richer had various aliases and false documents, that he didn't earn his living from the jewelry business but kept several brothels in Buenos Aires and Brazil, and that his wife, Leonor, also worked as a prostitute in a Rio brothel. Klara also told them that Richer had another wife, a woman named Vera Zalicoff, working in one of his brothels in Buenos Aires.

In the end, Klara's lengthy testimony did nothing to put an end to Richer's empire. He simply summoned the team of lawyers and police who were on his payroll, and Klara's testimony seemed to evaporate.

It's not clear what happened to Klara—whether she stayed in Rio de Janeiro or managed to return to the shtetl. However, after

Professor Kneizer's damning letter, Klara might have found it difficult to explain the truth to her family.

"When I found Klara my poor heart was broken," continued the letter that was sent to her parents in Poland. "But ever the gentleman I offered her a first-class ticket back home to her family. She refused and is currently living very happily with the Negro."

The letter, penned in Professor Kneizer's florid hand and signed "respectfully yours Sigmund Richer," ends with one of the professor's masterful laments: "I'm afraid your daughter is lost forever. She's a woman who belongs to everybody now."

THERE MUST HAVE BEEN times in her life when Sophia Chamys felt "lost forever," but on the voyage from Buenos Aires to Rio de Janeiro, she wasn't thinking about prostitution. Instead, she was obsessed about something she felt was far worse—the yellow-fever epidemic that gripped Rio de Janeiro.

She imagined widespread panic, respectable citizens dropping dead on crowded downtown streets, authorities piling the cadavers on the sidewalks because there was no longer any space in the morgues. She had convinced herself that she would meet a swift end as soon as she stepped off the ship. Which is probably why she had to be pushed off the boat by the steward—the one who had sown the fear of death in her in the first place with his dark jokes about the plague.

Trembling, Sophia clutched her battered carpetbag and walked down the stairs to the port with tremendous effort. Despite the scorching tropical heat, she recalled feeling cold—no doubt chilled by the prospect of instant death. Through hand gestures and the bits of Spanish she already knew, Sophia learned from her fellow passengers on the ship that "the fever" was transmitted by mosquitoes. How could she possibly guard against mosquitoes? Surely she would die as soon as she left the boat.

Her fears may have been partly justified. In the early 1890s, several yellow-fever epidemics ravaged the city of 250,000 people, resulting in thousands of deaths. The virus struck Rio's most impoverished residents first. Most of them lived next to open sewers, their stagnant water a favorite breeding ground for the *Aedes aegypti* mosquitoes, the prime carriers of the yellow-fever virus. The fever, whose symptoms included violent chills and vomiting, eventually worked its way into the kidneys and the liver. Victims in the final stages became jaundiced, their skin and eyes taking on a sickly yellow pallor before they died.

What would Sophia do if she was struck with yellow fever? Who would she turn to? What would happen to her baby? These difficult questions must have been quickly forgotten, for when she finally gathered the courage to look around her for the first time, she was pleasantly surprised by what she saw.

Her description of her arrival in Rio de Janeiro later amused the police officer who took her testimony. There were "men laughing, happy children eating candy, dogs chasing balls," and generally "great animation" at the port of Rio de Janeiro, Sophia said. "People weren't dying on the streets," she recalled years after her arrival. "The fever hadn't destroyed the city. I thought it was a terrible plague and I would find dead bodies on the streets. The other passengers told me such wild things!"

Perhaps she was also reassured by the natural beauty of her new surroundings. She could not have failed to notice the lush landscape, the verdant mountains that seemed to jut out of the sea, the radiance of the tropical sun as it warmed her face and sparkled on the blue-green waters of Guanabara Bay.

And she would have seen the street vendors who sat behind

rickety wooden tables piled with pyramids of oranges. An orange a day, that's what they had said in the shtetl. Rio de Janeiro must surely be the paradise they had spoken about.

Could this finally be America?

Confident that her luck was about to change, Sophia stepped boldly into the crowd and approached various passersby until she found someone who could read the address on the envelope that Chumpaisk had given her in Buenos Aires. The address, on Seventh of September Street, which commemorated the day in 1822 when Brazil achieved its independence from Portugal—was just around the corner from the port. Sophia didn't have far to walk, and it was with a mixture of hope and excitement that she knocked on the door of number 165.

Sophia's heart sank as soon as she saw the woman who answered the door. There was something about her that she immediately didn't trust. Perhaps it was the exaggeratedly painted red lips, the resigned expression, the cheap camisole that clung to her body, drenched in sweat. Or maybe it was the strong scent of rose water. The house, airless in the midday heat, with myriad wooden partitions, seemed all too familiar. It didn't take her long to figure out that Chumpaisk had betrayed her; this was just another brothel.

Overcome with despair, Sophia fell on her knees and began to sob. The woman who opened the door—the madam—ignored her, but the other women who worked in the house came running from their tiny rooms to see what was going on. The prostitutes seemed so moved by Sophia's story that they resolved to pool their resources to buy her a passage to a European port on the next ship sailing from Rio de Janeiro. Then she could travel by land to Poland and join her family.

Their generosity was overwhelming, but through her tears

Sophia immediately refused the offer. "I can't accept money from you because you are as miserable as I am," she told them. "I have already spent time in brothels, and I am going to do the same thing here. When I get enough money together, I'll go home."

It's not clear why Sophia felt she could make such a statement. After all, women in her position rarely had any choices. Most lived as virtual slaves, with most of their earnings earmarked for the brothel and to pay back the expenses they incurred. Perhaps Sophia still felt she was different from the other prostitutes, clinging to the illusion that the elegant businessman Isaac Boorosky was her legitimate husband. Or perhaps the reality was such that few pimps or madams wanted anything to do with a pregnant prostitute. Let her go wherever she wants to go, they might have said to one another. After the baby, she'll be back.

Sophia thought she had made all the money she needed after her first day in Rio. That night her second client, a well-dressed young man who arrived in the early evening, told her that he just wanted to sleep. The next morning he woke at dawn and pressed a gold coin into her hand. Sophia didn't recognize the currency, but when she saw the number 500 on the coin she fell to her knees and kissed the generous stranger's hands and feet. Then, throwing a shawl around her bare shoulders, she ran through the brothel, knocking on all the doors and screaming in her strange mixture of Yiddish and Spanish: "I have the money! I have the money! Find out when the ship is sailing. I want to buy a ticket to go home!"

But when the bleary-eyed prostitutes took one look at the five-hundred-reis coin, they fell over one another laughing. Five hundred reis was barely enough to buy a bunch of bananas, they told her. You need a lot more money to buy passage on a ship sailing to Europe, they said.

Dejected, Sophia returned to her room. Now more than ever,

she was determined to make the money she needed to return to Poland, no matter what it took. Let every man come. She would just shut her eyes and let them have their way with her. But how would she block out the scent of stale sweat, the sickly sweet aroma of sugarcane alcohol, the *cachaça* that seemed to envelop the rough, unshaven sailors and the drunken accountants and the office boys who made their way to her little room? Would she think of her husband, Isaac, when she felt other, rougher hands on her breasts, or prying open her legs? None of it mattered anymore. Let them come and leave their money. Sophia was finally going home.

IN THE EARLY 1890s, when Sophia Chamys arrived in Rio de Janeiro, Jewish women from Eastern Europe were considered the working-class prostitutes, their services sought after by sailors, small businessmen, and the legions of lonely immigrant men who began to arrive en masse from Europe.

White slavers from Europe gravitated to fin de siècle Rio de Janeiro, where they blended in easily with the new immigrants, and where, after arriving to evade authorities in Buenos Aires, they quickly realized the potential of the market for commercialized vice in what was then a rapidly industrializing city.

Rio's red-light district was then dominated by former black slaves who had only recently gained their freedom when slavery was abolished in the country in 1888. After abolition many desperate young black women turned to prostitution, although there were already dozens of their counterparts who had spent years toiling as sex slaves in the portside brothels. Ana Valentina da Silva, a fifty-something black woman known in the underworld as Barbuda, or the Bearded One, dominated the so-called slave brothels. A roly-poly matron who sported a beard and mustache,

Barbuda specialized in exploiting "beautiful, young black slaves" whom she had bought in the years before abolition. She had a brutal reputation among her charges, imposing "barbarous punishments" on women who refused to cooperate.

Although it was illegal to force female slaves or any other women into prostitution, the practice was quite brazen in Rio de Janeiro, where slave owners openly bought ads in the local newspapers extolling the amorous abilities of their female slaves: "For sale, a beautiful Negress, experienced in giving affection, with some education," noted one ad in the years just before abolition. Another ad offered "a very beautiful Negress as a present, knows how to sew and take care of children, with whom she is very attentive."

But while black slaves were the mainstay of Rio's red-light neighborhoods, the influx of new immigrants and the rapidly growing wealth of the white elite created a huge demand for foreign-born prostitutes.

The popularity of foreign prostitutes in Brazil was not new. The country already had a long history of importing prostitutes from Europe. Curiously, it was the Jesuits who had demanded that the Portuguese crown send the first boatload of foreign prostitutes to Brazil, in the sixteenth century. Manuel de Nóbrega, head of the Jesuit mission in Brazil, wrote the Portuguese king, imploring him to send prostitutes from Lisbon for the white colonists, who had apparently tired of the native women and were on the verge of insurrection throughout Brazil. "It would seem to me convenient, Your Highness, to send women who have little chance of marriage and who have erred to these parts, because here all of them will find husbands," wrote Nóbrega.

Over the centuries, prostitutes would be rounded up from other parts of Europe, principally the Portuguese islands of

Madeira and the Azores. By the 1890s, they were being plucked from the streets of Paris, but the most plentiful supply came from the shtetls of Eastern Europe.

Among the elite, French women were the most sought-after prostitutes in Rio de Janeiro. They were the favorites of cabinet ministers, politicians, and captains of industry, whose cultural and intellectual pursuits at the time were heavily influenced by French trends. In Rio, still considered very much a provincial outpost, having a *francesa* as a mistress added to the prestige of the men who formed the new aristocracy of coffee barons, politicians, and landowners. The French prostitutes were considered exotic. "But it wasn't because they held out the promise of sex with a white woman," noted one historian. "What was considered a great triumph was sex with a woman who had French cachet."

After 1894 the *cocottes,* as they became known in Rio, gravitated to the newly inaugurated Confeiteria Colombo, which they managed to turn into the city's most exclusive restaurant and meeting place. While it couldn't be called a brothel (there were no private rooms for trysts), the Colombo quickly became more than a restaurant and tearoom for the Brazilian elite. During the day, the Colombo hosted wealthy Brazilian ladies in white gloves who sipped English tea and wiped their mouths with dainty, embroidered linen napkins after taking delicate mouthfuls of flaky custard tarts. At night the Colombo's spectacular salons, adorned with Belgian mirrors and Italian-marble counters trimmed in dark jacaranda wood, became the meeting place of Rio intellectuals, newly minted coffee barons, and their *cocottes*. Every night after the theaters closed the French prostitutes headed to the Colombo, where they would appear "in a halo of importance and perfume." The *cocottes* would join their illustrious dates, many of them overfed older gentlemen in dark suits and monocles, and their "giggles would overflow, like the champagne they drank in crystal glasses."

The Jewish prostitutes were allowed entry to places like the Colombo only if they passed for French, which a lot of them did in order to improve their position in the hierarchy of sex workers in the city. But while French prostitutes could amass huge fortunes, wore expensive clothes, drank champagne, and were the confidantes of some of Brazil's most important leaders, their Eastern European counterparts, the *polacas,* lived in virtual bondage and squalor.

Still, the Jewish prostitutes, many of whom had white skin, blond hair, and blue eyes, were considered exotic because "they represented distant, imaginary regions in a country where the majority of prostitutes were still made up of black slaves."

As in Buenos Aires, Eastern European prostitutes were largely relegated to the port area and soon congregated in the bars and brothels clustered in colonial row houses near the urban canal known as the Mangue or "the swamp," so called because in the summer months the canal became a stagnant "focus of mosquitoes and putrid smells." The women worked out of "little houses, the residences of the poor who only survive because they are stubborn," wrote a Brazilian poet. "It was a miserable form of prostitution, humiliating and sad." One social worker, who worked among the Jewish prostitutes at the turn of the last century, described the area as "the worst part of the city, with poorly constructed houses with little electric light, poorly ventilated and nearly in ruins."

In the Mangue, a place one writer described as "the streets of the women," most of the impoverished Eastern European prostitutes dressed in nothing more than cheap lingerie and stood in front of the open windows of brothels in the sweltering afternoons and evenings to lure prospective clients. "In illuminated stores, there are women exhibited in the vitrines," wrote an Austrian writer on a visit to Rio. "Jewish women from Eastern Europe promise the most exciting perversities. . . . I saw almost five hundred women, among them young and old. Some of them appear indolent, others try to attract clients by dancing. Others, with a tired look in their eyes, seem totally indifferent."

Although there were Eastern European prostitutes in other parts of the city, where some of them even shared brothels with their more successful French counterparts, most were driven into the Mangue after 1870 following a spate of tawdry media stories and numerous complaints from "respectable" families who lived downtown and complained about them to police.

For the municipal authorities, "the principal objective was to maintain the prostitutes far away from the tram lines and commercial centers and away from the reach of respectable citizens." At the time, the police were simply acting in response "to the huge pressure generated by sensationalistic media campaigns and by medical and juridical authorities whose principal objective was to protect the 'honest families' and the international reputation of Rio de Janeiro." The Jewish prostitutes were considered the biggest problem—"an incessant danger to public health, and a threat to decent family values." In fact, the city's most important health officials in the 1890s blamed the Jewish prostitutes for "a serious lapse of morality," noting that these women had "few sentiments of modesty and self-esteem." According to the city's report on prostitution in the 1880s, "In general, the agents of evil come from outside our country. They are the foam of the putrid fermentation of the great cities of the Old World that has landed on our beaches."

In 1880, about a decade before Isaac Boorosky began to do busi-

ness in the city, more than seven hundred local merchants and industrialists signed a petition demanding that the authorities begin
legal proceedings against the Jewish pimps. It was a fit of anti-
Semitic hysteria, stoked by leading politicians and journalists to
blame the evils of local prostitution on the Jews. Some twenty-five
Jewish pimps were ordered deported. Many others were kicked
out of the city's Masonic orders.

But this anti-Semitic hysteria did not last. The deportations
and expulsions of the pimps proved little more than political
grandstanding. With the aid of their army of professors and
highly paid Brazilian lawyers, all of the pimps eventually fought
the deportation orders and most were readmitted into the secret
orders. The traffic of Eastern European sex slaves into the country
continued without interruption.

IN HIGH SUMMER, the mosquitoes swarmed at dawn and returned at dusk just as Sophia and the other prostitutes prepared to
take their posts at the windows, overlooking the still, dark waters
of the Mangue. Sophia was convinced that these were the yellow-
fever mosquitoes. After two weeks working the open windows at
dusk, her arms and legs bare, Sophia must have been covered in
inflamed red bites.

Would she die of yellow fever? Surprisingly, she seemed not to
care. Eight months pregnant, Sophia looked so bloated she could
barely bend down, and she was even more determined to return to
her home in Poland. She worked diligently and without complaint in order to make the money she needed for her voyage.

After about two weeks, the prostitutes took her to the ship's office, where she paid fourteen pounds sterling for a third-class pas-

sage to Hamburg on the S.S. *Weiser*. Not much is known about her journey on the ship, but soon after arriving at the port of Hamburg Sophia was rushed to a hospital, where, after several days, she gave birth to a baby girl. She was convinced her baby was Isaac Boorosky's child.

Sophia spent a month convalescing at the home of a local rabbi, who was summoned by the hospital staff after Sophia told them she had no family in the city.

It is not known whether the rabbi questioned why such a young mother was on her own in the world. Perhaps he attempted to find out about her hardships. Or he might just have given her the train fare to Warsaw, where she could be reunited with her family. The details are sketchy, but somehow Sophia and her daughter returned to Warsaw, where she asked in the Jewish ghetto if anyone knew the whereabouts of her family, who had moved since she sailed to Argentina.

Sophia's mother and sister went into a state of shock when they saw her enter the house with a newborn in her arms. A few days earlier Sophia's mother had lamented the fact that her eldest daughter was so far away. Her younger daughter, who lay sick with tuberculosis on the family bed, had calmly told her mother not to worry. "Don't cry, Mother," she'd said. "Sophia is on her way to see us. I can feel it. I know she is on her way, and soon we will all have the pleasure of hugging her."

Sophia's father also seemed to go into shock when he saw his daughter and new granddaughter. Perhaps he was overwhelmed with happiness. Still, there was something about his daughter that didn't seem quite right to him. Could he sense her sadness? Did he have any idea of how much she had suffered?

Sophia had never said a word to her family about her life as a prostitute in America. But the old man must have had his doubts. Perhaps that queasiness at the pit of his stomach, the feeling that had overwhelmed him during the negotiations with Boorosky in Castle Square, had returned. Perhaps in an effort to compensate for his lack of resolve a year earlier, Sophia's father demanded that she return to the shtetl, where the family could help her raise the child.

Sophia refused, and attempted to reassure her father that she was happily married to Isaac and was on her way to join him and introduce him to the new baby girl.

A few days after the emotional reunion with her family, Sophia left for Lodz and knocked at the door of the spacious apartment where she had first been employed. Isaac's mother answered the door and immediately recognized Sophia. She told her that Isaac had left for Africa, where he was attending to business, but that she would be pleased to look after the new baby while Sophia returned to work.

Sophia knew by the tone of her voice what kind of work she had in mind. But she didn't refuse. She meekly handed over her baby daughter to Isaac's mother, believing perhaps that the old woman would take good care of her new granddaughter. Sophia returned to the brothel, the one that had first seemed to her like a large hotel, where women were constantly coming and going.

After several weeks, Isaac returned from his journey to Africa and seemed genuinely pleased to be reunited with his wife. But as he began to make plans to return to Buenos Aires, Sophia's father arrived in Lodz, determined to bring his daughter and granddaughter back to the shtetl.

This time Isaac did not behave like the solicitous gentleman Sophia's father remembered. He ordered him out of his apartment, accusing him of wanting to return his daughter to the poverty of the shtetl so that she would end up like her younger sister, emaciated from consumption and near death.

Sophia's father was in tears as he began his long trek to the shtetl. Did he know he would never see his daughter again? Did he know his granddaughter had already died? Isaac never made it clear how the newborn perished. Perhaps Isaac's mother had taken the child to an overcrowded orphanage whose staff could barely cope with the dozens of abandoned children already under their care. In a place where many Jewish children did not survive to their first birthdays, the death of a baby girl was hardly a noteworthy event in Poland in the 1890s.

For her part, Sophia seemed more anxious about her husband than about the fate of her daughter, or at least that's how she conveyed the situation to police years later.

After Sophia had worked more than a year at various brothels in Lodz, Isaac told her that he was returning to Buenos Aires and taking her with him. Somehow he managed to convince her that they would finally live together as man and wife. But before this could happen, he needed to make the trip to Argentina alone, in order to deliver four of his latest recruits from the shtetl.

Sophia left for Buenos Aires a day after her husband, the man she still called her "protector." This time there was no illusion about what her arrival in America would be like. She knew she was destined for another brothel, but perhaps this time around Isaac would stay with her and take care of her as he always promised.

The next few years seemed a blur to Sophia as she related the comings and goings of her husband, who returned to Europe several times in order to recruit more women for his brothels in

Buenos Aires and Rio de Janeiro. On one of his return trips to Buenos Aires, Isaac arrived with another young woman he called his wife.

For Sophia it was the last straw. Overcome with jealousy and rage, she told Isaac she would work for him for another three months, but after that she wanted her freedom. He refused, which is when Sophia fled, returning to her old brothel on Seventh of September Street in Rio de Janeiro, where the prostitutes had once shown her such kindness.

Isaac had dealt with women like this before. They were all alike, after all. She would come back when she needed him. They always did. She couldn't go far.

BUT THEN AGAIN, what if she didn't return? Isaac Boorosky decided he needed to teach Sophia a lesson. A week later he arrived in Rio to fetch her. Perhaps he burst into her airless little room when she was with a client, and seeing her naked with another man was simply too much for him.

Was this lust or rage or a mixture of both that he felt? What crossed his mind as he grabbed Sophia by the hair, which he violently hacked off with his jackknife? He would teach her a lesson now, scarring her so badly that men would only look at her in pity.

Where were the kind prostitutes now? Perhaps they knew better than to interfere in what for many would simply have been characterized as a "domestic dispute" between a pimp and his "wife." Sophia, after all, was Isaac's property, and Isaac could dispose of his property at will.

Perhaps Isaac finally managed to calm himself down when he noticed pieces of black hair sticking to the sleeves of the white, broadcloth suit that his Spanish tailor on the very fashionable Rua do Ouvidor had just finished for him. Maybe it was the blood on his silk shirt cuff. Was that spittle on his black patent-leather shoes? *Damn these shtetl girls! Damn these stupid kurves!*

If he felt any remorse, he probably didn't show it. He brushed the hairs off his suit as best he could, smoothed back his shiny black hair, and turned to leave, his footsteps echoing loudly on the cheap wooden floorboards of the silent brothel.

IN THE EARLY 1900S, many impoverished Jews who immigrated to Rio de Janeiro settled in the Mangue neighborhood and found themselves living next-door to the brothels that exploited Jewish prostitutes. Did they ever hear the screams? Surely they were audible through the flimsy partitions that separated the dilapidated row houses in the Mangue.

Did they ever rush to help their fellow Jews?

"Sometimes we heard them, yes," said Freda Nagelsmander, who lived on one of the "streets of the women" with her Polish immigrant parents. "But we never associated with them. My father said that the prostitutes were a disgrace. They stood at their windows, wearing nothing but slips. We tried very hard never to go near them, never to look at them."

Fanny Futritsk, a Jewish immigrant from the town of Kracme, near Lublin, recalled that her mother forced her to cross the street immediately if they found themselves in the path of a Jewish prostitute. "The women from the Mangue always looked at us, tried to start up a conversation in Yiddish," she said. "But we were always told to ignore them, to look away."

In fact, respectable Jews like the Nagelsmander and Futritsk families did everything they could to leave the Mangue with "the greatest urgency," to settle in working-class neighborhoods far from the city center and far from the Jewish prostitutes. For ordinary Jewish immigrants the prostitutes were an embarrassment and "a black mark on the Jewish people," no better than "human garbage." As in Buenos Aires, the Jewish pimps and prostitutes were scrupulously barred from the community's religious institutions, cemeteries, and even cultural events.

Often huge fights erupted outside the Yiddish theaters in downtown Rio as Jewish community leaders chased away the pimps and prostitutes who wanted to attend the shows. Signs in front of the box office proclaimed ENTRANCE FORBIDDEN TO THE UNCLEAN ONES. So embarrassed were they by the presence of "the unclean ones" that the leaders of the Jewish community even set up a Community Defense Committee, a group of burly Jewish youths whose sole purpose was to prevent the pimps and prostitutes from entering the Yiddish theater. "During the nightly shows or the matinees, the white slavers and the prostitutes stood in front of the box office to buy tickets, by force if necessary," noted a witness to the numerous skirmishes in front of the theater. "Many times there were fights and the police were called in to prohibit their entry. It was never easy to explain to the police why these people were not allowed in the theater."

It can only be guessed how women like Sophia Chamys felt when they were treated with such scorn by their fellow Jews. And it's unlikely that they tried to appeal to them, to explain the sad circumstances under which they had been forced to work as prostitutes in America, even though surely it was a mitzvah to help a fellow Jew in distress.

But the truth is that nobody wanted to help the prostitutes, many of whom must have identified with Rosa, one of the most controversial characters in Yiddish theater, a Polish Jewish prostitute who finds herself working in a Rio brothel. The failed rehabilitation of Rosa is the main theme in Leib Malach's play *Ibergus* or "Remolding," which for the first time dramatized the battle between the "decent" Jews and the "unclean ones."

Rosa wants to leave the brothel she works in but realizes that she is doomed to life as an outcast because the decent Jewish community will never accept her. "When I go to a dance with the Brazilians, I'm treated with respect," she says. "But the Jews turn their heads away. I am not good enough for them and their honorable wives."

At one point Rosa laments that the Jewish prostitutes are so hated that they are even denied burial in the Jewish cemetery: "Their flesh and their entrails rot, thrown away in the trash. What sister was buried as a human being?"

In fin de siècle Rio de Janeiro, none of the Jewish prostitutes were buried as human beings, which was why death haunted them. When women like Sophia Chamys saw so many prostitutes dying in the yellow-fever epidemics that swept through the Mangue neighborhood, they must have panicked. Many lived in constant fear that they would die alone "in a foreign country abandoned in a hospital or the room of a brothel." They were also terrified by the fact that "there was no one to perform the Jewish ritual ceremonies in their hour of need, when they succumbed to the fever."

At the beginning many did die like that—destitute in public hospitals, buried in Catholic cemeteries run by the city. Still, at the hour of death even the most brutal of pimps allowed some form of Jewish ritual to take place, even if it was improvised by them, without the presence of a rabbi.

Olga, a Jewish prostitute who worked in the Mangue, succumbed to yellow fever in the 1890s. When she died, word spread quickly through the downtown red-light district, and dozens of prostitutes and pimps gathered by her bedside to pay their last respects. The pimps managed to form a minyan, a group of ten Jewish men that must be present in order to have a quorum for a prayer service. The prostitutes took turns washing the cadaver and wrapping it in a white sheet. Others tore at their clothes in mourning and confessed their wrongdoings to the dead woman.

"Olga, I have come to beg forgiveness!" wailed a prostitute in Yiddish. "I was the one who caused all the problems with Sarah. Forgive me, Olga, you were right. Please believe that I have repented."

"Olga! I have come to ask you to remember me to Joseph Salomon," cried a plump red-haired prostitute. "Tell him that my heart is still with him, and to save his heart for me!"

After the prayers, Olga's body was transferred to a cheap coffin and handed over to municipal authorities, who buried her with other indigents and black slaves in a public cemetery.

German Kaminer, a Jewish pimp from Odessa, attended most of the small ceremonies that passed for the prostitutes' funerals. A fleshy man with a receding hairline, German, carried out an important function. It was his job to make sure that any assets the prostitutes left would remain with the pimps. Those who died without a will had their assets seized by the Brazilian government. German, known in the Rio underworld as Griska, would force dying women to sign a last will and testament appointing him the sole beneficiary. If the women left any children behind, it was German's responsibility to make sure they were looked after, although it is not clear how this was done. Perhaps German, a busy man who managed women and brothels of his own, simply took the children to a local orphanage, or found them homes with other prostitutes.

However, in some instances the prostitutes took charge, and even men like German were not allowed to interfere. Max Muller, a Russian glassmaker who had immigrated first to Liverpool, worked as a cantor for the Jewish pimps and prostitutes and ended up officiating at many of their funerals, especially during the yellow-fever epidemics of 1896. In March of that year, as he lay dying of yellow fever, he pleaded with the prostitutes to somehow arrange for his three young children to return to Liverpool, where he had relatives who could look after them. Muller's wife had died of the same virus several weeks earlier, and Muller, who had recently arrived in the city, knew nobody else.

When he died, Sally Goldstein, a local madam, took charge of the two youngest children—Rosa, aged eight, and Moyses, five—guiding them through the ritual mourning process, buying them black funeral garments, and organizing a minyan to say Kaddish for Muller. Another prostitute took in twelve-year-old Adelia. Goldstein then collected donations from the community of pimps and prostitutes and bought three first-class passages for the children to return to England.

On April 2, 1896, at one o'clock in the afternoon, Moyses and his sister Rosa held on tight to Sally Goldstein as they arrived at the Rio port. Adelia, dressed in black, was waiting for them. When they boarded the *Orissa*, the same ship on which they had sailed from Liverpool to Rio only three months before, the ship's captain took one look at the three sad children dressed in mourning and immediately understood what had happened to their parents. He assured the pimps and prostitutes who accompanied the children that he would do everything to protect them on the ship.

Even the anti-Semitic authorities were moved by Muller's story and what they saw as the "generous act" of Sally Goldstein. The story made headlines in papers throughout the city, serving as an example that even criminals could behave decently, and that "the heart and human soul cannot be completely corrupted."

BUT WHEN IT CAME to business, men like Isaac Boorosky had no heart and no soul.

After he beat her, Isaac forced Sophia to return to Buenos Aires, where he kept her locked up in a *conventillo*. He hired one of his young ruffians to procure the most miserable clients for her. Even with Sophia in this state, without her beautiful long raven hair, her body marked by dark bruises and scars, Isaac was determined not to lose any revenue.

The next time Sophia escaped, Isaac initially had no more interest in looking for her. Perhaps it was because she had made a point of leaving 350 pounds sterling, which represented her earnings. It's not clear why Sophia left Isaac the money, but perhaps this was her way of buying her own freedom.

Isaac clearly had other things on his mind. It was May 1895, and he was heading to Poland with his new wife in search of more shtetl girls for his brothels. On his return to Brazil, a few months later, his wife died of yellow fever. For a man who had spent his professional career buying and selling women, treating them like cattle, Isaac seemed rather forlorn after the death of his wife. Maybe that's why he made a special search for Sophia in Rio.

When he found the brothel where she worked, he broke into her room, ripped open her drawers, and raided her closet. He found nothing of value, so he gathered all of her petticoats and camisoles to distribute to his other prostitutes, three of whom had just arrived in the city from the shtetls.

For a long time Sophia stood at the door, watching her husband ransack everything she owned. Had she really loved him once, this beast in a dark tailored suit? Did she love him still? How could she have loved a man who had betrayed her and her family at every turn, who had forced other men on his wife for profit? A man who had never thought to ask her about their child, the little girl he never saw. At that moment, perhaps Sophia came to a deep understanding of everything that had happened to her over the last few years. Isaac was not a good man. What did the prostitutes in Poland call him? *A ruffian.* Yes, Isaac was a ruffian, a beast without a heart, without a soul.

Perhaps the composure and confidence with which she walked the few blocks to the Fourth Precinct police station surprised her. In Yiddish-accented Portuguese, she calmly told the officer on duty that she wanted to file a complaint against her husband.

Husband? The police officer must have looked up at her with some surprise, but then again, maybe he was used to such complaints from these women, the *polacas,* who lived in the dilapidated brothels near the Mangue. There had been so many other complaints, so many other young women who had married these degenerate pimps and found themselves locked in a brothel and unable to return to their homes in Europe. The officers had surely heard other pathetic stories of these young, ignorant "wives" who were forced to work as slaves in the Mangue.

As she sat in the hard-backed wooden chair, Sophia must have thought back to her only other experience with the authorities in South America, when Madame Nathalia had taken her to see the police in Buenos Aires. What had they said to her then? That she needed to obey her husband. If he insisted that she work as a prostitute, well then, she had no other choice.

What would the police say to her now?

A few hours later, two officers escorted Isaac into the police station. His suit was rumpled, his shoes scuffed. But other than that, he looked much as he always did: beef-fed, prosperous, smug. "Everyone knows she's crazy," Isaac told the officers, whom he seemed to know by name. "You can't pay any attention to what she's telling you. She doesn't know what she's saying. She needs to go to a crazy hospital. She's sick in her head."

Is she your wife?

Did he pause before he answered that question? Did he look at Sophia one last time?

If he did, there was no tenderness left in his glance. It was hard, cold, and brutal. "I told her I wanted nothing to do with her anymore," he told the police. "She was my lover once. But I told her I wanted nothing to do with her anymore. Not until she straightens out. Not until her head gets better."

She was my lover once.

So this was all it was, just a lovers' quarrel, another domestic dispute that the police could file away. Perhaps Isaac had used this excuse before. Had his other women denounced him to the authorities? If they had, he was unperturbed. This was a man who was used to getting his way, especially with the authorities.

Sophia sat in silence. Could she really have been so naïve? She had been warned, but she had ignored all the warnings. Once she had truly believed in Isaac, her husband, her protector. But this was the way the pimps made their fortunes. They took advantage of girls who were young and naïve.

Several years ago, in Warsaw, Isaac Boorosky had preyed on a little girl who had felt the heat of his gaze and was flushed with excitement, or fear. Now the little girl seemed so much older as she sat bolt upright in a dingy police station in this strange and cruel land she called America. The memory of that distant meeting in that faraway country where she was born must have seemed like a fairy tale, a page from someone else's life.

For anyone who knew Sophia at thirteen would hardly recognize this emaciated figure wrapped in a shawl in the heat of a tropical summer. There were scars all over her body, where Isaac had hit her during his rages. The alabaster skin was sallow and pale, the raven hair limp and thinning. The breasts sagged in a wheezing chest, congested with disease.

Sophia was no longer afraid of yellow fever. Somehow she had managed to avoid the deadly mosquitoes. Now she had tuberculosis.

She must have known she was going to die, which might explain why she probably no longer really cared what happened to her or to Isaac, for that matter. Perhaps she wasn't seeking justice or retribution when she told her story to the police. She just wanted a record; not a life history invented by the professors but an honest account of a difficult life, which at the end was the only thing in the world that truly belonged to her.

This is my story.

It must have taken several hours, but she patiently told her story to the police officer, who typed it onto several sheets of carbon paper while he chain-smoked cheap Brazilian cigarettes.

How old are you now?

The officer might have looked up from the typewriter, lit another cigarette, and given her a good, long look. But he probably just kept on typing when she told him she was only eighteen years old.

CHAPTER FOUR

The Queen

Nobody knows why Rebecca Freedman volunteered to wash the dead bodies of the women.

Of course, it was a mitzvah, the greatest of the good deeds. As religious Jews they should all have been eager to help in the *tahara*, the ritual cleansing and preparation of the dead for burial. But the truth is few had the nerve to stand over the limp, naked bodies of their fellow prostitutes—most of them young women—dumped on the white marble table in the little house next to the cemetery. Few could bring themselves to clean the dried blood and excrement from the murder victims, or to gaze too intently at the tortured expressions of the suicides, many of whom seemed to face the end with the same startled daze, their eyes wide open as if they had only realized the full horror of what they had done when it was too late.

For some, the putrid odor of decaying flesh was simply too much. It seeped into their clothes, got under their skin, made them vomit. Which was why they were so grateful to Rebecca and never questioned her motives, her obsession with purification.

Rebecca handled the cadavers with great diligence and respect. With patient fingers, she removed the blood-encrusted gauze from the stab wounds, gently closed the jaundiced eyes of the yellow-fever victims, removed their sweat-soaked rags, straightened their long, matted hair with water and a brush, and even removed the dirt from under their fingernails. Then, with the help of another woman, she poured the water from several terra-cotta jugs lined up under the marble table, emptying them over the entire body. She knew it symbolized the final *mikvah* or ritual bath that Orthodox women underwent after every menstrual cycle, but for her it clearly had other meanings.

And I will pour upon you pure water and you will be purified.

They were the words of the prophet Ezekiel, and Rebecca repeated them in Hebrew as she watched the water splash over the dead bodies of these women, then drip from the marble table, forming dirty pools on the tiled floor before disappearing down the drain. For years she imagined that the water washed away the shame and the suffering of the shtetl girls—the women who had come to America so willingly to seek their fortune, only to find themselves so utterly helpless and alone.

Was there a worse fate than to die of fever, destitute, on a stinking mattress in a clapboard brothel so far from home? Yes, dying without dignity and with a sullied soul was far worse for a Jew.

How many Jewish prostitutes had died without the ritual redemption of the waters? How many had died *unclean?*

Sophia Chamys had died like this, in the years when the prostitutes did not yet have their cemetery or their Rebecca Freedman. Nobody purified her emaciated body. When she died in the late 1890s, she was hastily buried in a Catholic cemetery on the outskirts of Rio de Janeiro. No rabbi would officiate because, as a prostitute, she was unworthy of *tahara*. Perhaps a Catholic priest, hired by the city, performed the last rites, or perhaps there was no ritual at all, just the body of the dead girl who had expired of consumption, packed into a flimsy coffin and lowered into a freshly dug grave without a headstone or any other marker. In the end, nobody sat shiva, and nobody said Kaddish for Sophia.

The handful of Jewish prostitutes who always seemed to be present at what passed for the funerals of women like Sophia must have shuddered at the prospect of such a lonely death because at some point they resolved that they would not allow the same thing to happen to them. In life, they endured humiliation, abuse, and marginalization. But death was different. In the early mornings, when the brothels were quiet, how many of them lay awake in their small, metal-framed beds beside snoring clients thinking about death? Dying itself didn't haunt them. It was dying with dignity that obsessed them. Would anyone remember them? Would there be a marker on their graves? Would anyone say Kaddish for them?

Sometime in the early 1900s they began to whisper among themselves about forming their own burial society—a radical plan for a group of marginalized women to undertake on their own. But it happened just like that—in hushed conversations over the penny coconut sweets that they bought from the street vendors who worked outside the row houses on the mosquito-infested margins of the Mangue.

Then, on October 10, 1906, nearly ten years after Sophia's death and ignoble burial, a prostitute named Mathilde Huberger convened an extraordinary meeting in a down-at-heels brothel near the port. Mathilde and the eight other Jewish prostitutes who gathered for the meeting could barely read or write, but among them they somehow drafted a blueprint for an organization they called the Jewish Benevolent and Burial Association. Their goals were ambitious. In addition to founding a synagogue, these women planned to create a religious school for the prostitutes' children, and with the monthly dues that the association's executive would collect from its members, a special fund would be set up to provide the women themselves with everything they needed in old age: prescription drugs, physicians, hospital care, and even a third-class ticket to return to the shtetls, if they preferred to die there. Most important, the association sought "to bury members when they died, in accordance with the Jewish religion."

Rebecca Freedman was not present at that first meeting of what came to be known as Chesed Shel Ermess, which is Hebrew for the Society of Truth. She never met Sophia Chamys. But it didn't matter. Her service and obsessive dedication to the association earned her the reverence of the women, who would come to call her their queen.

Before or after they died, Rebecca came to know the stories of these shtetl girls whose dreams of America were shattered in the brothels of Rio de Janeiro. There was Sura Rachel Manchajm, who married her husband in a *stille chuppah,* or silent wedding, in her Polish shtetl when she was fourteen. The other women told Rebecca that Sura sailed with him to Buenos Aires, where she was forced to work in a brothel. Perhaps she was auctioned off in the back room of the Café Parisien, where the traffickers regularly gathered to view the new "merchandise" from Europe. Later she was transferred to Rio, where she may have been sold to another pimp. In any case, she ended up a madam, managing a brothel full of shtetl girls like herself until the day she died, when they deposited her in a heap on the white marble table.

When she lifted the white sheet that covered Sura's dead body,

Rebecca probably saw an elderly woman with deep brown eyes, her hair completely gray and her arms covered in liver spots. It was difficult to believe that this woman, who looked like a kindly grandmother, had ever worked as a prostitute. But then again, all of the women looked like someone's grandmother when they began to get that old. Perhaps Rebecca detected a sadness in Sura's open eyes, or she might have questioned why a successful madam no longer dyed her hair or rouged her lips—just to keep up appearances, to serve as an example to her girls. Maybe she had simply given up, reached the point in her life when dying came as a relief, and life without family, without children and grandchildren to dote on you, became too sad to face anymore. In the 1950s, when the first ones started to die, Rebecca saw a lot of the old women with that same sadness and resignation in their eyes.

Feiga Nossenchug, known in the Rio underworld as "the Little Turk," had looked like that. When she went to clean her fingernails for the last time, Rebecca surely noticed that Feiga, a green-eyed prostitute from Russia, was missing a finger on her left hand. How did that happen? she may have wondered. Was this the result of a childhood accident, or something far more sinister? Rebecca knew the stories of the demonic torture practiced on the shtetl girls who refused to do the bidding of their "husbands." Perhaps Feiga had at first resisted the brothels and then had been taught a lesson by a brutal pimp. In any case, Feiga was lucky. There were no scars on her smooth face, no telltale cigarette burns on her body. Not like Perla Ajdelman, from Warsaw, who died with fresh scars on her chin, her cheeks, and all over her body. Feiga lost a finger; she hadn't been so disfigured that she had to stop working or could only attract the misery clients—the tubercular black men and the diseased sailors who sought out the cheapest street-corner prostitutes, the ones who had been kicked out of the brothels, forced to wander the dark streets. No, Feiga was lucky.

Estera Gladkowicer had not been so lucky, as everyone said when she died. But at least she had taken care of herself, worried about her appearance. Her hair was dyed black, and she was still wearing the pearl choker that Rebecca must have admired when she placed her hands under Estera's limp head to unclasp it. It may have been a gift from her boyfriend, the wiry bohemian musician with the white hat who drank little glasses of *cachaça* and tapped out samba rhythms with the palm of his hand on the counters of the grimy bars that dotted the red-light district. But he never looked like the kind of man who had any money, certainly not enough to buy a double strand of cultured pearls. Still, he knew how to sing, and he sang so beautifully about the shtetl girls, or at least Estera. Everyone knew he was hopelessly in love with her, but what was the point of that? You couldn't live on samba, after all.

"In her eyes, full of love and poetry, sleeps the mystery of the night" went the lyrics to the samba he wrote for Estera. But there was no mystery in Estera's eyes now. The moment she killed herself, she extinguished the love, the poetry, and now there was nothing left but a numbing, blank stare—the same vacant look that Rebecca must have seen on some of the other suicides. Did she stare into those eyes before she forced them shut with her fingers, or could she not bring herself to look too closely? It didn't matter. What was important was that she prepared the body to receive the waters that would wash everything away.

In the end, it was for all the shtetl girls that Rebecca and her assistant poured the waters in a continuous motion so that they cascaded over the dead women, submerging them completely, if only for a brief second.

She is pure. She is pure. She is pure.

Rebecca always said the ancient Hebrew prayer three times. Perhaps she wanted to make sure that God was paying particular attention to these hapless women, whom she began to feel strongly bonded to and later would call her sisters. Or perhaps she somehow wanted to purify herself by performing the greatest of God's mitzvoth—the one for which there would never be any earthly thanks because the recipients were dead. For Rebecca Freedman knew she had sinned, and she may have been asking God's forgiveness for herself whenever she addressed the wet cadaver.

Estera, we ask forgiveness from you if we did not treat you respectfully, but we did as is our custom. May you be a messenger for all Israel. Go in peace, rest in peace, and arise in your turn at the end of days.

Rebecca carefully dried and wrapped the bodies of her fellow prostitutes in white linen shrouds, then sprinkled bits of earth that symbolized the land of Israel over the women's eyes and hearts. She also placed the earth at the bottom of the caskets.

When it was all done, when the bodies were lowered into the simple caskets, Rebecca removed the blood-splattered white robe she wore over her clothes. With hot, soapy water, she rinsed her tools: the tweezers she used to scrape away the dirt under the fingernails, the linen rags she used to clean the bodies, the steel-toothed comb she used for the hair.

Outside the little building where she performed the *tahara,* the tropical air would have been stifling, heavy, as if before a storm. Under the shade of a large mango tree, she washed her hands in the fountain. She knew that the simple gesture broke the bond between her and the dead sisters she had worked so diligently to purify. In Judaism, the hand washing after *tahara* is a reaffirmation of life, a return to the land of the living. She spent a long time like this, feeling the cool water splash over her hands, washing away death. Perhaps she wanted to avoid, for a few minutes at least, the inevitable return to her own life.

But she was a practical woman, and after she dried her hands on a stray piece of white linen shroud, Rebecca Freedman walked alone to a nearby bus stop and returned to her brothel.

REBECCA FREEDMAN HAD ARRIVED in Rio de Janeiro on August 30, 1916, sailing third-class from New York on the *São Paulo,* a ship full of Syrian merchants, American businessmen, and German immigrants.

Unlike the other shtetl girls who arrived in the city on the arms of their new "husbands," the pimps who would exploit them in the brothels, Rebecca came alone, with her dreams of a new life in America long since shattered. The Lloyds of London shipping agent who recorded her information on the ship's manifest in his tight, officious script noted that Rebecca was thirty-five years old and an American citizen, even though she was born in a shtetl near the port city of Szczecin, on Poland's western border with Germany.

There was no official documentation of her occupation, no reason given for why she had made the journey to Brazil at the height of the First World War. Nobody seems to have asked those questions. Perhaps the reasons Rebecca was planning to settle in a place where she had no friends or family, or other means of support, might have proved too difficult, too embarrassing, to explain.

Then again, if anyone had bothered to ask, she could have just started at the beginning, but Rebecca was not fond of talking about herself. Years later, when she was on her deathbed in one of the dark rooms of the brothel she owned near Rio de Janeiro's central train station, her remaining friends seemed truly surprised when they found out that Rebecca had lived in New York, and that she was already "unclean" by the time she sailed to South America.

Rebecca arrived in New York during the massive wave of Jewish immigration to the United States. Between 1881 and the beginning of the First World War in 1914, more than 1.5 million Jews arrived in the United States, to escape extreme poverty and anti-Semitic violence in Eastern Europe.

It is difficult to know why Rebecca ended up in New York as a young woman, or how she felt when she arrived in the city around the turn of the last century. Was she disappointed when she first saw the stinking tenements where newly arrived immigrants from Eastern Europe lived much as they had in the shtetls?

Where were the riches that the shtetl elders had spoken about? Did she recognize the faces of the men who had returned to the shtetl after making their "fortunes" in America? They had landed in the shtetls reborn—wearing silk hats and frock coats of the finest wool, and were considered millionaires by the peasants. But now, here in New York, she saw their bleak reality. They worked in the factories, lived difficult lives in the rat-infested tenements, while their wives watched over broods of children, taking in piecework to help their families survive.

In the fabled America, land of opportunity and riches, the Jewish peasants still wore their coarsely woven garments, and most lived in a single room, cooking their meals of shredded cabbage and potatoes over coal-fired stoves. Few of their children ever went to school. As soon as they were able, the older children were forced to toil fourteen-hour days in the garment factories that dotted the immigrant neighborhood of New York's Lower East Side.

It's not clear whether Rebecca Freedman was forced to take a job in a garment factory as a young woman to help her family survive. If she was typical, she might have spent hours at a time in an airless building, sewing shirtwaists, earning less than five dollars a week, barely a living wage. She may have returned home along darkening streets, averting her eyes from the Jewish street toughs who preyed on even the youngest girls. She would certainly have seen the prostitutes, lounging with their lit cigarettes on the stoops of the tenement buildings, "naked under their flowery kimonos, occasionally flashing chunks of breast and belly, slippers hanging from their feet," always ready for "business."

Rebecca could not have avoided these women who called out "their wares like pushcart peddlers." The *nafke,* as the old-timers called them in Yiddish, were everywhere on the Lower East Side. They were such an embarrassment to respectable Jews that in 1898 the *Forward,* a Yiddish newspaper, warned its readers of an "official flesh trade in the Jewish quarter" and told them to avoid Allen, Chrystie, and Forsyth Streets, "if you go walking with your wife, daughter, or fiancée." On those streets and others scattered throughout the Lower East Side, Jewish prostitutes "occupied vacant stores, crowded into flats and apartments in all the tenements," where they typically charged between fifty cents and a dollar per client. In one such tenement, investigators discovered a *cheder* or Jewish school directly above an apartment used by prostitutes.

Like Rebecca, the Jewish prostitutes were illiterate girls from the shtetls who had arrived in New York with few prospects. At first they may have headed to the sweatshops. But when they tired of the slavelike conditions in the factories, many went looking for the pimps or "cadets" who prowled the streets and the dance halls.

Everyone knew the *nafke* were rich, that they easily earned at least twenty-five dollars a week. Even the youngest girls knew that. "It's a good business, easy, and you can dress and eat and live," said an unidentified little Jewish girl who regularly watched a prostitute servicing her clients because the window in her tenement flat looked directly into the flat used by the prostitute in an adjoining building.

A good business. Perhaps that's why Lizzie Dannenberg, a thirty-four-year-old German immigrant and cleaner, encouraged her fifteen-year-old daughter to become a prostitute. Between 1888 and 1892, Rachel Marks also sold her daughters to various brothels.

Did Rebecca Freedman seek out the "easy" life of the prostitutes when she entered the dance halls where, every Saturday night, she paid her nickel to dance with the other shtetl girls? Did she see the pimp approaching her, casually flicking the ashes from his cigarette onto the worn, wooden floorboards? She may even have approached him—shyly at first, flushed, the adrenaline rush giving her a headache, clouding her vision, confusing her emotions. Maybe she never really understood the implications of her actions, or perhaps she understood them too well.

Are you here by yourself?

In the dance halls, the seduction and entrapment of the shtetl girls started with an innocent question, and often ended with rape in a dark alley or a tenement stairwell.

Rebecca Freedman might have been procured for the brothels of the Lower East Side just like this—following a rape, after some moments of shy, awkward flirtation. Was she excited by the cigarette the stranger offered her when they were alone on the dark sidewalk? Only the *nafke* smoked cigarettes. How free they looked when they were smoking, not caring what anyone said about them, laughing when the pious Jewish mothers rushed their children to the other side of the street to avoid them.

Perhaps Rebecca longed to be free like that. Why save herself for a poor Jewish man like her father? Why continue with the drudgery of the sweatshop where the young shtetl girls lost fingers and suffered other horrible accidents when they fell asleep at the machines? And then there was the terrible fire at the Triangle shirtwaist factory in 1911. How many of those poor factory workers had died? Many of the shtetl girls had been burned alive running for the fire exits that were locked by the owners to prevent theft; others had plunged to their deaths when the fire department's ladders could not reach them on the building's top floors. They cried for help, the fire engulfing their bodies, and then they died with a thud, reduced to a heap of clothes and broken bones on the cold sidewalk below.

In New York, nobody cared what happened to the factory girls. *Are you here by yourself?*

Yes, Rebecca Freedman was by herself, and that was why she may have decided to follow the man, to smoke a cigarette for the first time in her life. Perhaps she longed to feel a man's kisses on her neck. Maybe, when he was raping her, he whispered about untold riches and promised her a better life, away from the mind-numbing drudgery of the factories. Or maybe it was just a pair of silk stockings, a package of cigarettes, a meal in a restaurant.

This is the way girls like Rebecca lost their purity. This is how they became *nafke*.

Unlike their counterparts in South America, the New York Jewish pimps had no need to marry and lure their innocent victims from the shtetls. Marriage in the shtetl? an incredulous New York pimp might have asked. Who went to that kind of trouble when you had hundreds of dumb, impoverished shtetl girls already here? These girls would do anything you wanted, and they were so naïve all you had to do was speak to them nicely and offer them presents.

"By apparently kind and generous treatment, and by giving the young girl glimpses of a standard of living which she never had dared hope to attain," the pimp quickly gained the confidence of young factory workers and recently arrived shtetl girls. In a groundbreaking report on prostitution in New York at the turn of the last century, investigators of the Committee of Fifteen of the Chamber of Commerce found that pimps, many of whom also moonlighted as petty thieves and pickpockets, would seduce the young women, sometimes offering them drugged drinks. Then, "through fear and promises of marriage she would cast her fortune with her companion and go to live with him." The "companion" conveniently managed to disappear, leaving the girl "an inmate of a house of prostitution."

The desperate poverty of the women on the Lower East Side made them easy targets. Hunger eroded tradition and allowed them to ignore the warnings of their parents and the rabbis. "Living in most crowded districts, with the burden of economic pressure on them, these children of Israel had almost lost that spiritual basis of life which has been their very birthright," noted a probation officer who worked with dozens of Jewish prostitutes through the city's night court. Among the immigrant women who went into prostitution in New York in the years before the First World War, most were Jewish. The authors of a report prepared by the United States Immigration Commission in 1910 found that "Hebrews exceeded all other ethnic groups in convictions for soliciting on the streets and of being inmates of disorderly houses."

In fact, some pimps insisted that the young women came to them voluntarily in search of work. A pimp identified only as

Harry compared himself to a social worker and a "philanthropic businessman" when he told a neighbor that he provided all the impoverished women who came to him with food, clothing, and education for life. "I teach them manners," he said. "I teach them to be sober and to save their money. I make something out of them. Many of my girls have saved enough to bring their parents from the old country."

Of course, most of the older generation despised the flesh trade, but what could they do? Perhaps Rebecca Freedman's parents panicked when they saw that their daughter was going down the path of no return, or perhaps they chose to be ignorant of her business, asking no questions, grateful for the few extra dollars she might have sent them every week.

In many instances, when shtetl girls were raped by pimps, their parents forced them to marry their assailants. In 1901 Dora Rubin Schneiderman was raped by a pimp when she was seventeen. Her horrified parents forced her to marry him, unwittingly committing their daughter to a brothel for the rest of her life.

New York social workers documented one case of a seventeen-year-old Jewish girl who tried to obtain a divorce after she had been abducted, raped, and forced into marriage without the knowledge of her Russian immigrant parents. Once married, the unidentified young woman worked for three weeks in a brothel. When she was diagnosed with venereal disease, her husband simply kicked her out. The case came to the attention of the city's deputy assistant district attorney when the girl approached the city's Legal Aid Society to help her obtain a divorce.

Although the seventeen-year-old girl managed to obtain her divorce and was saved from a life of sexual slavery, such outcomes were rare. Most women procured for the brothels never left them, even though many of their parents did try to save them. The truth is that the pious Jews were helpless; there was little they could do to save their "wayward" daughters. Complaining to their landlords about the prostitutes who worked in their tenements never changed the situation. Often the landlords simply sided with the prostitutes. "Yes, those girls are whores," said one of them. "But they pay three times the rent you do, and they pay promptly."

Although many upright Jewish families complained about prostitution, many were forced out of economic need to rent space to local streetwalkers who were not affiliated with a brothel. Reformers and investigators who conducted numerous studies on "the social evil" were often horrified to find prostitutes living with young families in the tenements. One investigator described how a Jewish couple with three small children ended up subletting one of their rooms to a prostitute: "The other member of the household was an immoral woman who received men both night and day in one of the two rooms in which the family lived." During the day, the mother, baby in her arms, offered to leave the flat when the prostitute received clients. At night, when the other children were home from school, the whole family "remained in one room while the other was being used by this immoral woman." The only division between them and the prostitute was a flimsy curtain.

Jennie Silver was a notorious prostitute who worked out of her home. When police accompanied her back to her tenement they found two men and a two-year-old girl on the couch of her small room. The little girl was Jennie's daughter, and one of the men was Jacob Silver, her husband and pimp. The police officer noted in his report that Jennie "has been living with him for the past ten years. He never works. If she does not make enough money for him, he kicks and beats her."

Horrified by what they saw all around them, desperate immigrant parents appealed to the authorities, writing anonymous letters to investigating officials and providing them with a list of brothels in their neighborhood. Jacob Siebowitz, a Polish immigrant, denounced a brothel at 145 Ridge Street, noting that he had "tried every particular way to get the disorderly house across the street from me away from here but without avail."

Out of desperation, some Jewish parents who feared that their daughters were straying into prostitution took them to women's night court in order to have them charged with "incorrigibility." Of course the young women were usually discharged immediately, but for many parents it may have been "the final recognition" that their Old World methods of family control were simply useless in America.

Although a young woman may have earned more in the brothels than in the sweatshops, life as a prostitute in the early-twentieth-century in New York was far from glamorous. Most of the Jewish prostitutes worked out of so-called fifty-cent and dollar houses that were, in the words of New York's Bureau of Social Hygiene, simply "unfit for human habitation." The "loose and creaking floors are covered with matting which is gradually rotting away, the ceilings are low, the windows small, the air heavy and filled with foul odors."

As in South America, most of the Jewish prostitutes serviced the lower-class clientele—"usually longshoremen, truck drivers, street cleaners, coal heavers, soldiers and sailors, recently landed immigrants of low moral standards, and laborers of all kinds." They worked under slavelike conditions, subject to what one inspector called the "brutal" treatment of the pimps. The account books for one fifty-cent brothel note that one prostitute saw 273 men in two weeks, "an average of 19 per day (her high was 28 in a day), earning $136.50 for the house." Two other prostitutes in the same brothel serviced an average of between 120 and 185 men per week, with one of them seeing 49 clients in one day. Perhaps some of the women who had traded the sweatshops for the brothels bitterly regretted their decision when they found themselves strapped to another kind of assembly line.

Of course, most of these prostitutes suffered from all sorts of venereal diseases. Hygiene studies conducted in the city at the turn of the last century show that some 80 percent of all of the prostitutes working in Manhattan carried a sexually transmitted disease. But in order to frustrate the health authorities who regularly checked the conditions of the brothels, pimps furnished falsified medical certificates attesting to the good health of their prostitutes. These certificates were also brought out for the perusal of skeptical would-be clients, to prove that the women were clean.

How did Rebecca cope with being a prostitute under such conditions? How many men did she see each day in her tenement on Eldridge Street, in the heart of the Lower East Side's red-light district, where the rank odor of rotting fish and old vegetables from the markets below hung like stale air in her apartment, numbing her nostrils, settling into her clothes? Rebecca was a pragmatist, and she rarely bemoaned her lot. Not like the weaker shtetl girls, the ones who decided to take their own lives rather than face life in the fifty-cent brothels.

The *New York World* was full of such cases—shtetl girls who swallowed carbolic acid. The reports always carried a graphic description of what happened to a person who swallowed the sweet-smelling antiseptic that was mostly used to clean wounds. Rebecca could not read the news reports, but she seemed to know all the symptoms associated with death by carbolic acid, so frequent were the suicides of girls she knew. It was a horrible death. First there was excruciating pain in the mouth and throat that made breathing nearly impossible, followed by convulsions, uncontrolled vomiting and diarrhea, blue fingernails and lips, and finally a coma from which one never awoke. Rebecca had seen its effects too many times.

Lena Meyers, a twenty-eight-year-old prostitute, took carbolic acid. She was found dead in her room at 193 First Avenue. Her lips and fingernails had turned blue. Authorities found her lying in a pool of her own vomit. They also found a recent letter from her mother, who lived just outside Kraków, in Poland. From her earnings as a prostitute, Meyers had regularly sent money to her parents but had obviously never told them how she made it. Two weeks before her death she had received a letter from her mother, who asked her, "Lena, why don't you get married? Do you want to be an old maid?" The police who arrived on the scene and must have had the letter translated from Yiddish concluded that Lena could no longer face the shame of working as a prostitute, and had decided to kill herself when she received the letter from home.

Susie, a young prostitute who was determined to leave the business and go back to the sweatshops, also committed suicide with carbolic acid. "There lay Susie, writhing like a cut worm. 'See momma,' she gasped. 'I am getting out of the business at last.' The ambulance came for her, and she died the next day in hospital."

Perhaps Rebecca's condemnation of girls like Susie and Lena, the weak ones, was unduly harsh. Most did not have her resolve, her ability to survive under the worst possible circumstances. "I have never been ashamed of what I do," she boldly told a journalist when she was on her deathbed in Rio.

Perhaps the bravado was necessary for her, a way to cope with the reality that there may have been very little that separated her from Lena and Susie. She was trapped, just as they were trapped. After all, they had nowhere to go. They couldn't appeal to their families, for whom they were probably a source of deep shame. They couldn't go back to the sweatshops, and they couldn't appeal to the authorities—not in turn-of-the-century New York City, where hundreds of police officers were on the payroll of a group of ruthless criminals who controlled gambling and prostitution on the Lower East Side.

The pimps and the other criminals acted with impunity because they shared the profits of their trade with the corrupt officials of Tammany Hall, a powerful political force in the city since its founding in 1789. Tammany political bosses were strongly linked to the Democratic Party and made huge profits skimming off the proceeds of gambling and prostitution. Big Tim Sullivan, the Tammany boss who ruled the working-class neighborhoods of the Lower East Side with his extended family, made more than three million dollars a year (fifty million in current dollar terms) from the city's vice networks, which were controlled by Irish, Italian, and Jewish mobsters.

In the Jewish neighborhoods, gangsters Jake Wolf, Max Hochstim, Martin Engel, and his brother Max were feared by the local population, shaking down those who had managed to set up small businesses, later dividing these "tributes" with Tammany political bosses and the police. For many of the recently arrived Jewish immigrants, the mention of these men "made them shiver."

When a Russian Jewish widow named Caela Urchittel refused to pay Max Hochstim fifty dollars in "protection" fees soon after she opened a small restaurant in Brooklyn, she was devastated by the repercussions. Caela soon found herself hauled to the local police station, where she faced trumped-up prostitution charges. Later, when she was deemed by the police an unfit mother, her children were taken to an orphanage—a savage act that appears to have provoked Caela's nervous breakdown. By her own account, she spent six months in the Sixty-sixth Street Hospital before she managed to regain custody of her children.

In order to strengthen their hold on the New York underworld, the Jewish mobsters incorporated a trade association of local ward politicians, brothel owners, real estate agents, and saloon owners under the rather innocuous-sounding title of the New York Independent Benevolent Association (IBA). Like the Zwi Migdal in Argentina, the organization, whose membership counted between 135 and 600 criminals in its heyday, was set up as a mutual-aid association and burial society for Jewish pimps and other gangsters. Soon after its incorporation the IBA acquired a plot of land at a Jewish cemetery in Brooklyn, where some of its members are now buried.

Although IBA members may once have had grand ambitions for the cemetery, in the end it was a small, forlorn plot, with only a handful of graves, tucked into the back of the Washington Park Cemetery. A rather lofty stone arch, which seems too large for the plot, bears the organization's name in carved block letters. Perhaps the criminals had pretensions of greatness, like their counterparts in Argentina. Perhaps they also had plans to construct a great synagogue with the profits from white slavery.

If these were in fact their ambitions, their hopes were dashed. These men who had built an empire on the suffering of the shtetl girls and who acted with total impunity would soon find their organization in ruins.

REBECCA FREEDMAN MAY NEVER have learned Mordke Goldberg's real name, even though, in hindsight, he would have such a profound effect on her life. To her and the other Jewish prostitutes on the Lower East Side, he was simply known as "the King."

A tough-talking gangster who spoke English with a heavy Yiddish accent, the King operated his lucrative business from the back room of a delicatessen on Seventh Avenue. Between the barrels of sauerkraut and the slabs of curing pastrami, he waited every morning at a small table for his collectors—four of his most trusted men, who arrived with several black bags full of money. The money, which represented the proceeds from the King's eleven houses of prostitution, each of which employed fifteen women, was dumped on his table in the deli's back room. The men counted the coins before digging into steaming bowls of cabbage soup, its sweetly fermented smell no doubt reminding Goldberg of the slums of Warsaw where he grew up.

On the Lower East Side, everyone knew the King was ruthless. All the prostitutes he controlled knew the story of his "wife," Rosie, the young shtetl girl he had seduced when he was a soldier in Russia. Mordke traveled with Rosie to South Africa, where she "earned thousands of dollars for him" in a Johannesburg brothel. When he arrived in the United States, he took Rosie from city to city until he collected enough money to open his first brothel in New York.

By 1912, he reigned over the New York underworld. The so-called Vice Trust that he controlled became an important rival to the IBA and had interests in more than forty brothels and hundreds of prostitutes throughout New York. Goldberg and his associates cleared more than a million dollars a year (approximately fifteen million in today's dollars). No pimp could open up a brothel in the city without first consulting Goldberg, who had high-level connections in city government and among the police.

It's not clear whether Rebecca Freedman ever met Mordke

Goldberg, but their fates were strangely intertwined after a series of police raids on the Jewish underworld that left both the IBA and Mordke's empire in ruins—and Rebecca without a job.

From the summer of 1912 through 1914, city officials conducted sweeping raids of brothels and gaming houses after a Jewish mobster named Herman Rosenthal became the victim of a gangland shooting. Rosenthal operated a gaming house on the Lower East Side and was closely connected to Tammany Hall. After he suffered what he described as undue harassment from police lieutenant Charles Becker, Rosenthal exposed Becker, in an article in the *New York World,* accusing him of being his former partner in a gambling operation.

Rosenthal complained that Becker had sent police officers to harass him at his midtown gambling establishment when he refused to pay him protection fees. Newly installed Republican city officials committed to cleaning up Tammany corruption seized on the Rosenthal case. Dozens of Jewish mobsters were rounded up for questioning, and in exchange for immunity from prosecution, many readily confessed what they knew about the slaying. Some of them said that Becker threatened to put them all behind bars on trumped-up charges unless they participated in the crime. Becker and four Jewish hoodlums were eventually arrested and charged with Rosenthal's assassination. In 1915, after appeals had been exhausted, they were all sent to the electric chair.

The police, who "had the heat of public opinion on them" and needed "to demonstrate their trustworthiness" after the scandal, went on a purge of the brothels with a vengeance. At first the mobsters seemed confident that the increased police vigilance would blow over shortly. But it only got worse. The situation became so intolerable that the mighty Mordke Goldberg had to shutter his brothels and flee the country. It was during these police raids that Rebecca Freedman likely first heard the words South America, whispered among the pimps who worked for the King. Dozens of pimps and prostitutes later scrambled to buy passages to anywhere in South America in order to escape prosecution.

When most of Goldberg's brothels were closed by the police, he may have thought of returning to Johannesburg, where he had first learned how to live off the proceeds of prostitution. But South Africa might have seemed too far and too complicated to reach, especially once the First World War began, restricting transatlantic shipping lines. South America was different. The shipping routes were completely open, and Goldberg must have heard the rumors of "easy" money to be made in the red-light districts of Buenos Aires and Rio de Janeiro, the largest centers for the white-slave trade in the Americas.

When Mordke Goldberg sailed to South America, dozens of pimps and prostitutes fled with him, or just after him. Among them was Rebecca Freedman.

REBECCA FREEDMAN ARRIVED in Rio de Janeiro just in time for the funeral—the first proper Jewish burial of a shtetl girl who had slaved for years in the city's brothels.

Helena Goldatrin, who was born in a tiny shtetl somewhere in the Austro-Hungarian Empire (no one was quite sure where), had died suddenly in childbirth. Her funeral was a sad occasion to be sure, but for the Jewish prostitutes of the Society of Truth it was also a victory and a time for celebration.

For five years they had lobbied local authorities to grant them a plot of land to establish their cemetery. Perhaps José Dias Cupertim, the city hall bureaucrat who eventually stamped the documents establishing their cemetery, had had enough of these heavily rouged women, with their harsh accents and their sloppy Portuguese. They invaded his office, baked him sweets, brought him *cachaça,* and pressed delectable walnut cupcakes and jam biscuits on his secretaries. Or perhaps they offered him other favors. Not that he would have taken anything untoward. José Dias Cupertim was an upstanding civil servant, entirely devoted to the rules. Even the sweets seemed too compromising, which is why he always left them on the desks of his underlings. He had to set an example. He could not be corrupted like this. No, the girls, as he called them, would have to wait their turn just like everyone else. Yes, there were many corrupt officials in Brazil, lesser men than he who would crack under such a barrage of attention. But for Dias Cupertim, the law was sacred. These foreign women would have to fill out the forms, pay the processing fees, and abide by the laws of the republic, just like everyone else.

And so they waited, taking turns making the pilgrimage to Dias Cupertim's office, leaving their offerings wrapped in a starched linen napkin on the jacaranda-wood reception table, chatting with the receptionists, asking about their families, listening to their problems. The receptionists eventually figured out that these beautiful women with their blond hair, their green eyes, and their provocative dresses were prostitutes. But after five years of eating their cakes and drinking their *cachaça,* nobody really seemed to mind what they did for a living.

Then, on a rainy afternoon in August 1916, Dias Cupertim finally got the approval from above to stamp the documents, which he placed on the table to await the regular afternoon visitors. He may have retreated to his office after that, no doubt relieved to be rid of the flamboyant albatrosses who had been swooping down on him for five years.

In the end it wasn't a particularly attractive location, or a good piece of land for that matter. It was a sizable enough plot, but it was way out, in Inhaúma, a blistering hot, unkempt suburb of overgrown banana plants and mango trees on the industrial outskirts of the city. The place was as bleak as the Mangue, where the brothels were located. Maybe that's why the prostitutes felt immediately at home there. The women didn't waste any time. As soon as they acquired the land, they hired a group of black and mixed-race laborers, who worked for several days to clear it for a cemetery.

When Helena died suddenly, the cemetery was still not finished. The little building for the *tahara* ceremony was not yet complete; there were no fountains where the mourners could wash their hands; no proper gate or stone wall separated the cemetery from the steep dirt road that the locals called Piragibe Street. "There were no walls, no place to wash the bodies before they were swathed from head to toe in vast white cloths, like a cocoon," noted a Brazilian journalist sent to cover what must have seemed a strange curiosity—the inauguration of a cemetery reserved for prostitutes. Jewish prostitutes. Surely there was no other place like it in the world, the editors of *The Night* may have said to one another at the editorial meeting in their downtown offices where they decided what would be the newsworthy events of the next day.

What kind of cemetery would this be? the editors may have wondered. Would it be a grand place, with huge family crypts and elaborately carved tombstones? Everyone knew that the Jewish prostitutes and their *caftens,* as the Jewish pimps were derisively called, were rich. They lived an easy life, they had gold teeth, and their clothes were fashioned by the finest tailors on Ouvidor Street. This cemetery was surely something special.

They were probably disappointed when their reporter returned, with no scoop, no elaborate description of riches or grandeur. "There was nothing, really," wrote *The Night* reporter describing the cemetery. "Nothing except a level field, solitary and sad."

To the prostitutes who had put aside a portion of their earnings each month for five years to purchase the sad plot of land, that didn't matter. For now, they were determined to give Helena Goldatrin a proper Jewish burial, even if they were forced to perform the purification rites in one of the airless rooms of a brothel before bringing the white-shrouded body to the cemetery. They resolved that in the future the *tahara* would be conducted in a proper building, with a marble table and a drain in the floor to wash away the waters.

She is pure.

This, of course, went right over the head of the Brazilian reporter, no doubt a Catholic, who stood dumbstruck. For him, the Jewish funeral rituals must have seemed as foreign as the Afro-Brazilian religious ceremonies practiced in secret by former black slaves throughout the city.

Still, it must have been a strange gathering on that sunbaked parcel of land, so far from the city center: the tearful prostitutes, heads covered in lacy shawls, standing next to their pimps, reciting rapid-fire Hebrew prayers and tearing at their garments in their grief as the young woman was lowered into a freshly dug grave.

"They lit many candles and stuck them in the earth," wrote the reporter, going on to describe in detail the sacrifice and burial of a small, white lamb on the new cemetery grounds before the funeral began. The men, who wore small black hats that covered the tops of their heads, recited what appeared to him "complicated prayers while the women moaned and wept, the tears rolling down their cheeks like the drops of wax falling off the candles, battered by the wind."

But after the weeping and the prayers—"the horrible chorus of lamentations"—there was a decidedly festive air as the mourners produced jam biscuits, sugarplums, and cupcakes from their pockets and proceeded to have a party. As they "feasted ravenously" on the sweets, actresses from Rio's Yiddish theater, who moments before had been weeping inconsolably, flitted among the mourners "like sucking bees," handing out tickets to that evening's performance. It may have been a "macabre party," but for the Jewish prostitutes who had fought for several years for their own cemetery, that first burial must have seemed like a reason for celebration.

Admittedly, the mourners were terribly saddened by Helena's death. The thirty-three-year-old prostitute had died the day before, shortly after the birth of her child, a girl the prostitutes had named Eva. But the Brazilian sailor who was the infant girl's father didn't like the Old Testament name. According to *The Night* article, he had wanted to name her Iracema, a Tamoio Indian name.

No one knows whether Rebecca Freedman attended Helena's funeral, but she would surely have been aware of the cemetery, which was celebrated as a great victory among the community of Jewish prostitutes even as it was condemned by the nascent community of respectable Jews who began arriving en masse from Eastern Europe after the United States closed its doors to Jewish immigration.

The day after Helena's funeral, the article about the inauguration of the Jewish prostitutes' cemetery was published on *The Night*'s front page, along with a black-and-white photograph showing the "sad" plot of land surrounded by a barbed-wire fence and a prominent stone tablet that featured a Star of David and the identification "Cemetery of the Jewish Benevolent and Burial Association." Rio's Jewish leaders, who presided over a small but growing community of Jewish immigrants from Eastern Europe, the Middle East, and North Africa, were livid with the newspaper's editors, pointing out that they did not distinguish between the prostitutes who made up the Jewish Benevolent and Burial Association and the respectable Jewish community. The cutline under the photograph identified it simply as the "Cemetery of the Jews."

Three days after the article appeared, *The Night* published a letter from David J. Perez, editor in chief of *The Column,* a Jewish community newspaper in Rio. He argued that the prostitutes and the pimps had no right to inaugurate their own cemetery, and that such an act was the sole responsibility of the Chevra Kadisha, the sacred Jewish burial society that had not yet been convened in Rio de Janeiro. It would only be established in 1920, four years after the inauguration of the prostitutes' cemetery, and its members would be forced by municipal authorities to establish their cemetery in São João de Meriti, on the distant outskirts of Rio. "If those exploiters were in a city where my brothers lived in an organized fashion, they would surely be in jail by now, paying for their crime," wrote Perez. "We are not connected with them, either in life or in death."

The pimps and the prostitutes had already raised the ire of respectable Jews like Perez. Three years before the inauguration of the cemetery, they had attempted to set up a makeshift synagogue downtown, and then had the nerve to invite leaders of the respectable community to its opening. When the pimps decided to take to the streets holding aloft a Torah scroll, for the dedication of the synagogue, they were savagely attacked by young men from the respectable community. By the end of the mêlée, which the newspapers called the Torah riot, the new Torah scroll was in tatters on a sidewalk. Police were called to the scene, where they found a group of about a dozen pimps, some holding silk handkerchiefs to their bleeding noses, some pointing in the direction in which the respectable Jews had long since retreated. The police officers, who were well acquainted with the work of the pimps, did nothing.

Still, despite the enmity they felt toward the Jewish pimps and prostitutes, the mainstream Jewish community leaders had to admit that they were pioneers. They had arrived long before the Sephardic immigrants from Morocco and Syria and well before the wave of Ashkenazi Jews from Eastern Europe. Despite their upstanding character, the respectable Jews were hopelessly divided and their community disorganized. A rabbi sent to Brazil under the auspices of the Jewish Colonization Association confessed to a group of his colleagues in New York that "it was not so easy . . . to gain the confidence of the Jews" in Brazil. "A miasma of distrust and even hostility filled the air."

The pimps and prostitutes, on the other hand, were extremely well organized. They founded their cemetery long before the Jewish community set up its sacred burial society, and as early as 1906, when the prostitutes founded the Society of Truth, the Jewish gangsters were already performing improvised Jewish rituals, in order to hold on to the vestiges of their religion. A Rio newspaper reported on a bris carried on in a brothel by a notorious trafficker named Mauricio Arkmann, who was "dressed in white robes, with his long hair neatly braided."

So visible were these underworld Jewish rituals performed by Jewish gangsters that one British Jewish traveler to Rio de Janeiro remarked in 1913 that "while nobody could speak to me about the existence of a respectable synagogue and so few people knew anything about the respectable Jews, everyone could speak about this [the gangsters'] synagogue. Jews as well as non-Jews knew of its existence."

Rebecca Freedman also found out about the synagogue of the prostitutes as soon as she arrived in Brazil in 1916. Did she hesitate before knocking on the door of the brothel on Luís de Camões Street on a breezy Friday night in September? This was the site of the underground synagogue, the place where the women met to celebrate the Sabbath. After the services, performed by anyone they could get to act as a cantor, the women sat together in the kitchen or the grimy front parlor, passing around plates of homemade sweets, which they washed down with orange juice or, when the occasion called for it, tiny glasses of syrupy liqueurs.

Perhaps Rebecca felt uncomfortable, hard-pressed to recall the last time she had been inside a synagogue. The room with its Torah scroll sheathed in burgundy velvet and its lit candles may have reminded her of the *shtibl*—the clay-floored synagogues in the tiny rooms of the thatch-roofed shtetl houses.

Had she ever entered a synagogue in New York? Did she attend what passed for the funerals of women like Lena Myers, who ended their sad lives with a gulp of carbolic acid?

The truth was that Rebecca Freedman, poor, illiterate, schooled only in the art of cheap seduction, had never been a particularly pious woman. God was not in the shtetl, otherwise how could he have permitted so much suffering and death? Was He present on the streets of New York? Surely not when women were plunging to their deaths from a burning factory building or stepping gingerly over piles of rubbish on the Lower East Side as they attempted to attract the men who carried the cigarettes and could provide them with their next meal.

Rebecca Freedman might not have felt particularly close to God, and years later she could not remember how or why she had made her way to the colonial-style door on Luís de Camões Street. She might have stood for a long time examining the chipped white paint, the embroidered linen curtains, that covered the small windows.

It was a simple gesture: a gentle knock on the door, then another one, a little more insistent than the first. Yes, a small, simple, everyday gesture. But for Rebecca Freedman, it would change her life.

CHAPTER FIVE

The Work of Sisyphus

Sally Knopf noticed the woman right away. She was standing alone in the crowd at the port of Amsterdam, clutching a stack of papers in her arms. She was small, slight, and dressed almost completely in black—black stockings, black leather shoes, an elegant black woollen dress. Was she on her way to a funeral? Sally might have wondered, as she glanced in the direction of the woman, whose wispy white hair was pulled back in a bun, giving her the air of a stern schoolteacher, someone who inspired respect but perhaps also her share of cruel spinster jokes whenever her back was turned.

The woman stood on tiptoe, craning her neck like a startled black swan, scrutinizing the crowds of travelers who rushed past her: beefy businessmen with worn leather valises and rolled-up newspapers under their arms, porters weighed down with the baggage of a wealthy Dutch couple off to their holiday in America, and a group of bedraggled peasants who stood in the middle of the port, obviously in a state of shock at the bustle all around them. Sally might not have given her a second look, except that she had the impression that the woman might be waving to her. No, it wasn't an impression. It was real. The woman was waving to her, and she began to walk briskly through the crowd as if she had something urgent to communicate to Sally.

Are you traveling alone?

The woman seemed breathless as she addressed her in Yiddish, which must have surprised Sally, who had been told that people in Amsterdam spoke another language. Yes, Sally Knopf, sixteen, was traveling alone. She was on her way to America, to a small town in the Brazilian interior to live with her Uncle Joe, her mother's older brother. A few months before, Sally's family in Poland had received a surprising letter from Uncle Joe, who bemoaned the fact that he had no heirs, and would very much like it if his eldest niece would consent to live with him and his wife at their hotel in Brazil. He needed someone to take over the business and would teach Sally everything she needed to know. In exchange, he would make her his sole heir. To prove his good intentions, he enclosed a first-class passage for Sally to travel to Rio de Janeiro, where he would meet her after the three-week voyage.

But perhaps this was simply too much information to give a stranger. What had her mother said about talking to strangers on the journey? Still, Sally needed to talk. It eased the fear of being away from home, of traveling so far from her mother and brother. But she must have regretted divulging so much so quickly, even though there was something about this officious older woman that made Sally trust her immediately. The woman, who might or might not have identified herself (Sally couldn't remember), seemed to give Sally a pitying look, and then she held up one of the pieces of paper from the stack in her arms.

Don't talk to strange men. Don't believe any of their promises.

The warnings must have frightened her, because at some point in the conversation Sally dug through her carpetbag, her nervous fingers brushing past the old linen nightdress that her mother had ironed for the journey, past the woollen stockings for the cold nights on the ship, and past her precious bottle of rose-water cologne that she had purchased—so foolishly and so impulsively—with the money that Uncle Joe had sent the family for her journey. She pulled out the letter of introduction that her uncle had written for the Brazilian authorities at the port of Rio de Janeiro. But neither the woman in black nor Sally Knopf could read what was typed in official Portuguese on the white vellum sheet.

Whether Sally had heard the stories of what often happened to young women traveling alone on ships to America is not known. In any case, none of it applied to her. Yes, she was traveling alone, but she was going first-class, and she was going to live with her family.

Flustered, Sally must have also shown the stranger her first-class ticket. But the stranger seemed unmoved. Clearly, she had seen this before. How did you convince these naïve young girls that they could be in grave danger? How did you convince them to stay in Europe, to stay away from America, a place that for most of them would only bring hardship and suffering? The prospect of another Jewish girl going off to America to become a prostitute must have depressed the woman in black. Even in the mid-1920s, when women throughout most of Europe and America had won the right to vote, the right to take charge of their destinies, these shtetl girls were still being sold into slavery.

But what could one do when they seemed to go so willingly, so blindly, without any concept of geography, not knowng "whether

America is a city in the vicinity of London or how long it will take to reach a certain destination?"

Throughout Europe and across America there were dozens of these officious women in black who scoured the ports and the train stations for girls like Sally. The women, all of them volunteers, were affiliated with various Jewish feminist organizations that began to monitor European train stations and ports as early as 1907. In some cases they were identified by their yellow armbands, emblazoned with the motto "Help by Women for Women." Their placards, visible in most of the European ports, featured a Star of David and proclaimed "Combat White Slavery." The volunteers approached the naïve peasant girls who appeared to be traveling alone and offered to provide them with job counseling and placement services on the spot.

They were committed to stopping the trade, one shtetl girl at a time. In 1924, as Sally made her way to South America, the anti-white-slavery movement was gaining a great deal of momentum in many European Jewish communities, as a direct result of a resolution passed by the League of Nations demanding that the international community work together to fight the traffic in women and girls, "arresting it at the frontiers and mercilessly suppressing it when it succeeds in crossing them and penetrating into the countries where a demand exists." So the Jewish volunteers coordinated their efforts around the world, arriving at some of the busiest ports in Europe with their stacks of flyers and their posters, which warned women in several languages of the dangers that awaited them abroad. Occasionally they were successful and managed to catch up to unsuspecting girls before they boarded transatlantic ships. In 1919 a volunteer at the port of Boulogne saved an unidentified young Jewish woman who had left her home in London with the intention of sailing to Buenos Aires.

Are you traveling alone?

The young woman might have appeared skittish because, upon questioning, her statements were found to be "contradictory." The Jewish volunteer in Boulogne decided to notify the police immediately. Later, authorities found that her parents in London had no idea of the girl's whereabouts. Jewish social workers in Paris took over her case and eventually helped her find legitimate work.

Sometimes, if they were particularly vigilant, the volunteers could save women at their port of arrival. In September 1926, a Jewish community official named Selig Ganopol stationed at the port of Buenos Aires watched passengers disembark from a ship that had arrived from an undisclosed European port. Shortly after taking up his position, he saw "a girl looking about anxiously and who hardly seemed to know where to go." A few minutes later she was approached by a woman who had "already aroused suspicion." When he approached the two women, they told him that they were aunt and niece. But Ganopol had his doubts, and while the aunt went to claim the girl's luggage, he gave the girl the address of his organization. He warned her that she might be entering into a white-slavery ring. After a few days, when it became clear to the girl that her aunt and uncle wanted her to work as a prostitute, she immediately recalled the meeting at the port and began to plan her escape. "Then the uncle by marriage tried to violate her so as to reduce her self-respect," noted the report of the Jewish volunteer who investigated the case. The unidentified woman managed to communicate her plight to a neighbor, who contacted Ganopol's organization. The young woman was one of 925 "unprotected girls," including 85 non-Jewish women, whom Ganopol's organization, the Ezras Noschim, aided that year. The figure had almost doubled from the previous year, when the organization helped 525 young women arriving in Argentina destined for the white-slave market.

But the work was never easy, and the circumstances under which many young women ended up as prostitutes rarely clear. In Argentina an activist known only as Madame Arslau confessed that after three years of meeting just about every transatlantic ship that sailed into the port of Buenos Aires, "taking the gangway by assault, and ransacking the ship in search of young ladies gone astray," she had given up. Most of the women she met arrived with all sorts of delusional ideas about quick wealth in America and were simply not interested in being saved, she said. "It was their destitution that defeated me," she told a reporter. "They always chose their 'man' in preference to me. 'I know what I have come to do,' they say. 'I don't want morality; I want food.'"

The woman in black at the port of Amsterdam questioned Sally Knopf for what seemed like a long time. Perhaps this shtetl girl was in fact telling the truth about this mysterious uncle in America, but she still felt uneasy. In the end it might have seemed a feeble gesture—handing Sally a flyer in Yiddish, warning of the perils of white slavery on the other side of the world, telling her to contact the authorities immediately if she felt she was in any danger.

Maybe Sally would take the time to read the flyer when she settled into her cabin. Maybe she would be smarter than the others. One had to hope.

Don't talk to strange men. Don't believe any of their promises.

Sally politely took the piece of paper without giving it a glance, absentmindedly stuffing it into her carpetbag. With a pounding heart, she rushed to board her ship to America, a place she imagined steeped in permanent sunshine. What other fantasies had she concocted about her future life there? She would dress like a lady and sip tea on the terrace of her rich uncle's hotel. She would ride horses in the nearby forests and give orders to the hotel staff. Sally was certain that she would live happily with her rich Uncle Joe. She knew him to be a generous, good-hearted man who regularly sent packages of clothing to her family in the shtetl.

She knew that, but nothing else about him.

Sally was probably too busy daydreaming about her new life in Brazil to take a hard look at the warnings, printed in large black type on the piece of paper that languished somewhere at the bottom of her carpetbag.

Combat White Slavery.

But on a stormy night as her ship ploughed through the South Atlantic, Sally suddenly recalled those warnings with an icy clarity. That was the night she stood rigid with fear, the screams stuck in her throat, as she attempted to extricate herself from the embrace of the bald, Dutch ship's officer who groped her savagely, his hands furiously unbuttoning her dress, his wet lips on her neck. Although she managed to fight him off, years later she would look back on the encounter as a sign, like the black-clad stranger at the port—premonitions that things would not turn out well in America.

BERTHA PAPPENHEIM SAT bolt upright in an uncomfortable chair in the rabbi's waiting room. It was March 1911, and the fifty-two-year-old Austrian Jewish feminist was on what she called a "working tour" of Eastern Europe and the Middle East, to see for herself the conditions under which many shtetl girls were living, and why so many of them were so easily duped by the traffickers.

"The rabbi let us wait for a long time," she noted in her diary later that night. "Without a word, stonelike, he then let me look at his non-distinguished profile."

At the meeting with the unnamed rabbi, "a tall, dapper gentleman in Hungarian clerical garb" identified only by his initials, "H.A.," in her diary entry, Pappenheim boldly asked him to help her and her Frankfurt-based women's organization, especially in warning the young shtetl girls in Hungary of the dangers of getting caught up in the white-slave traffic to America. "I did some research, listened . . . and I learned something not only terrible, but also something shameful: many Jews are traders, many Jewish girls are goods," Pappenheim told just about every Jewish leader she met on her journey.

But not everyone wanted to be confronted with this harsh reality. Perhaps the Hungarian rabbi resented being talked to like this, by this *haute bourgeoise* with the snow white hair and the schoolmarmish disposition, who spoke impeccable German and had the manners of an aristocrat. For despite her good breeding and family connections, everyone knew Bertha Pappenheim was a troublemaker, an upstart in the Jewish community, and, worse— what did they call those women?—a *feminist*. Besides that, wasn't she mad, afflicted by nerves? In fact, Pappenheim had spent a few years in a sanatorium, her madness documented in Sigmund Freud and Josef Breuer's *Studies in Hysteria,* in which she appears as a central case study, under the pseudonym Anna O.

It's unlikely that the Hungarian rabbi knew so much about Pappenheim's personal medical history and its role in the development of psychoanalysis, but there was something about this woman that he obviously didn't like. In any case, he had no time for mad feminists. He was the spiritual leader of Budapest's Jewish congregation. He had more important things to think about, more important things to do than to speak to this diminutive spin-ster with the acid tongue. "The issue [of white slavery] doesn't in-terest me," he said.

When he was reminded of his role as the chairman of the Soci-ety for the Protection of Children, the rabbi seemed to shrug off his responsibilities to protect them from slave traffickers. "Yes," he said without batting an eyelid. "But only of children up to twelve or thirteen years of age. The older ones are not my business."

Just as Pappenheim was about to counter his arguments, the rabbi abruptly ended their meeting by "forbiddingly" raising his hand. "I shall not be converted," he said.

It wasn't the first time, and it would surely not be the last, that Bertha Pappenheim would sit openmouthed and wide-eyed at the total disinterest of her coreligionists, most of them men who by their "indifference and a frivolous philosophy of life that only rec-ognizes acquisition and pleasure as worthwhile goals" were little better than accomplices to what she called "the immoral com-merce" of impoverished shtetl girls. For Pappenheim, who be-came the most influential advocate for the shtetl girls who were forced into sexual slavery in America, the indifference of these revered Jewish leaders was difficult to swallow.

Pappenheim, who had grown up in a wealthy Viennese house-hold, decided while she was still in her twenties to devote her life to helping women and children in the Jewish community. In 1906 she rescued 120 Jewish children from the Russian pogroms and arranged for them to travel to Germany, where she found homes for all of them. In addition to setting up an orphanage in Frank-furt, where she lived after the death of her father and her bouts with hysteria in the 1880s, she founded the Judischer Frauenbund, a Jewish feminist organization whose members spent much of their time raising awareness of white slavery.

Although she started organizing against the traffickers at the turn of the last century, dispatching volunteers to European ports, finding placements at vocational schools for the young women her organization saved, by the mid-1920s when Sally Knopf was making her way to America, Pappenheim had made almost no headway in what was a complex and extremely unpopular issue. The problem was that most Jews just didn't want to hear about white slavery because they felt that drawing attention to the issue stigmatized all Jews. "We Jews talk so much about the Traffic that the world is beginning to believe that it largely exists among us and that we are greatly responsible for it," said one leading German rabbi in the late 1920s. "We rabbis are of the opinion that it is dangerous to talk so much about the Traffic and to be incessantly proclaiming our sins to the world."

Even most of the Jewish press was clearly against speaking too openly about white slavery, condemning the international gatherings of Jewish leaders that were convened by anti–white-slavery activists in London to come up with ways to suppress the Traffic. "Unhesitatingly, we are of the opinion that such a gathering ought not to have been held," noted an editorial in a British Jewish newspaper, in reference to one such gathering in 1927. Another newspaper noted that "over the suitability of the Conference, opinion in Jewish circles was strongly divergent." As a result, the conferences were not open to the public, and reports were heavily censored.

Despite the opposition to her cause, Pappenheim wasn't deterred. She was a fixture at these international gatherings, where she wasn't afraid to call for the emancipation of Jewish women in the shtetls and demand funds for public-awareness campaigns.

She also accused official Jewish leaders of "turning a blind eye" to the problem, and told of the poverty she had seen in the shtetls on her trips through Eastern Europe, where in most places "the

A dedicatory stone at
the Inhauma cemetery
in Rio de Janeiro.
(PHOTO BY ZORAN
MILICH)

BRAZIL AND RIVER PLATE SERVICES — ROYAL MAIL LINE — "A" and "D" VESSELS

NOTICE

Young Women Travelling Alone.

All Royal Mail passenger vessels are met on arrival at Buenos Aires by a lady representative of The National Vigilance Association who will be pleased to render advice and assistance to young women travelling alone. The lady can be met at the Purser's Office after the steamer has docked, or at the following address:

LAVALLE, 341 (Office 315).
BUENOS AIRES.

PASTABA

JAUNOM MOTERIM VAŽIUOJANČIOM VIENOM

Visus Royal Mail keleivinius garlaivius, kurie atvažiuoja į Buenos Aires, sutinka moteris kuri atstovauja Tarptautinio Apsaugojimo Draugijai, maloniai suteiks pagelbą jaunoms moterims kurios keliauja vienos. Šią moterį galima rasti laivo kasininko raštinėj, kuomet laivas sustoja uoste, arba sekančiu antrašu:

LAVALLE, 341 (Kontoras 315)
BUENOS AIRES.

NOTICE

Dames et Jeunes Filles Voyageant Seules

Une dame de confiance de l'Association Nationale de Vigilance (The National Vigilance Association) se rend à bord des paquebots de la Royal Mail, à leur arrivée à Buenos-Aires, et se fera un plaisir de conseiller et d'assister les dames et jeunes filles voyageant seules. On peut trouver cette dame au Bureau du Commissaire après l'accostage du navire ou à l'adresse suivante:

LAVALLE, 341 (Bureau 315).
BUENOS-AIRES.

UPOZORNENIE

MLADÝM ŽENÁM SAMOTNE CESTUJÚCIM

Všetky osobné lodi spoločnosti Royal Mail sú pri príjazdu do Buenos Aires očakávané zástupkyňou spolku "Národné Ochranné Sdruženi," ktorá ochotne podá radu i pomoc ženám samotne cestujúcim. Táto zástupkyňa môže byť vyhladaná po prístáni lodi v kancelárii pokladného dostojníka (Purser's Office), alebo pod následujúcou adresou:

LAVALLE, 341 (Office 315)
BUENOS AIRES.

A warning to women about traveling alone aboard steamers to South America and the dangers of the white slave trade. Warnings were printed in several different languages on placards and posted at ports in Europe and South America. (COURTESY OF FAWCETT LIBRARY, CITY OF LONDON POLYTECHNIC)

Sophia Chamys, who was bought by a Jewish pimp on a Warsaw street, was trafficked to brothels in South America. (SKETCH BY THE RIO DE JANEIRO POLICE FORCE, CIRCA 1890)

Rachel Liberman in a photograph taken Warsaw when she was nineteen years ol

Ferber, Rachel Liberman's first husband, en route to Argentina. Jacob sailed to South

Jacob Ferber's passport issued in Poland in 1921.

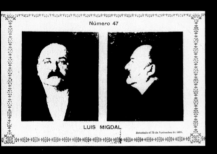

(above) Police photo of Luis Migdal, reportedly the founder of the Zwi Migdal criminal enterprise in Argentina.

(right) The photo shows Rachel Liberman, center, on October 22, 1922, the day she arrived in Buenos Aires. She is greeting her husband, Jacob, and her sister-in-law, Helke Milroth. Years later, Helke was arrested as a member of the Zwi Migdal for trafficking women.

Sophia Chamys and her pimp/husband, Isaac Boorosky, in a photograph taken just before Isaac dispatched her to a brothel in Buenos Aires.

Rachel Liberman and her two sons, David and Mauricio. When newspapers reported her involvement in the downfall of the Zwi Migdal, Rachel deliberately kept her family hidden from the press.

(right) "We need a broom to clean up the evil elements that traffic in women," says an editorial cartoon from the Argentine daily *Critica,* which was published as police raided brothels throughout the country in 1930.

Hace Falta una Escoba

Por Rojas

Este simbólico dibujo de Rojas fué publicado hace tiempo en CRITICA. Reclamábamos entonces la necesidad de empuñar "la escoba" para limpiar al país de elementos tenebrosos dedicados a la trata de blancas

The drawing shows how young naive shtetl girls were often recruited into brothels by wily pimps. (COURTESY OF TAMIMENT COLLECTION, NEW YORK UNIVERSITY)

The red light district in Buenos Aires. Photograph was taken by the dramatist Peretz Hirschbein in the 1920s. (COURTESY OF YIVO INSTITUTE, NEW YORK)

The prostitutes' synagogue and administrative offices of the Society of Truth on Afonso Cavalcanti Street in Rio de Janeiro. (COURTESY ZEVI GHIVELDER)

(below left) Police file of the Russian Jewish prostitute Estera Gladkowicer who arrived in Brazil in 1927, and commited suicide years later. She is buried at the Inhauma cemetery in Rio de Janeiro. (COURTESY BEATRIZ KUSHNIR)

Nome: ESTERA GLADKOWICER
Nacionalidade: Russa (Brasil.nat.) Nat. Russia
Pai: Izaak Hersz Gladkowicer
Mãe: Hinda Basia Gladkowicer
Nascido em 20 / 5 / 1907 Res. Avenida N.S.Fatima, 42 - ap.504
Profissão: domestica Estado civil: solteira Instrução: Primaria
Côr: branca Cabelos: oxig. Olhos: castanho Dossier N°.
Sinais característicos: visiveis, não tem.
Documentos: Carteira de Identidade n° 170.343 - I. F. P.
Histórico: Veio para o Brasil em 1927.

ARA 108 TENEBROSOS SE HA DICTADO PRISION P

Cuatro Famosos Tenebrosos

on los Socios de la Migdal e los que el Juez R. Ocampo lalla la Prueba del Delito

(right) The front page of the Argentine newspaper *Critica* proclaims the arrest of some of the most notorious members of the Zwi Migdal following police raids on brothels in September 1930. Most of those arrested later used their connections with the judiciary and police to escape justice.

(right) The Superior Sister Fanny Suszman, a prostitute and one of the early directors of the Society of Truth, in an image affixed to her tombstone at the Inhauma cemetery in Rio de Janeiro. (COURTESY BEATRIZ KUSHNIR)

(above) The Superior Sister Angelina Schaffran, a prostitute and one of the legendary presidents of the Society of Truth. The photo is taken from her tombstone at the Inhauma cemetery in Rio de Janeiro. (COURTESY BEATRIZ KUSHNIR)

(right) The only surviving photograph of Rebecca Freedman, the last president of the Society of Truth. (COURTESY OF THE NATIONAL ARCHIVES, RIO DE JANEIRO)

(left) The interior of the prostitutes' synagogue on Afonso Cavalcanti Street in Rio de Janeiro. (COURTESY OF ZEVI GHIVELDER)

(above right) The *tahara* room at the Inhauma cemetery in Rio de Janeiro. The bodies of Jewish prostitutes were cleansed on the marble table as per the Jewish purification ritual before burial in the cemetery. (COURTESY OF ZEVI GHIVELDER)

(left) A dedicatory stone at the Inhauma cemetery in Rio de Janeiro. (PHOTO BY ZORAN MILICH)

weekly wages of some fathers are just sufficient to buy the Sabbath bread and candles" and where most Jews "live worse than cattle." While Pappenheim noted that she could forgive the impoverished Jewish women of Eastern Europe who resorted to prostitution as a means of survival, she could never forgive her coreligionists for ignoring the social conditions that caused their plight in the first place.

Still, Pappenheim was a realist. She knew her entreaties fell on deaf ears, and so was fond of calling her work on behalf of the shtetl girls "Sisyphus Arbeit," or the work of Sisyphus, after the Greek mythical hero who was condemned to an eternity of frustration in the underworld. Fighting white slavery was clearly a losing battle because every time she seemed on the verge of a breakthrough, "her appeals for help would go unanswered and again she had to push the rock of her appeals up the mountain of indifference."

There were, however, some exceptions—a handful of influential Jews in Europe who rallied behind her cause, treating it as nothing less than "holy warfare."

Claude Montefiore, the British theologian and leader of Reform Judaism in Britain, was clearly on Pappenheim's side. He was determined to do his part to end the white-slave trade when he assumed the presidency of the Jewish Association for the Protection of Girls and Women at the turn of the last century. The organization was the most influential in its campaign against white slavery. Montefiore was so committed to ending the trade that he volunteered to go to the ports to counsel women traveling alone—an effort that did not meet with great success. With his elegantly cut English suits, aristocratic manner, and good looks, he was clearly more suited to diplomacy than social work, judging from his encounter with two Jewish prostitutes at the docklands. "Without knowing precisely what occurred when this distinguished, scholarly gentleman arrived at the docks, it is reported that the effort failed with the result that he decided to leave the more practical aspects of his charitable work to others."

Montefiore focused his efforts on drafting international legislation against the traffic of women and children, and agents for his organization traveled around the world compiling reports and trying to raise money for their efforts. At the conferences of the Jewish Association for the Protection of Girls and Women, he brought together Jewish delegates from Europe, the United States, and South America and forced them to take on such difficult issues as how to end the practice of *stille chuppah* in the more backward parts of Eastern Europe, and he called for equal rights in marriage and divorce for Jewish women. Montefiore and others also demanded increased funds for vocational training schools across Europe and suggested that more women be recruited into the police forces to deal with the victims of white slavery.

"Many of our sisters are victims, sometimes wholly unwittingly, sometimes half-wittingly, half consciously, sometimes tempted, sometimes under the pressure of poverty and privation," Montefiore argued. "We know that to ignore the evil is not only cruel to the victims—actual and future—but an injury to our cause." His advice to the delegates was not to cower behind the fear of provoking the anti-Semites but to fight them head-on and to work to help the young women forced into prostitution.

It was an eloquent speech, and it might even have received a standing ovation at the 1927 London conference on the suppression of the Traffic, the largest and also the last conference of its kind in Europe. But in reality Montefiore's passionate entreaties fell on deaf ears. For despite the warnings, the volunteers, the meetings, and the countless studies that were commissioned on the topic of Jewish white slavery, the respectable Jewish community did little to stop it.

Bertha Pappenheim continued to volunteer her efforts to fight the Traffic well into her sixties and seventies. Sometimes she went to the ports, to see for herself the still-steady stream of shtetl girls who were making their way to America. Perhaps she even met Sally Knopf in Amsterdam. In any case, she gave away the leaflets, tacked up the posters, and tried her best to warn the shtetl girls of the horrors of the white-slave traffic.

Sisyphus Arbeit.

Sometime in March 1924, when Sally Knopf sailed from the port of Amsterdam to join her Uncle Joe in America, Bertha Pappenheim must have returned from a particularly bleak day of work. She might have been talking to the shtetl girls at the ports or trying to convince yet another Jewish leader of the importance of the work she considered her duty. "All I discovered," she wrote, "was that a *single* voice, the voice of an unknown woman, produced no effect."

SALLY KNOPF COULDN'T STOP CRYING when her ship finally docked in Rio de Janeiro. After almost three weeks at sea, during which she was mostly confined to her cabin, terrified that she would be the victim of rape, Sally must have felt a strong sense of relief. Perhaps after her encounter with the Dutch officer, she would have taken the time to read through the pamphlet given to her by the Jewish volunteer at the port of Amsterdam. Or, if she didn't know how to read, maybe she sought out a young, sympathetic woman on the ship with a better education to read it for her.

Zima, a young woman from Poland who was sailing to Rio de Janeiro to meet her fiancé, might have read the pamphlet, for the two young women became constant companions on the trip.

In any case, by the time her ship docked at Rio de Janeiro, Sally must have understood the dangers, known everything there was to know about white slavery. Or at least enough to be careful.

Don't talk to strange men. Don't believe any of their promises.

"I don't know why I started to cry when my ship sailed into Guanabara Bay," she would later confess. "But when I saw that city bathed by the sun and the blue sea I felt as if I had been re-born. I felt free."

But there was also lingering uncertainty, a premonition that something was simply not right. She had arrived in a city she knew nothing about to meet a relative who a month earlier had seemed little more than a distant family legend. She had left behind poverty and violent discrimination in Poland, but she had also left her family, and for the first time in her short life, she felt alone, unable to communicate, totally helpless.

Sally blinked at the crowds on the dock as she prepared to leave the relative safety of the ship. Dozens of passengers nudged her with their bags in their haste to meet their waiting relatives. "Everywhere, people were crying when they found their relatives," said Sally, recalling her arrival dozens of years later. "When I saw those sun-tanned people, I told myself, 'These are happy people.' You had no choice but to be happy in a country with such a brilliant sun."

Rio might have seemed like a happy, sunlit land, but for decades before Sally's arrival the city had served as a horrible prison for hundreds of young shtetl girls. What would Sally have thought if someone had told her the story of another Polish girl, Sophia

Chamys, brutally exploited by Isaac Boorosky, a fellow Jew and Pole?

As for Boorosky, the Brazilian authorities had deported him along with nearly 120 other Jewish pimps just before the First World War. Yet the unprecedented sweep seemed to have had little effect on the trade in Brazil. "It is to be regretted," noted a prominent Jewish volunteer, "that the major part of the immoral trade in the towns is in the hands of women, who are amassing fortunes and proving themselves very dangerous." In order to preserve their wealth in Brazil, Isaac and many other pimps entrusted their business to madams until they could return to the country. It is not clear whether Isaac Boorosky managed to return to Brazil after his deportation, but many of the other pimps did return, and resumed their businesses as if the police raids had never occurred.

Through all of this, and even through a world war that disrupted travel and shipping lines, the shtetl girls continued to arrive. And now, arriving at the port, they were on their own. Unlike the European and Argentine ports, where Jewish volunteers regularly met the ships searching for single girls like Sally, in Rio there was no one to meet them. There was no one to search them out and warn them of the well-dressed men who lingered at the port, who spoke Yiddish and were too quick to offer their services. If young women arriving alone claimed that they needed to reach a relative in the city, the pimps were only too glad to oblige, bundling their unwitting victims into the backseat of a taxi, after which many were never heard from again. At the port of Rio de Janeiro there were no "Combat White Slavery" placards, translated into several languages, no women in black.

Even the Jewish activists in London admitted that they had a problem with Rio. "There was never any determined effort to fight the evil," said one of them. There were no societies of organized Jewish volunteers in the city, and the London activists were often forced to rely on consular officials or European business travelers to Brazil "to give up their leisure time in order to further the movement against white slavery" whenever they had urgent business—a young woman who needed to be saved from a brothel—in the country.

In one instance the British consul general was called upon to save a young British Jewish woman who had been forced by her husband to become a prostitute in the city. The unnamed husband returned to London with the couple's children, leaving his wife to work in a brothel. He had treated her "so badly that friends in Rio took her part" and sought out the authorities, the police report said. The woman was eventually saved, after a coordinated action by the Jewish Association for the Protection of Girls and Women in London and the British consulate in Rio. She was repatriated to London and eventually managed to regain custody of her children.

Not only were there no Jewish volunteers waiting for Sally Knopf at the port of Rio de Janeiro, there was no Uncle Joe. Not that she knew what Uncle Joe looked like. She had seen him once in a family photograph, but in her agitation she could no longer remember anything about him. Did he look like her mother? Was he tall, short, heavyset? Did he wear a hat? Did he have a mustache?

Sally began to panic, so much that she misplaced the letter of introduction that Uncle Joe had written to the Brazilian immigration authorities. In her agitated state, she might have handed them the only other piece of paper she had in her carpetbag, but it's not likely the Brazilian authorities could understand enough Yiddish to read what was written on the "Combat White Slavery" pamphlet, although they surely had seen hundreds of young women like Sally arriving alone, scanning the waiting crowds for signs of a familiar face.

Sally eventually found the letter at the bottom of her carpetbag, but she was about to give up hope of seeing Uncle Joe at the port. What to do? Where to go? As she stood transfixed, Zima, the young Jewish woman she had met on the ship, gave her a card with her address on it. She told Sally to contact her in case no one arrived at the port to meet her. Then she left, on the arm of her Brazilian fiancé, who had arrived earlier to meet her.

When Sally finally heard someone calling her name through the crowd, she thought she was dreaming. But it wasn't a dream, it was her heavyset Uncle Jenkel, whom she did know, and who had sailed to Rio a week earlier. He was running in her direction, followed by a young woman who must have been about the same age as Sally. Uncle Jenkel apologized for his delay and told her that Uncle Joe had been unable to meet her ship. "Business," he said. Sally nodded, without pressing him for more details, so happy was she to see a familiar face.

But who was this thin teenager who accompanied Uncle Jenkel? Rachel, a shtetl girl, was the daughter of Uncle Joe's friends in the city, Uncle Jenkel explained when he caught Sally staring at his young companion. Uncle Jenkel did not bother to explain why she had accompanied him to the port to meet Sally.

Uncle Jenkel took Sally's carpetbag, and the three piled into a rickety taxi, driven by an old black man, who kept a long strand of colorful beads wrapped around the rearview mirror and a small postcard of a black woman with flowing robes. Who was that woman? Sally may have wondered. Years later, she found out it was the goddess of the sea, worshipped by Brazil's former slaves.

"I had never seen so much beauty in one place," Sally recalled

of soaring palm trees, pale pink and whitewashed colonial mansions, and black women who balanced baskets of exotic fruits on
their heads. "As I sat in the taxi I saw mountains, a blue sea, beautiful gardens and soaring buildings."

By the time Sally arrived in Brazil in the mid-1920s, the country was already well known to thousands of Jewish settlers, who
had sent messages back to Europe about the rich and beautiful
land they had discovered. Brazil was the richest part of America,
they claimed. "It was no longer the land of the monkeys, but a
land of prosperity and little religious conflict." Brazil proved such
a popular destination for Eastern European Jews that many "even
concocted a complicated scheme to gain passages and visas." First,
they applied to work on one of the Jewish colonies in the southern
state of Rio Grande do Sul, a commitment that earned them a free
passage to the country from the Jewish Colonization Association,
which had bought up land for agricultural colonies in Argentina
and for Jewish settlement in southern Brazil. Once the new immigrants arrived in the agricultural colonies of the south, however,
they took a train to São Paulo after agreeing to work on coffee
plantations. Many simply hopped the train when they reached the
large cities where they would look for work in their own professions.

Riding in the taxi, the warmth of the sun beating down on her
face, the salty ocean breeze tossing her hair, Sally must have
thought she had arrived in paradise. Her backseat companion,
Rachel, said nothing on the journey to the colonial house on Marquês de Sapucaí Street, in a lower-middle-class district near downtown, where Uncle Jenkel deposited both girls. Sally spent ten
days with Rachel at the house, waiting for her Uncle Joe to arrive.
At first she seemed astonished by her good fortune. "We ate
chicken every day, which was a real surprise because in Poland

such a luxury was only possible on the big religious and national holidays," she wrote many years later.

But something was not right in the house on Marquês de Sapucaí Street. For one thing, Rachel seemed to go out every night, unchaperoned. When Sally asked Rachel what she did in the evenings, Rachel just shrugged. She seemed tired and defeated, and spent much of the day locked in her room sleeping. And a couple who occupied the bottom floor of the house also behaved quite strangely. The husband seemed not to work, and the wife also went out at night, returning in the mornings.

It's not clear when Sally realized that she was an occupant of a house of prostitution. Was this the white-slave trade that she had been warned so much about?

Don't talk to strange men. Don't believe any of their promises.

Was Uncle Jenkel one of these men who trafficked in shtetl girls? One night, struck by her own boldness, Sally decided to ask him. Uncle Jenkel seemed to evade her question and instead offered to return her to Poland. He would be sailing for Europe next week "on business," and if Sally felt uncomfortable and wanted to return to the shtetl, he would be happy to arrange her trip.

But after more than a week of basking in the warmth of Rio de Janeiro, of eating chicken every day, Sally must have thought the journey back to the muddy shtetl would seem like defeat. "I left Poland full of hope because Uncle Joe promised he would also send for my family," she told Uncle Jenkel. "I think I can do a lot if I stay in this country. So, I'll make you a deal: I won't ask you anything more about your line of work in Brazil, if you stop talking about sending me back to Poland."

Uncle Jenkel returned to Poland just as Uncle Joe arrived in Rio de Janeiro to meet Sally.

"He was very handsome," recalled Sally. "He was tall and sun-tanned and he dressed very well. Even though he was older than my mother, he looked much younger than she did."

Uncle Joe seemed overwhelmed by his beautiful young niece, and a few days before they boarded a train to the interior of the country where Uncle Joe ran his inn, he took Sally to what seemed like the city's finest boutiques. For Sally, who had felt guilty for spending part of the money for the journey on a bottle of rose water, the beautiful silk dresses and leather shoes that she tried on and modeled for her uncle left her head spinning.

Wearing a new suit that her uncle had bought her for the train journey to the state of Minas Gerais, Sally seemed to be living her daydreams, the ones in which she starred as the beautifully dressed proprietress of a fancy hotel in the country. Any girl would be ecstatic to be riding on a train wearing new clothes in the company of such a good-looking and obviously wealthy relative.

Any girl but Sally Knopf.

Did her uncle sit too close to her on the train? Did he stare at her too longingly?

It's not clear what happened on the journey to Poço das Caldas, the small town in the Brazilian interior where she once imagined she would be spending the rest of her life. But on the train and after her arrival, something went terribly wrong. "Uncle Joe," she recalled years later, "revealed himself to be a different man."

Perhaps it started with his lingering kisses, uncomfortably close to her lips. Then he might have resorted to groping her waist, reaching for her breasts, in the dark recesses of the hallways on the long, oppressively hot summer afternoons. As she held her breath and tried to repel her uncle's advances, Sally could hear her aunt chatting animatedly to the guests who lounged on the white-washed wicker chairs on the terrace, where black waitresses poured tea. "Uncle Joe started to chase me, making romantic advances, even though I was his niece and underage," she wrote. "It became torture for me. I started to avoid him every way I could, but the situation didn't get any better because he always found ways to get close to me when my aunt was not around."

She knew Uncle Jenkel was a trafficker, and now she had the feeling that Uncle Joe was one as well. This was the family business, the white-slave trade. The woman in black had warned her about the strange men and their empty promises, and the placards in Amsterdam had even listed the names and locations of the most infamous Jewish slavers; but nobody had warned her about her own family.

When he wrote her unsuspecting family in Poland promising to make Sally his heir, Uncle Joe clearly had other plans for his niece. She didn't wait to find out what they were. With the help of one of the housekeepers at her uncle's hotel, she escaped from Poço das Caldas dressed as a man, determined to return to her family in Poland. Sally made her way back to Rio, where she went to live with Zima, the Jewish woman she had befriended on the ocean crossing from Amsterdam. Hysterical, Sally told Zima the entire story, and asked for help in returning to Poland.

"You shouldn't go back," said Zima. "If you go back now you'll just have to deal with all the same problems that we thought were behind us, especially the hatred of our race."

Months later Sally sought out a Jewish group that helped new immigrants in Brazil. She had decided that it was her duty to denounce both her uncles, to warn the anti–white-slavery activists. It was excruciatingly embarrassing to tell her story to a stranger, but Sally felt she had no other choice—not if other shtetl girls were to be saved a similar fate. What if she hadn't managed to escape? Would she be working in one of her uncle's brothels in the interior of Brazil? How would anyone have found her there?

The Jewish volunteers listened patiently to her story, but they had clearly seen this all before—traffickers who induced their own relatives into prostitution, inviting them to come to America from Eastern Europe. It was nothing new to them. The seduction, if you could call it that, usually began after the girl's first few weeks in America. "First through gentle suggestions, and then by more forceful ways of persuasion—which included raping the girl so she would acquiesce once her virginity was destroyed—her life would become doomed to the brothel."

"Where have you been, my girl!" remarked one of the Jewish volunteers who helped Sally settle in Brazil. "That man [Jenkel] is not accepted in the Jewish community in Rio de Janeiro because he works with white slaves. Your Uncle Joe is his partner!"

Sally never told her family in Poland about the kind of business her uncles were involved with in America. It was simply too embarrassing, too difficult to explain. Besides, her confession to the Jewish volunteers in Rio de Janeiro did nothing to end their business, nothing to protect their other victims. Nobody contacted the authorities; her uncles were never brought to the police for questioning. In the end, Sally decided that nobody was really interested in combating white slavery, and both uncles continued to bring the shtetl girls from Poland to work in their brothels.

For her part, Sally tried her best to get as far from them as she could. After her marriage to a respectable Jewish entrepreneur in Rio de Janeiro, Sally and her new husband headed deep into the Amazon rainforest to work on a ranch.

Years later, when she recalled her brushes with her white-slaver uncle in her diary, which was published in Brazil in the late 1970s, the poisonous snakes and hostile native tribes she encountered in the middle of the jungle seemed like minor nuisances by comparison.

. . .

REBECCA FREEDMAN KNEW BETTER than to trust the people she called the respectable Jews. Perhaps, like Sally Knopf, she had tried to seek their help in the past, and perhaps they had let her down.

Or perhaps she knew that most of the Jewish immigrants were afraid of women like her, afraid that the Jewish prostitutes with their heavily rouged cheeks, their tight skirts, and their high heels would influence their precious daughters. From her window in the brothel she occupied in the Mangue, Rebecca could see these respectable Jews, who covered the eyes of their daughters as they rode the trams that rattled outside her door. "They were a huge stain on our immigration, because they were flamboyant and they never tried to hide who they were," recalled a Jewish social worker whose organization refused to work with the Jewish prostitutes. "We were not even permitted to talk about them."

Perhaps this is the reason there were no Jewish volunteers to meet Rebecca Freedman's ship from New York, or Sally Knopf's from Amsterdam. Not that it's likely anyone would have thought to stop Rebecca Freedman. Unlike Sally, Rebecca didn't look frightened, didn't look confused. And if they had approached her, had dared to hand her a leaflet or offer her a job as a seamstress or a shop attendant, she probably would have told them the truth. She didn't need to be converted, didn't need a job, and didn't need the Jewish busybodies to tell her she was "unclean."

Rebecca Freedman knew in her heart that she was clean, but she had no illusions about her clients; she knew they were *treif,* or unclean, as she liked to say, using the Yiddish word for emphasis. But why shouldn't she accept their money? The money was kosher, she was fond of telling anyone who dared ask.

Rebecca had little time to worry about what the wider Jewish community thought of her. As soon as she arrived in Rio, and made the fateful decision to knock on the door of the colonial house on Luís de Camões Street, she became inundated with work for the Society of Truth. It's not clear when she volunteered to perform the *tahara* ritual on her dead sisters, but she seems to have joined the organization as a full-fledged dues-paying member soon after her arrival in Rio de Janeiro in 1916. Later she was elected to its board of directors, overseeing the organization's finances for years to come.

"There was nothing else for us to do," said Rebecca when she was well into her nineties and confined to her bed. "Nobody else would help us. We had to do everything for ourselves." They couldn't turn to the respectable Jewish community to help organize their lives, and they surely couldn't turn to their oppressors, the pimps, who raped and tortured them when they refused to do their bidding. Instead, they sought to foster strong ties among themselves, and created an organization that was ahead of its time.

In exchange for monthly dues that amounted to the equivalent of a few dollars, women who belonged to the society elected a board of directors every January by secret ballot to oversee their collective affairs. Board members, such as Rebecca Freedman, were treated with reverence, and called the Superior Sisters by the other members. Wearing light blue sashes of office, they presided over meetings, which in the early days were held in one of the clapboard brothels in the Mangue. The inauguration of a new board of directors was a festive occasion, celebrated with speeches, baskets of freshly cut flowers, and a table piled with homemade delicacies and liqueurs.

There were other occasions for celebration, of course. Weddings were particularly joyous occasions, for which the members would decorate the brothel with red roses and red carpets. If the bride could not afford a small dowry, as was the custom, the prostitutes took up a collection for her at the end of their monthly meetings. Of course, no self-respecting rabbi would preside at such a wedding, so the prostitutes had to find other ways to marry their daughters, who, in the early days at least, always married within their own small community. They hired a cantor and invited their male friends. "We danced the Tora, and it was beautiful," said the daughter of a prostitute who was married at one of the society's makeshift synagogues.

But the organization's most important functions were focused on old age and death. "When a member became gravely ill they automatically rendered their power of attorney to the board, which in case of death took on the responsibility of distributing their assets among their heirs." The organization also took care of their medical expenses and burials when they died.

We had to do everything for ourselves.

And yet, for nearly fourteen years their power was usurped, after the Jewish pimps took over the organization and the cemetery that the women had fought so long to establish.

It's not clear why the pimps decided to take over the Society of Truth in 1918. Perhaps they were feeling their mortality, entering old age, and wanted to die with dignity as Jews. Where else could they do that except at the cemetery at Inhaúma, the one controlled by the women they had treated so brutally? And maybe there was a more sinister motive—keeping the women under their thumbs. Maybe the men had more cash to donate, and were reluctantly admitted by the original board members when they offered to put up the money to buy their cemetery.

For years the pimps had tried to infiltrate the respectable Jewish organizations in America, never quite accepting the reality that as rich as they became they would never be accepted by their core-

ligionists. At one point Jewish pimps in Argentina offered to contribute huge sums of money to the local Chevra Kadisha, or sacred
burial society, in order to be buried in the Jewish cemetery. Although the organization was deeply divided between the Ashkenazi members who wanted nothing to do with the pimps and the
Sephardic Jews who welcomed their contribution, the Ashkenazi
sentiment prevailed and "the separation between purity and im-
purity was extended even to the dead."

So great was the fear of admitting the "unclean ones" in any
form that one rabbi threatened to write in his testament that if the
pimps were allowed into the Jewish cemetery, he should be in-
terred in the municipal cemetery, preferring "to lie among honorable gentiles than among our *tmeyim*."

When they finally gave up on the illusion of becoming respectable members of Jewish society, the pimps decided to storm
the organization created by the prostitutes, who were, after all,
their own landsmen, their own people. They had all come from
the same part of the world, were all in the same business. Every
good Jew needed a Chevra Kadisha, especially when they were
living far from home. Since ancient times, the burial society had
been an essential component in the lives of immigrant Jews. It was
essential to the Jewish ideal of community, "reflecting the
poignant reality, that for more, America was now home, the burial
society symbolized too the fear of being buried among strangers as
well as the continued maintenance of one of Judaism's most enduring traditions."

The women of the Society of Truth may have been in an up-
roar at the forced entry of their pimps and oppressors, but perhaps
there was little they could do. They were all Jews, and to deny a
fellow Jew burial in a Jewish cemetery seemed to go against all of
their principles. (In 1924, at the founding of the prostitutes'

mutual-aid organization in the city of São Paulo, the all-woman board took an important lesson from their sisters in Rio when they expressly prohibited pimps from being elected to their board of directors, which throughout its history was dominated by women.)

Still, the pimps brought nothing but trouble, and Rebecca Freedman and the other women seized on every opportunity to get rid of their leadership. One opportunity came in July 1929 after Jacob Weinstein, a pimp who had muscled his way onto the board, was arrested after the attempted suicide of Fanny Weinstein, his eighteen-year-old "wife." Fanny had immigrated to Rio from Russia with her mother, who sought work as a prostitute in order to support her daughter. Fanny drifted into the underworld of the Jewish pimps and brothels, where she met Jacob, a wealthy and well-known pimp. In December 1928, as she was recovering from childbirth, Jacob suggested, gently at first, that she work for him so that they could make enough money to return to Europe.

The blows began when Fanny refused to work in the brothels. Jacob began to treat her as he did his other "acquisitions." He repeatedly raped her, threatened to take away her newborn baby. After months of abuse, Fanny fell into a deep depression and tried to kill herself, swallowing poison as her newborn wailed on the bed beside her.

It's not clear why police arrived on the scene. Perhaps the neighbors suspected something was amiss when they heard the incessant, piercing screams of the child. Whatever or whoever alerted them, police reached Fanny just before the effects of the poison set in, and rushed her and the baby to hospital. When Jacob Weinstein was confronted with the attempted suicide, he told police that Fanny came from a family of prostitutes, and that everyone knew that she had been raped by her mother's pimp.

Those girls are all alike. No morals. No sense of shame.

A native of Constantinople, Jacob Weinstein had arrived in Brazil in 1916, sailing from Turkey the same year Rebecca Freedman journeyed from New York City. By the time police hauled him in for questioning after Fanny's attempted suicide some twelve years later, Jacob was already a Brazilian citizen, spoke the language fluently, and, more important, knew how to deal with the cops. He had friends in high places, he wore fashionably tailored suits, he was a Freemason.

Those girls are all alike.

But the police didn't believe his story, and after medical examinations found evidence of long-term violence, Jacob was charged with rape.

It was at that point that Rebecca Freedman and her sisters saw the opportunity for a coup d'état. They immediately evicted Jacob Weinstein from their organization for having violated their by-laws, for having committed a serious breach "against the security and honor and honesty of the family." For despite the fact that the members of the Society of Truth lived on the margins of respectable society, the board would simply not tolerate its members breaking the law. Other members had been kicked out for lesser infractions. A year earlier Bertha Wernick was suspended from the São Paulo branch of the prostitutes' organization after she physically attacked a board member in a meeting. Although the details of the incident are vague, Wernick appears to have been suspended for two months, during which time she was prohibited from attending any social or religious functions in the community of the Jewish prostitutes.

But compared with Jacob's offense, Wernick's was relatively minor. Although many Jewish prostitutes had been raped by their pimps in the past, by the late 1920s it was no longer tolerated, especially if the offender was a dues-paying member of the Society of Truth. Perhaps Jacob Weinstein was surprised by his harsh treatment. Shortly after his arrest at the end of July 1929, twenty-eight-year-old Jacob, registered member 185, found himself summarily kicked out of the organization he and other pimps had so desperately tried to control. Even his highly placed friends in local government and the local branch of the Masonic order could do little to help him.

But Weinstein's exile was short-lived, and when his friends in the Masons, police, and local government finally came to his defense a year later, he was acquitted of charges of aggravated assault, rape, and procuring his ex-wife for a brothel. He was readmitted as a full member of the society following his acquittal in September 1930. Perhaps board members decided that they could not afford to lose a member who paid his dues on time, or perhaps they simply did not feel they had the right to deny a Jew, no matter what he had done in the past, the right to be buried in their Jewish cemetery.

Jacob Weinstein remained a full and active member of the society until his death in 1970. Perhaps it's a testament to his wealth and power in the Rio de Janeiro underworld that his is among the largest tombs at the Inhaúma cemetery. Instead of a Star of David, there are Masonic symbols carved into his black granite headstone, along with the following inscription: "In life you were our love and comfort. In death you are missed by your companion, son, sister-in-law and grandchildren." There is no mention of his "wife" Fanny Weinstein, and no documentation of what happened to her and her baby.

Two years after the Jacob Weinstein incident, Rebecca Freedman and her sisters were able to regain control of the Society of Truth. It is not clear why or how this happened, but almost as soon as it did, the new all-woman board saw fit to pass a series of bylaws establishing new rules of conduct with respect to financial issues. The most important of these was Article 27, which stated that "those who divert funds or other assets while occupying the position of treasurer will be immediately eliminated and will have to indemnify the association."

Had the previous all-male board tried to embezzle funds? Had they violated their own articles of incorporation? It's difficult to say, since the surviving minutes offer no explanation as to why the ten-member male board was replaced by the same number of women. Perhaps the abrupt changes also had a great deal to do with the death of two of the organization's key male leaders, Abisch Klinger, the president, and Jonas Izkovitz, the first secretary. It's difficult to believe that a diversion of funds could have occurred in an association that had such a strong commitment to internal rules of ethics.

We had to do everything for ourselves.

In the end, they did do everything for themselves. As oppressed as they were in the brothels, the Jewish prostitutes would accomplish what the diligent Jewish volunteers, the women in black, and the authorities on two continents had failed so miserably to do. For Rebecca Freedman and her sisters it would come as little surprise that one of their own would quietly rise up and almost single-handedly put a stop to their oppression, unleashing a chain of events that would spell the end of the white-slave trade in the Americas.

CHAPTER SIX

The Miracle

It must have taken a tremendous effort of will for Julio Alsogaray to remain calm throughout the lengthy interrogation. Not that the federal police commissioner was known for outbursts. To anyone who worked with him he was a sober, conservative professional, carefully weighing the facts before he proceeded with an arrest or hauled anyone in for questioning.

He was careful, but he was also passionate, a man obsessed with cleaning up the crime and corruption that dominated his beloved country. He was singularly devoted to his job, often the first to arrive at precinct headquarters and the last to leave, the kind of person who always seemed to show up late—if at all—for family gatherings. So it really should have been no surprise that Alsogaray was spending New Year's Eve 1929 in his office in the cavernous precinct building, the headquarters of the so-called Seventh Section of the Federal Police in downtown Buenos Aires.

It's not that the commissioner made a conscious decision to

spend the evening in his office, his shirtsleeves rolled up, a pen in his hand, his profile illuminated in the glare of his desk lamp. As he often told his family and his fellow officers, he had no choice. Crime never took a holiday, and neither should the law.

Still, he must have heard outside his window the revelers who took to downtown streets to usher in the new decade. But if he was aware that it was New Year's Eve, it's likely Alsogaray would have treated the loud merrymaking as little more than a nuisance. Despite the summer heat, he would surely have shut his window, turned on his small metal fan, and refocused his attention on the woman who sat in a straight-backed wooden chair on the other side of his desk.

With her discreet pearl earrings, dark dress, and brown hair pulled into a bun, Rachel Liberman looked more like a prosperous homemaker than a prostitute. If Alsogaray had seen her running for the tram, or buying vegetables at the market, he probably wouldn't have given her a second look, assuming that this heavyset woman was a well-to-do *porteña*. Of course, it was the image Rachel wanted so desperately to convey. In all her years working in the cheap brothels of La Boca near the port, Rachel eschewed the high heels, the cheap lingerie, the heavy makeup of her trade. She might have had to work as a prostitute to survive, but at some point she must have resolved that she never wanted to look like one.

A twenty-nine-year-old Polish immigrant who had arrived in Buenos Aires with so much hope seven years before, Rachel dreamed of reclaiming the small antiques shop that she had only just managed to open in a well-to-do enclave of the federal capital. Unlike most of the other Eastern European prostitutes, Rachel had made a deal with her pimp and managed to leave the brothel after a few years. But middle-class respectability eluded her, especially since her pimp reneged on his promise, reluctant to let go of one of his most profitable women. He must have thought she understood what he meant when he sent the thugs to burst into her shop. It was revenge, they said, just in case she missed the point. To prove they were serious, they smashed ornate glass bowls, knifed expensive oil paintings, broke wooden chair legs. And next time, they warned, they would do the same to her.

Perhaps anyone else in the same situation would have been frightened, but the threat of violence just seemed to strengthen Rachel's resolve. It's not clear why she was so determined to tell her story to the police. She had worked hard in order to save the money to open her antiques business, and she was not about to let a group of ruffians, no matter how powerful they were, take it all away from her. Especially now, when she was so close to realizing her dream of living a respectable life.

Yes, this also was revenge, Rachel might have thought as she slowly told her story to the commissioner in Polish-accented Spanish.

She spoke hesitantly and softly at first, but Alsogaray hung on her every word, occasionally interrupting her in midsentence to make sure he had the correct spellings of names, asking her to confirm addresses. He knew that Rachel's testimony, if she was brave enough to go through with it, could signal the end of the mighty Zwi Migdal organization, which had been a major player in the Argentine underworld for nearly half a century.

A man who had spent most of his professional career fighting the Jewish pimps and the corruption of his fellow officers, Alsogaray felt that Rachel Liberman's testimony was the long-awaited "miracle" he needed in order to take swift and determined action against them. None of the Jewish prostitutes under the control of the Zwi Migdal had dared to speak out against them in the past.

Rachel's detailed testimony, which implicated most of the Zwi Migdal hierarchy, was the weapon he needed to act. Having waited nearly a decade for such a breakthrough, Alsogaray insisted that the testimony be recorded immediately, just in case Rachel had a change of heart.

As he sat scribbling notes in his policeman's shorthand, did Alsogaray remember the other poor Jewish women he had tried to help in the past?

Did he recall Brony Spigler's body, covered in cigarette burns and bruises? When his men found her in 1926, she was so badly bruised and beaten that she was unconscious and had to be carried out of the brothel. Spigler had been brought to Argentina by agents of Abe Marchik, the man the other pimps called the king of the Buenos Aires underworld. Marchik had made his fortune recruiting impoverished shtetl girls to work as prostitutes for German soldiers during the First World War. After the war, he brought them to Argentina.

There was also Ita Kaiser, the young woman with the haunted expression and the heartbreaking limp. How had the pretty girl from Warsaw been crippled so? It was one of her clients, moved to pity, who had contacted Alsogaray's men. Kaiser, a plucky nineteen-year-old who had fiercely resisted working in the brothels, walked with a limp from the continuous beatings she had received from her pimp, a man named Victor Smieten. No amount of makeup could hide the bruises on her face and body. After meeting Ita and examining her wounds, Alsogaray had personally gone after Smieten, ensuring that the corruption that permeated the police forces didn't allow the criminal to slip through the cracks. Smieten was sentenced to twelve years in the notorious prison in Ushuaia, at the frigid southern tip of Argentina, for the pain and suffering he inflicted upon Kaiser and the other women he controlled. But he served only a portion of his sentence before returning to the streets of his native Warsaw, where he continued to buy and sell women for the brothels of America.

In the end all the pimps escaped justice, even Arnaldo Noyman, who had been so cruel to his own niece, the Polish girl named Perla Pezeborska. For some reason, it was Perla's case that seemed to haunt Alsogaray the most. When he was exhausted at the end of a long day, it was always Perla's face—her sad eyes and emaciated frame—that seeped into his thoughts, made him work even harder in his mission to put the Zwi Migdal out of business. A year earlier, when he found the twenty-two-year-old shtetl girl stretched out on the tiny metal-frame bed in a downtown brothel, Alsogaray thought Perla was dead. "Her body seemed not to feel any pain, but deep in her eyes we saw the tragedy," wrote Alsogaray in his black police notebook.

Perla's aunt and uncle had kept her locked up in the brothel and would not even permit her to walk on the patio, for fear that she would manage to escape. She had arrived from a shtetl in Poland to live with her uncle Arnaldo Noyman, one of the Zwi Migdal's most notorious pimps. When Perla refused his advances, he and his wife confined her to a room in one of their filthy brothels.

Desperate, Perla wrote a note in Yiddish, which she tied to a rock. In the early morning hours when the brothel was quiet, she threw the rock through her window, hoping that someone would find it. "To the society that protects women: I beg you to come get me from Noyman's house," the note said. "I beg you to come at once and save me as soon as possible, because I am in danger of disappearing. Perla Pezeborska. Lavalle, 2038."

In danger of disappearing.

Perla's words must have struck Alsogaray hard. So many of the shtetl girls had disappeared into the brothels of Buenos Aires. Alsogaray read Perla's hand-scrawled note several times, pondering its message, before he decided to act. The note, written on a torn piece of paper, had been passed on to him by a Jewish newspaperman named Mathias Stoliar. The editor of the Yiddish daily *Di Presse,* Stoliar had called Alsogaray immediately after one of his reporters brought him the note, which a passerby had found outside Perla's brothel.

Alsogaray personally led the raid that saved Perla. "I resolved then and there to take her violently from the claws of those repulsive criminals," wrote Alsogaray, who helped his men lift the body of the semiconscious young woman out of the bed.

Perla survived her ordeal, becoming one of the only shtetl girls who was saved before she was raped and forced to work as a prostitute. The Noymans were arrested on the spot, but thanks to their "godfathers and defenders" in the Argentine government, the case against them was dropped.

Corruption was Alsogaray's biggest challenge, even as he was promoted to head the Seventh Section of the Federal Police, with the sole responsibility of destroying the Zwi Migdal. He knew that many of his colleagues in the police force were on the pimps' payroll, knew that the Zwi Migdal enjoyed almost total impunity. In addition to the police, they had bribed everyone from leading politicians to high-court judges. They also retained some of the city's craftiest lawyers. For years, fighting against them had been a losing battle—"the struggle of a Lilliputian against Hercules" was how Alsogaray put it. Still, there were a handful of honest men in high places in Argentina, particularly in the military, men who wanted to end the white-slave trade and lead a revolution against high-level corruption in their country.

Alsogaray had seen how the pimps made their important friends. They gave them envelopes full of bills and wined and dined them. They threw lavish parties at their Beaux Arts mansion, framed by stately imperial palms, on Córdoba Street. The pimps, members of the Zwi Migdal hierarchy, mingled with the city's most corruptible elite while waiters in tuxedoes and white gloves served champagne and canapés.

Had Alsogaray been invited to one of these soirées? Had they offered him a car, an apartment in the fashionable Recoleta neighborhood, as they had done with his predecessors? Had he been tempted by the women they sent his way, the ones who smoked cigarettes and eyed him suggestively outside the precinct headquarters? Or did the envelopes thick with bills that he regularly found among the files on his desk give him pause? It's just a small *propina,* Commissioner, a tip from your admirers, the pimps liked to taunt him.

Or perhaps they had tried other ways to get to him. Perhaps the threats came late at night, while Alsogaray worked at his desk. Did the loud, sudden ringing of the telephone in his office at the precinct headquarters jolt him awake, perhaps just as he was drifting off to sleep at his desk? Did the voice on the other end of the phone ever threaten to kill him, to hurt his family? It is not known what kind of pressure the pimps might have exerted over Alsogaray, but he was not one to be moved. He was an obsessive cop, a strong nationalist, committed to the cause of justice and to purging what he called these "foreign elements" who were "polluting the great Argentine nation."

"Their attitude was to pay out and be insolent," said Alsogaray of the traffickers he pursued for years. "They thought themselves gentlemen because they always paid well, and because they lived without fear of repression. Their sense of impunity knew no bounds."

In order to fight against the organization, he assembled his best men and forged alliances with the only other group of people in

the capital who hated the pimps more than he did. The respectable
Jews were only too glad to help the commissioner, a worthy man
and their only ally among the authorities. They passed on tips they
received about women being held in brothels against their will
and gave him intelligence reports on the pimps' activities that they
culled from other Jewish organizations around the world.

Alsogaray obsessively studied the pimps' habits, compiled complex charts that showed the movements of the Zwi Migdal's enormous wealth through foreign banks and legitimate business
ventures in America. He knew they controlled some three thousand women in one thousand brothels scattered throughout Argentina. He also knew that their empire included gaming houses
and numerous smuggling operations. They had their hand in
everything from diamonds to silk to canned beef and French
wine. One of the pimps, who shamelessly drove around the capital
in the car of a leading parliamentary deputy, brazenly advertised
his smuggling venture, El Japon, in one of the leading Jewish
weeklies. When police cracked down on his operations, they
found "twenty-four promissory notes for enormous sums and
mortgages on expensive properties and a quantity of gems" in a
safe-deposit box.

But the pimps were always quick to show their business in the
best light, treating it as a kind of altruistic endeavor instead of the
cruel factory of exploitation that it really was. "We take them and
wash them and scrub them," said one pimp of his work with the
prostitutes. "We dress them properly and give them a taste for
clean linen. We teach them economy and their duty to their family. As soon as they have a man, they send money regularly to their
old grandmother, their sick father, or their little sisters; or rather
we send it for them."

Alone in his office, Alsogaray may have chuckled as he recalled such ridiculous rationalizations. Or perhaps he wasn't in the mood for humor as he reflected on the ugly side of this immoral mentoring program.

Maybe if the pimps had not treated their "assets" with such brutality, their illicit business would have prospered relatively unfettered by the authorities. But in the end it was their violence against the women that proved their undoing.

Alsogaray chronicled all the cases of abused women in his collection of black, well-thumbed police notebooks. By the time he was ready to strike in 1930, he knew that Noyman and Marchik were among his biggest targets. Still, he also wanted to ensnare the others—José Solomon Korn and Simon Brutkievich, members of an elite group among the traffickers who controlled some 17 brothels and 202 women throughout Argentina.

But how could he put these men behind bars unless the prostitutes came forward? Perhaps he could convince Brony Spigler or Ita Kaiser to testify against their pimps. Perla Pezeborska had agreed to testify, but because she had not actually worked as a prostitute under the auspices of the Zwi Migdal, her testimony would not be enough to convict any of the high-ranking members of the organization. Alsogaray was not a particularly patient man, but he had no choice other than to wait for a miracle. It took a year, but on New Year's Eve 1929, when "the miracle" finally walked through the commissioner's office door at the Seventh Precinct headquarters, Alsogaray knew exactly what he had to do.

He offered Rachel Liberman a chair and calmly instructed her to start from the beginning.

"DESTINY HAD RESERVED for her a mission," wrote Alsogaray about his encounters with Rachel Liberman. "Tenacious and determined, she would knock down the foundations of the powerful criminal organization that threatened our society."

Rachel would probably have been surprised by the lofty way the commissioner described her in his memoirs. For while she was certainly "tenacious" and "determined," she wasn't really motivated by a sense of justice. It's not clear whether she even understood the importance of her testimony in the prosecution of the Zwi Migdal's most important members. Perhaps Alsogaray had kept this information from her, fearing that if she knew how much he and his colleagues were counting on her evidence, she might buckle under the pressure.

But in the end Rachel Liberman gave Commissioner Alsogaray everything he wanted, even if it was only the official history. Rachel hated the pimps and wanted nothing more than to see them locked up for the rest of their lives. But unlike Alsogaray, she didn't have the same messianic resolve to see justice done. She knew the terrible plight of the shtetl girls who ended up in the brothels of America, but it wasn't to ease their suffering that Rachel decided to give evidence against the pimps. Rachel had her reasons, and she was determined to keep them to herself. The truth, she might have thought, was far too complicated, and probably wouldn't interest anyone in the end.

So in the official version of the story, the one that eventually made its way into the Argentine newspapers, Rachel told the commissioner that she had been duped into becoming a prostitute by Jaime Cissinger, a tall, well-dressed fellow Pole with "intense blue eyes." According to Rachel, they fell in love while Cissinger was on a business trip to Warsaw. Rachel, a seamstress with few prospects, agreed to accompany him back to Buenos Aires, where he told her he managed several "businesses."

Of course, once they arrived in Argentina in 1922, Cissinger, a member of the Zwi Migdal, installed Rachel in a brothel and forced her into prostitution.

"After I was 'initiated,' I felt totally disgusted with myself and the people around me," said Rachel. "I thought I was not going to be able to put up with it and my days were numbered. I began to think about what would be the best way to kill myself." Later, it was the hope of seeing her mother again in Poland that prevented her from taking her own life. At least, that's what she told Alsogaray.

After five years of working as a prostitute, Rachel was able to save enough money to turn her life around. She opened up her small antiques business on Callao Street in downtown Buenos Aires, and prepared to put the past behind her for good. Her independence was short-lived, however. Two months after opening the shop, Rachel met José Solomon Korn, yet another impeccably dressed Polish Jew, with a boyish expression, who said he was an art collector. He visited her shop regularly and told her that he was in love with her. Korn proposed, and Rachel quickly agreed to a hasty marriage.

Alsogaray knew Korn extremely well. He was one of the Zwi Migdal's wealthiest traffickers. Why had she agreed to marry Korn so soon after being rid of Cissinger and leaving the profession?

Rachel seemed to anticipate the question, and told Alsogaray that she was duped. She claimed that she had no idea that the synagogue where she was married on Córdoba Street was controlled by the Jewish traffickers. Nor did she know that the man she was marrying was one of the group's most important traffickers, the man known in underworld circles as "the Bolshevik" because of "his menacing and dominant manner."

Perhaps Alsogaray was so caught up in Rachel's testimony that he didn't think to question how someone so intelligent could possibly be duped into marrying one of the city's most notorious Jewish pimps. But he recorded the information without question, then told Rachel to continue with the story.

A few days after the wedding, Korn seized Rachel's life's savings—an undisclosed amount that she had put away for her antiques business. He also forced her back into the same brothel where she had worked when she was under Cissinger's control. Finding herself enslaved yet again, Rachel might have recalled what one of the older prostitutes had once said to her several years before. "The traffickers," she said, "never allow a woman to go free, especially if she is still capable of earning money. They are like dogs; they never leave a bone as long as there is something left to chew."

But for Alsogaray there was another, perhaps even more important motive for forcing Rachel back into the brothel. "His [Korn's] purpose was to set an example for the other prostitutes . . . , to show them that any kind of resistance they showed was easily suffocated," he said. Alsogaray knew that independence and competition were simply not tolerated within the Zwi Migdal.

Of course, Rachel was furious, and it was then that she resolved to take her story to the police. The pimps had used blackmail on the shtetl girls in the past; now Rachel Liberman was determined to use it on them. She would threaten them with police action unless they returned her money.

Instead of threatening Korn, the man who had sent her back to the brothels and stolen her assets, Rachel went to the top of the organization and demanded a meeting with Zwi Migdal's then president, Simon Brutkievich. In his bow tie and English-tailored suit, Brutkievich immediately understood the gravity of Rachel's threat. A *polaca* who was determined to tell all to the authorities was simply not good for the Zwi Migdal. Even the organization's highly placed friends in government would be hard-pressed to help them under such a threat, especially if she was in league with Commissioner Alsogaray, a man they had already tried and failed to bribe.

I'll make you a deal.

Perhaps Brutkievich agreed to Rachel's demands on condition that she withhold her testimony to Alsogaray. While it is not known what kind of deal Brutkievich eventually made with Rachel, it is clear that he at least tried to persuade Korn to return the stolen money. At Brutkievich's urging, Korn agreed to meet with Rachel, but in the end the Bolshevik ignored his instructions. Korn simply had no intention of returning anything to a harlot. Besides, everyone knew the money was his. Rachel was working at *his* brothels. It was thanks to Korn that she got back into the business. That was just the way it worked, Korn might have thought; the women had no right to any of the money. Korn simply could not believe that a whore and an immigrant would be able to topple an organization as powerful and as wealthy as the Zwi Migdal. But he didn't want to appear to go against Brutkievich's orders, and agreed to offer Rachel a small percentage of the total amount he had taken from her. Those stupid whores will take anything you give them, he must have thought.

But Korn underestimated Rachel's anger, and in the end that would be his undoing. When Korn refused to return everything he had stolen, Rachel told him that she would denounce him and everyone else in the Zwi Migdal to the police commissioner.

That's when the pimps decided they had had enough of Rachel Liberman and sent a fleshy pimp in a sober business suit to teach her a lesson.

Mauricio Kirstein was new to the profession, eager to impress his bosses at the Zwi Migdal. He thought he knew how to deal with prostitutes, even former prostitutes. When he first barged into Rachel's store, Kirstein tried to rape her, awkwardly kissing her on the lips and grabbing her breasts. When that didn't work, he told her that he would kill her. When he saw that Rachel didn't take his threats very seriously, he destroyed the objets d'art in her shop, beginning with the glass bowls and ending with the antique chair legs. He returned a few more times, sometimes in the company of other thugs, to break more objects and threaten Rachel again. At one point he even offered to return a larger portion of the money Korn had stolen if Rachel gave up the idea of going to the police.

But Rachel shook her head. Like Alsogaray, she couldn't be moved. As she watched them break everything in her tiny shop, she became even more determined to seek revenge, to get her money back and to make them all pay for everything they had done to her.

Were you frightened?

Alsogaray's question must have given Rachel pause, and perhaps her answer, blurted out with little thought, surprised even her. "You only die once," she told Alsogaray. "I am not backing down."

THE RAIDS BEGAN at dawn on May 10, 1930, as Alsogaray's men pounded on doors throughout the city. They began at the Jewish-owned brothels in La Boca and spread out through the more fashionable neighborhoods where many of the pimps owned lavish apartments. As his men went methodically from door to door, Alsogaray sat in the backseat of his car, with the windows open. Perhaps he smoked a cigarette as he watched men such as Simon Brutkievich and José Solomon Korn complaining loudly in their Yiddish-accented Spanish as Alsogaray's men led them away in handcuffs.

It was Korn, his old nemesis, who seemed to make the biggest impression on the commissioner. The Bolshevik was known for his particularly brutal way with the women. Yet as he was led away from his home, he had the look of a frightened child. How could such an innocent-looking man, with such a smooth, clean-shaven baby face, be such a notorious pimp? Alsogaray might have pondered this as he smoked cigarette after cigarette, all the while watching Korn blink in the early-morning light. Perhaps the question occurred to Korn himself, because as he was escorted into an idling police car, he appeared startled. Perhaps he had been caught off guard by the photographers' flashbulbs, or perhaps he was thinking of everything he had ever done to Rachel Liberman, the woman who was supposedly his wife. For the look on his face suggested that he just couldn't quite believe that he was being arrested. Was that whore responsible for *this*? he may have asked himself. Could this really spell the end of his lucrative underworld career? The end of the Zwi Migdal?

But if Korn was tormented by such thoughts, he was probably the only one among the dozens of pimps who were arrested throughout the city that day. The other pimps appeared as they always did—supremely self-confident, in finely tailored suits and polished shoes. They must have seen the photographers and newspapermen assembled on the sidewalks outside their elegant apartment blocks, their expensive townhouses. The underworld madam everyone knew as Ema the Millionaire, one of the few female traffickers to be arrested, seemed determined to look good for the cameras. As she emerged in handcuffs from the front doors of her Art Deco apartment building she was the very image of an upper-middle-class matron, wearing a dark coat trimmed with mink and a stylish cloche hat, and carrying a smart leather purse.

Alsogaray followed the raids, working from the neatly typed list of addresses that he rhymed off to his driver. Would the pimps find their usual creative ways to block his efforts? But there were no legal loopholes to crawl through this time, Alsogaray might have thought. With Rachel's testimony and the raids, all of the pimps would be exposed, and many of them might even go to jail for the rest of their lives.

In all, there were 424 arrest warrants issued against members of the Zwi Migdal. Alsogaray's men burst into brothels not just in Buenos Aires but throughout Argentina, rounding up Zwi Migdal members and charging them with "illicit association" under the Argentine criminal code. The raids took more than ten days to complete, and on May 20 police broke into the Zwi Migdal mansion on Córdoba Street, seizing valuables, banking records, and other important documents that incriminated some of the country's highest-ranking politicians and civil servants. Other "offices" of the Zwi Migdal were raided throughout the city and in the suburb of Avellaneda, where the traffickers had established their own cemetery years before. In Avellaneda, police found a rather pathetic office "made up of two wooden rooms in a terrible state of repair."

Of those charged in the historic raids, only 112 were captured, and few of them were high-ranking members. Some of the most important members of the Zwi Migdal had been tipped off by their friends in high places and had escaped to Uruguay and Brazil in advance of the raids. Seventy of those named in the warrants had already died. Still, Alsogaray must have comforted himself with the fact that he had finally netted men such as Korn and Brutkievich and Cissinger, who had played such key roles in Rachel Liberman's terrible ordeal.

Although the Jewish community threw its unconditional support behind what some called Alsogaray's "sacred mission to destroy the shady organizations," many believed that the pimps would simply find another way to evade justice. "Everyone, especially those in the Jewish community, is very pessimistic," noted one observer. "They feel that nothing will eventuate. They mention the police are in the pay of the traffickers."

But a few months after the May raids, the political situation in Argentina changed dramatically with the coup d'état led by General José Felix Uriburu. The coup was the beginning of Argentina's long flirtation with fascism, and the new ruler purged the police forces and the judiciary and "brought vital conservative support to the campaign to obliterate the white slave trade." Although many government officials in the early 1930s "continued to appall Alsogaray by their venality, the more puritanical atmosphere of the nation under Uriburu's moralistic rule helped to curtail the trade in women."

Still, a year later, when the Zwi Migdal cases went before the appeals court, most were thrown out. Despite Rachel's testimony, Alsogaray had not been entirely successful in showing that the Zwi Migdal "acted against the morality of the state."

All but three of the Zwi Migdal prisoners were ordered released, and Argentina was left with "the sad reputation of being the world's biggest market for the white slave trade." Despite the coup, some corrupt officials still ruled the Argentine judicial system and many police officers who were sent to deport Zwi Migdal fugitives who had escaped to Brazil simply allowed the procedural deadlines for their extradition to pass, allowing the fugitives to go free.

Although some were later deported by the Uriburu regime, the wealthier pimps simply transferred their operations elsewhere and began shipping women to Brazil, Mexico, Cuba, Venezuela, and Colombia. But despite the fact that they continued to trade in desperate women, the Zwi Migdal enterprise would never again attain the kind of power and influence that it had had in Argentina.

Jaime Cissinger, the pimp who had first forced Rachel into prostitution, managed to flee the country soon after the May raids. But he was apprehended by police when he tried to disembark in Lisbon. Authorities later deported him to Poland, where there is no record of what happened to him. Many of the other leading members of the traffickers' mafia, including José Solomon Korn, ended up escaping to Brazil, where they continued to exploit young women until the Brazilian authorities cracked down on the brothels.

In the end Alsogaray may not have succeeded in bringing each member of the Zwi Migdal to justice in Argentina, but he did destroy their business by making it nearly impossible for them to operate with the same level of impunity that they enjoyed before the raids. "In spite of such circumstances," he wrote, "I used all means to defeat them in their own fortress, defended by money from pandering and by the collaboration of servile and unworthy officials. Against all the painful setbacks, I continued to believe in the sanctity of the laws and in the good character of a few men."

And at least one woman.

After the sensationalistic reports of the brothel raids died down, Rachel Liberman simply disappeared from public view. Only one newspaper wrote in depth about the importance of her testimony, but the reporter described her simply as "a woman who led a depraved life."

In the end, that's all anyone ever really knew about Rachel Liberman, that she was a Jewish prostitute from Poland, that she worked in the down-at-heels brothels in La Boca. But had the reporters decided to dig deeper, they would have found a completely different story, one that was truly heroic.

Destiny had reserved for her a mission.

Did Alsogaray know the truth about Rachel Liberman? Did she give him any other details of her life, and did she make him promise to keep it to himself? It's unclear what transpired in Alsogaray's office at the Seventh Precinct headquarters on New Year's Eve 1929. Alsogaray was a consummate professional, and if he had made a deal with her on that steamy night when the shouts of the revelers seemed to overwhelm their tête-à-tête, he took the truth to his grave.

IT'S NOT CLEAR why Rachel Liberman kept the letters and the photographs that exposed the real story about her life. Perhaps she secretly hoped someone would find them one day and tell her story, the one that revealed her as much more than "a woman who led a depraved life."

It's clear in the first photograph taken of her in Buenos Aires that Rachel Liberman was not the depraved prostitute of the tabloids. A handsome woman with brown hair, she stands stiffly for the camera, her gaze strong, resolute, and steady.

It is October 22, 1922, and Rachel has just arrived in the city after a long trip from Warsaw, via the port of Hamburg. In the photograph she is standing at a respectful distance from her husband, to whom she extends her right hand in a rather arch attempt at a greeting. In her cloche hat, the smart ankle-length suit that she had made for the journey, and fox fur stole, she looks every inch a middle-class European matron.

But maybe, if you look closely at that first black-and-white photograph of Rachel in America, there is already a hint of that tenacity and heroism in her expression.

Her Polish passport identified her as Ruchla Laja Liberman, a twenty-two-year-old Jewish seamstress and mother of two little boys. She was born in Kiev on July 10, 1900, and married a Polish tailor named Jacob Ferber nineteen years later. Although little is known of her life in Warsaw, where she immigrated with her family when she was a little girl, Rachel began dreaming of Argentina soon after she married. Helke, her sister-in-law, had settled in the interior of Buenos Aires province years before and had invited the young couple to live at her home. To Rachel, who had few prospects in Poland, Argentina must have seemed a world out of a fairy tale, where, she had been told, she could practice her religion without fear of persecution and live happily ever after with her young family.

Rachel's husband left for Buenos Aires in July 1921, two years after their marriage. Like so many other immigrants to America, Jacob planned to make his way in the new country before sending for his family. He left his one-year-old son, David, and his pregnant wife in the care of his sister-in-law in Warsaw and made his way to the port of Marseilles to board the ship that would take him to America.

In the letters that he wrote to his family in Warsaw, Jacob gave few details about his life in Argentina. He did, however, describe the country as a prosperous land of opportunity. "I'm . . . sending you a peso so that you can see what Argentine money looks like," he wrote in one letter. "But don't throw it away because here they pay 1.200 Polish marks for every peso."

For her part, Rachel couldn't wait to make the journey and be reunited with her husband. "Dear husband, I don't have to tell it to you nor to repeat it to you, since you are a faithful husband and I am a faithful wife, to hurry your papers and see what you can do so we can reunite soon," she pleaded in one of the first letters to her husband in Argentina.

During their yearlong separation, Rachel wrote letter after letter complaining to Jacob about her situation in Warsaw, where she was forced to move in with her sister in order to save money for her passage. The living arrangements proved intolerable, especially after Rachel delivered her second child, born a few months after Jacob's departure. "My darkest sorrow is that there is no place anywhere for me and my little sons," she wrote on March 16, 1922. "I am being pushed every day from one place to another. I am being insulted and cursed. Do I have to bear how my sister goes about with a long face without saying a word to me? I have to put up with my brother-in-law shouting and insulting me and my sons, and see how our older son David sits all day, pounding his mattress; and at night he's never allowed to run around the house, as a boy needs to do . . . My heart bursts!"

Finally, a few months later, Jacob sent Rachel enough money for the trip, instructing her to try to board a boat called the *Polonia,* "one of the best ships in the world," from the port of Hamburg. The letter was chatty and full of practical advice: Bring enough money for the trip—at least $10—"in case you wish to drink a glass of beer or another drink and buy chocolate and oranges for the boys"; check at the port to make sure the luggage arrives; ask the crew for blankets and pillows, especially for the children, because it is cold on the boat at night. "Don't be frightened if you get seasick," Jacob told his wife. "Try to have warm clothes for the children and for yourself. Don't sell your clothes; pack everything, clothes and household items. Buy yourself and the children coats and shoes. And when you arrive, *beshalom* [in peace], I will buy you such clothes that no one will guess that you are a green [foreigner], but that you are a native."

Rachel was clearly ecstatic when she received the letter, and she wrote to her husband a month later that "my happiness is boundless. . . . My two lovely and adored children and I will be patient because we know what a splendid future brightens our eyes and renews our strength, to withstand everything else more easily. I see our salvation coming closer."

For Rachel, stepping off the ship at the port of Buenos Aires must have seemed like stepping into a new life. Perhaps that's why she stared into the camera with such determination, even defiance. In contrast, Helke, her heavyset sister-in-law, who is also in the photograph at the port, seemed wary and uncertain. And then there is Jacob, unsmiling in his new clothes—a silk-lined suit, fedora, dark overcoat, and black shoes. "I have also purchased a pair of patent leather shoes and a foreign-made hat, because I looked too much like a gringo in my *kapelush* hat," he wrote to his wife soon after arriving in Argentina.

The camera failed to register anything remotely resembling happiness in Jacob's expression; only a kind of resignation showed on his face. Perhaps his wife's arrival in this strange new country reminded him that the year he had spent away from his family had been pretty much a failure. Jacob had worked as a tailor in Warsaw, but in the village of Tapalqué, where he went to live in the house of his sister and brother-in-law, he could find little work in his profession. "I started to work with a tailor, but I worked for two weeks only, and I don't work any longer because I don't understand the language and they don't understand me," wrote Jacob in a letter to his wife. "And the pay is very low."

He earned a little money doing odd jobs—fishing in a nearby lake and tying horse carriages. He had yet to learn Spanish and had not managed to make enough money to afford a place of his own, which meant that his wife and two children would have to move into his sister's home and live much the way they had in Warsaw. Which may explain why Jacob's letters to his wife are full of statements about his responsibilities as a husband and a father. Reading between the lines, one gets the feeling he is chastising himself for not living up to his promise or reminding himself of his duties when he wrote: "Nevertheless, my dear ones, you can see I do my utmost to comply with my duty as a husband and as a father. I know full well I did not leave there [in Poland] a lover, but my wife and my sons. I believe I have acted as any faithful husband would act."

The reality in the early 1920s was that many of the men who immigrated to America on their own ignored their families back home. Surely Jacob was surrounded by many young men in his position who had simply chosen to abandon their families in the Old World and start new lives in America.

Perhaps he was making subtle reference to the temptations he faced on a daily basis in Argentina. Why worry about his family in Poland when there were other women and other opportunities in Argentina? Or maybe he was feeling terribly impotent because almost as soon as he arrived in Argentina, he became gravely ill. During the yearlong separation from his wife, he was paying regular visits to a local hospital to treat what appeared to be tuberculosis.

"A healer told me my troubles were caused by the evil eye,"

noted Jacob in a letter to his wife written months before her arrival. "And I think she was right on the mark because I already
feel, thank God, almost well. I hope to be completely well soon."
In the same letter he noted that although their situation was bleak
and "the water came almost to the neck," everything had changed
and "all our sorrows and our anguish will end soon."

But it all proved to be wishful thinking. Less than a year after
Rachel's arrival in Argentina, Jacob was readmitted to the hospital
in Buenos Aires, where Rachel and Helke took turns visiting him.
By July 1923, it appeared that he would not make a full recovery.
In a letter written to him by his sister Helke, she is startled by the
seriousness of his condition: "I received your dear letter from the
hospital. We were all standing up when Rachel read it. You can't
imagine the emotions everyone felt when we received it. We all
shouted in one voice, 'Good God, help us! Put an end to our wor-
ries and our anguish!'"

Jacob died soon after, and Rachel was left without money or a
proper home in a new country where she could communicate only
in Yiddish. Faced with no prospects for employment in Tapalqué,
Rachel entrusted her children to a neighbor (her sister-in-law was
an invalid and could not take care of the children on her own) and
made the decision that would change the rest of her life.

Perhaps she boarded the train to Buenos Aires intending to
search for employment as a seamstress among the city's rapidly
growing Jewish community. At least she could communicate in
Yiddish among her own people, and eventually learn Spanish. It is
not known whether Rachel was aware of the dangers that young
women traveling alone in Buenos Aires faced in the mid-1920s, by
then a bustling metropolis of nearly two million people with its
wide avenues and cafés that must have reminded her of Warsaw.
The city was teeming with thousands of immigrants from Italy,

Germany, Poland, and the Middle East—"Babel multiplied a thousand times." Did Rachel know that in the Argentine capital, where men greatly outnumbered women, an unchaperoned woman was the object of all sorts of taunts and harassment? Did she know anything of the white slavers who wandered the ports and the train stations looking for young, vulnerable women for their brothels?

In her testimony to the police, Rachel claimed she knew nothing of the Zwi Migdal when she arrived in Buenos Aires, but she was probably not being entirely honest.

It is unclear how or why Rachel hooked up with the Zwi Migdal, but shortly after arriving in the Argentine capital in 1924, Rachel Liberman did meet a man named Jaime Cissinger, although the encounter probably did not occur by chance.

Rachel's in-laws in Tapalqué were both traffickers, and in the raids of May 1930, Helke Ferber Milroth was detained by Alsogaray's team "for her links with the activities of the Zwi Migdal." Earlier, Helke and her husband, Moshe, had also appeared on Alsogaray's list of most-wanted white slavers in Argentina.

At some point, Alsogaray must have known about Rachel's family connections with the Zwi Migdal. Did Rachel's husband lure her to Argentina to work as a prostitute? Surely he must have known the kind of business his sister and brother-in-law were running in the village of Tapalqué. Perhaps the knowledge that his family trafficked in women explains the gloomy look on Jacob Ferber's face when he was photographed with Rachel at the port of Buenos Aires. How would he ever explain to his wife that he had brought her to America to live among such people?

But Jacob, who was rushed to the hospital almost as soon as Rachel arrived, probably didn't have time to go into the particulars of his sister's business affairs in America. Rachel, however, would find out in due time. For after her husband's death it was surely Helke who must have organized the meeting with Cissinger in Buenos Aires. Helke might have told Rachel that it was the only way she could make a living in Argentina and the only way in which she could provide for her two small children. Besides, no one back home would ever know, she might have reassured her. Helke must have thought that a voluptuous woman like Rachel could make a tidy profit for her and her husband. The Buenos Aires pimps would surely be excited by such a recruit.

The problem would be convincing Rachel to leave her children and work with Cissinger in Buenos Aires. Perhaps Helke told her that unlike the other women exploited by the Zwi Migdal, she would be able to leave the profession as soon as she saved enough money to buy a small house and open a business—maybe a boutique or a gift store. If she worked hard, she could get rich quickly, Helke might have said.

Buoyed by her sister-in-law's support, Rachel must have gone willingly to meet Cissinger in Buenos Aires. For his part, Cissinger must have agreed to Rachel's conditions to split her profits with him. Perhaps she told him that she would stop working as a prostitute for the Zwi Migdal as soon as she had the money to open up a small business.

Although Cissinger seemed to have kept up his side of the bargain, things clearly turned sour when Jose Solomon Korn appeared on the scene and decided to steal her assets. Did he bother to marry her at the Zwi Migdal synagogue, or did Rachel meekly agree to do his bidding because he threatened to hurt her children?

It's not clear why Rachel made the decisions she made in the years that she worked on the streets of Buenos Aires. But one thing is certain—that she desperately wanted to protect her children, David and Mauricio, from the Zwi Migdal.

The boys adored their mother, even though she appears to have been frequently absent while they were growing up. Their childhood is chronicled in the black-and-white photographs that Rachel left behind. In the ones taken with their mother, they appear as children of privilege, wearing matching sailor suits, shorts, and polished leather shoes. In fact, they are always impeccably dressed. In one of the photographs, Rachel sits on a chair flanked by her two boys in their school uniforms. She wears a long strand of pearls and a dark woollen dress and looks every inch the respectable, doting mother. Behind them is an ornate tapestry— perhaps in her antiques shop—and she hugs both children around the waist.

Are they eating properly? How is David's cough? Does Mauricio need a new pair of shoes? Rachel might have asked in the frequent letters she wrote the women she hired over the years to look after her children. Even as she worked in some of the worst brothels in the city, her mind was clearly on her children. On weekends, when she managed to visit them in the country, perhaps Rachel came loaded with presents that helped her to appease the guilt and anguish she felt over leaving them with a stranger. Leaving them was always the hardest thing she ever did, harder than working in the brothels, more difficult than fighting the most powerful members of the Zwi Migdal.

In one letter to Rachel, her eldest son, David, wrote, "Dear Mamita, I would like to see you soon by my side, but since that is impossible, for the moment I live happily with your memory and with the knowledge that you love me, just as I love you." In a separate letter Mauricio, the youngest, wrote, "Dear Mamita, David loves you no less than I do. And although I am little, my love for you is great."

It is not clear whether Rachel ever told her boys what she had to do for a living in order to support them, but on some level they must have suspected something was not right about their mother's activities in Buenos Aires. When David won first prize in a singing contest, he was too ashamed to pick it up, since he would be forced to show his identification papers. Perhaps he feared being tied to the "depraved" prostitute whose name was well known in Argentina in the 1930s.

David, it seemed, preferred to remember his mother another way. For the photo he most cherished is a studio portrait taken in 1919, when Rachel was nineteen years old and still living in Warsaw. The faded black-and-white photograph shows a young woman in an elegant and chaste high-collared dark lace dress, a long string of pearls around her neck, clutching a white rose. She is beautiful, but it's her eyes that are her most striking feature. They don't look at the camera but seem focused on something beyond. How many times did David stare at those eyes and wonder about his mother? Nearly a half century after the photograph was taken, David, well into his forties, wrote the following inscription on the back of the photo: "Picture in homage to the most sublime person on earth, THE MOTHER."

A month after the raids against the Zwi Migdal, Rachel returned to the streets, registering again with the municipal authorities in Buenos Aires in order to work legally as a prostitute. Despite her testimony, Rachel never received her money from Korn and was forced to work as a prostitute to put her life back in order.

Defense lawyers for Korn and others used her return to the brothels to try to discredit her testimony. They wrongly claimed that she had worked as a prostitute in Poland and "continued practicing it since arriving in Buenos Aires, making the obligatory visits to the Municipal Health Office even as she set up her business so that she would not lose the authorization to work as a prostitute."

Rachel did nothing to correct them, since any correction would have forced her to report the real circumstances under which she had arrived in the country. The last thing she wanted to do was reveal her true identity, exposing her sons to ostracism in the Jewish community. Let José Solomon Korn and his lawyers say what they wanted to say about her. In the end, she could easily sacrifice herself, not her precious children.

Three years after the trial, when her name had long faded from the headlines, Rachel continued to work in a Buenos Aires brothel while putting money aside to resurrect her antiques business. In letters written during this period, Rachel seemed constantly preoccupied with her two boys, who continued to spend most of their time away from her. "Your children are very well," wrote Eugenia Elisa, an Argentine woman who looked after David and Mauricio in 1933. "They behave and study very well."

In 1934, when her sons were entering adolescence, Rachel was slowly putting her life back together. She had managed to save enough money to reopen her antiques business and was even planning a family trip back to Poland to visit her elderly mother, who was on her deathbed.

In a letter of good conduct written on her behalf to the Polish consulate in Buenos Aires, where she needed to apply for a visa to return to her country of birth, the writer notes that members of the Jewish Scientific Institute visited Rachel at her home and "received a pleasant impression."

"The name Rachel Liberman is very well known for her partic-

ipation in the case against the Zwi Migdal," said the letter. "Anyone who saw her now, in these new healthy surroundings, would
be far from surmising that this was the same woman who had
once spent a licentious life for several years. The stigma [of prosti-
tution] generally leaves an indelible seal in the faces of many
women who had the misfortune of surrendering themselves continuously to vicious practices. But Liberman made a favorable impression on us. She insisted that her regeneration was a real fact."

Rachel was approved for travel to Poland, but as she was
preparing for her trip, she became gravely ill. She died in a Buenos
Aires hospital on April 7, 1935, three months shy of her thirty-fifth
birthday.

CHAPTER SEVEN

"Burning Ground"

Once a year, the white candles were allowed to burn night and day.

They were lit by Rebecca Freedman and the other prostitutes under a temporary shelter, a canopy made of white canvas, erected behind the brick, two-story building that housed their synagogue. The candles commemorated the anniversaries of the deaths of their sisters—a kind of collective *yahrzeit,* honoring their memory.

Orlando, the handyman who maintained the synagogue, was also the custodian of the candles. It was his job to watch them day and night, to make sure that a sudden gust of wind didn't send the flames flying out of control, in the direction of the white canvas canopy or the nearby mango trees. Orlando often brought his nephew Alberto along with him, in case he nodded off while on duty. Both of them used to refer to the candle ceremony as the Jewish day of the dead, even though there is no such holiday in Judaism. "Back then, when we started working for them, we didn't know anything about their religion," said Alberto da Costa, Orlando's nephew. "We didn't even know who they were."

But Alberto and his uncle must have known they were prostitutes. Everyone in the neighborhood knew the business of these women with the pale skin and the red lipstick who spoke a harsh, guttural language that few people understood. But the two men seemed not to care. Under the canopy that smelled of melting wax, they shifted uncomfortably on metal chairs and gulped down sugary coffee from a battered Thermos to keep themselves from dozing, from being mesmerized by the flames that they guarded for the dead.

Alberto was twenty-five years old when he began working alongside his uncle for the Society of Truth in the early 1950s. He was hired by Angelina Schaffran, the charity's president, on the recommendation of Rebecca, the woman who became his mentor and by his own account the most important person in his life. Perhaps this is why Alberto, a trim black man with an efficient, professional air, decided to stay with the society, long after its members could no longer afford to pay his salary. It wasn't about the money, he liked to say, it was about everything he learned, about the respect and admiration he had for the sisters, who would become closer to him than his own family. In the end it was Alberto who became the society's final custodian, and keeper of its secrets.

It's unclear whether Alberto approved of how the women made their living, where they obtained the money to pay his modest monthly salary. He quickly learned that discretion was an important component of his job, and he vowed many times to Rebecca Freedman to take the sisters' secrets to his grave. But sometimes he felt a need to talk, to defend their honor. They may have been prostitutes, but to Alberto they were—what was the word he liked to use? They were *noble*. Perhaps he knew it sounded strange, calling a group of aging prostitutes noble, but there was something about these women—a humanity, a serenity perhaps—that influenced his life in a fundamental way. "My uncle and I never spoke about what they did to make a living," said Alberto. "In the end, it never seemed to matter. We always respected them and their religion. We always saw them helping other people."

One of the people they helped was Alberto himself. Perhaps these women who lived as pariahs, on the margins of society, felt a special bond with Alberto, a young man trying to make his way in a city where the color of his skin was a huge impediment to advancement. They must have admired Alberto's ambition, his dedication and efficiency. Shortly after he began working for the society, Rebecca and some of the other women decided to pay for his studies, helping him to complete his degree in accounting.

Their motives weren't entirely altruistic; they had their own reasons for helping Alberto. Most of the women were illiterate and knew little about budgets and financial planning. But they were smart enough to realize that if the society was going to survive into the future, they needed someone to administer their assets, someone like Waldemar Mirandella, their first accountant, who died about the same time Alberto was hired.

Alberto never really understood why Rebecca and the other women took such a keen interest in him, but before he knew it they were all playing an active part in his life. They invited his family to their High Holiday celebrations at the synagogue—grand occasions when the long wooden conference table was laid out with handmade lace tablecloths, platters of homemade sweets, and bottles of *cachaça*. When Alberto confessed that one of his relatives had a weakness for matzo, Rebecca made sure that he received a box every year at Passover. "She never forgot," said Alberto. Their relationship became so close that when Rebecca was on her deathbed, it was Alberto who was her trusted confidant; it was Alberto who was in charge of drafting her last will and testament.

In return, Alberto took care of the Society of Truth, becoming as passionate about its work as some of the women themselves. In the early days he doubled as an office boy and what the Brazilians call a *despachante,* literally an expeditor. He stood in long queues outside banks and municipal offices in downtown Rio to pay the society's bills. When the members, most of whom were not naturalized Brazilians and still maintained their status as foreigners in the country, had to appear before the Federal Police for routine fingerprinting and renewal of their Brazilian visas, Alberto stood in line for them (sometimes for days) until it was their turn to meet with an officer.

Alberto was also in charge of the cemetery maintenance and painstakingly compiled the minutes of the monthly meetings in his tight, economical script, taking the final copies to a series of nearby notaries who stamped and initialed each page, per the Brazilian laws governing corporations. For some of the women it was a struggle just to sign the minutes. But Alberto always waited patiently as the directors of the corporation labored over their shaky primary-school scrawls.

When a burial occurred at the Inhaúma cemetery, Rebecca always called on Alberto to help her with the final arrangements. He and his uncle would fetch the prostitutes' bodies from the hospitals or the brothels where they died. The two men would deliver them to Rebecca, who washed and rewashed her tools in preparation for the purification ritual. The door of the small building where the *tahara* was performed was almost always bolted shut after Alberto and his uncle delivered the bodies and deposited them on the white marble table. Rebecca never allowed non-Jews to be present at the purifications.

On the High Holidays, when there were more than the usual handful of visitors to the synagogue, Alberto also became the society's official doorman. Perched on the doorstep and always neatly dressed, he would give out black yarmulkes to the handful of male visitors when they arrived for services, and make sure that they surrendered their weapons at the front door. He would lock the guns in the society's safe and only return them after the ceremony, when the men were preparing to leave the building. Alberto said he didn't know the identities of these men, although he guessed some must be police officers and close friends of the prostitutes.

Most of the other men who came were elderly. Alberto often wondered why they frequented a synagogue that was reserved for women. Were these grizzled, stoop-shouldered men, with ill-fitting suits and crumbs on their ties, former pimps? Perhaps they were former lovers, or simply good friends. Alberto would never think to ask such questions, and for him it never really mattered all that much. The men treated him with respect. They shook his hand, slapped him on the back, and sometimes they tipped him, awkwardly stuffing a few bills in the breast pocket of his white cotton shirt. Only a handful of these men came regularly on the High Holidays, and in the years immediately preceding the charity's demise, they stopped coming altogether.

Alberto might not have known much about the Jewish religion, but he knew that the women could never get a rabbi to officiate at the services. Rebecca had once told him that the rabbis hated the prostitutes, considered them traitors to the Jewish religion. But she also said it was the women's independence the rabbis hated most, their love of their own religion. Somehow, Rebecca managed to convince a Jewish tailor who lived nearby to act as their cantor. Alberto never quite understood the difference between a cantor and a rabbi, but he knew it was a victory. Yes, that's what Rebecca called it: a victory.

Which is probably why Alberto always thought it fitting that the synagogue, for which the women paid the full asking price in cash in 1942, was located in Rio's Eleventh Square, a district that commemorated victory. Every Brazilian schoolkid studied the battle that took place on June 11, 1865, in which the Brazilian navy triumphed over invading forces from Paraguay on the Paraná River. Perhaps Alberto told Rebecca about the battle, comparing it to the fight for dignity waged by the prostitutes against their neighbors, the respectable Jews who excluded them from their community.

But setting up a synagogue for prostitutes in the heart of the Jewish community was more than a victory, Rebecca might have thought, it was also revenge against the respectable Jews who shunned the prostitutes at every turn. Now the respectable Jews would be forced to acknowledge them. They could still avert their eyes and cross to the other side of the street when they heard the click of their high heels on the cobblestones or caught a scent of their cheap rose-water perfume. The prostitutes, who for years had been confined to the nearby Mangue, were now in their midst; there was no getting rid of them.

For immigrant Jews arriving in Rio after the First World War, Eleventh Square became what the Lower East Side was for Jewish immigrants to New York. The neighborhood of neat, colonial row houses painted in pastel hues was once the heart of Jewish cultural and commercial life in the city, with Yiddish theaters, Hebrew schools, delis, restaurants, and stores where young boys hawked a myriad of Yiddish-language newspapers on the street corners. "The neighborhood was a point of convergence and was host to a dynamic Jewish life," noted one immigrant who arrived from Eastern Europe with his family in 1923. "In the twenties and thirties, [it] was like an enormous ghetto, but without walls or any restrictions."

Later, many established Jewish families left Eleventh Square for the more affluent parts of the city, such as the beachfront Copacabana district or Tijuca, in the north. By the 1960s, as most of the respectable Jews began to move away, the streets around Eleventh Square began to fill up with impoverished Brazilian families who migrated from the rural northeastern states in order to seek a better life in the city. These wide-eyed pilgrims, with their oily bundles and ragged clothes, might have reminded the Jews of the peasants from the shtetl. They were just as poor, and had fled the horrors of drought and starvation. Arriving in Rio de Janeiro, they resembled refugees from a war or natural disaster as they walked through the old Jewish neighborhood and began the patchwork construction of shantytowns that still cling to the hills on the outskirts of downtown.

Shortly after the women of the society established their offices in Eleventh Square, the neighborhood began to show signs of serious decline. For Alberto it was a strange irony that their synagogue, despised by the wider Jewish community, became the last vestige of Judaism in the neighborhood.

Alberto knew that only Jews whose families were members of the society, and who had paid their dues, were allowed to enter the synagogue. But every Friday night a group of non-Jewish prostitutes would gather outside the synagogue to listen to the cantor, whose melodious voice wafted through the red-light district at dusk, momentarily rising above the calls of the street vendors, the faraway rattle of the trams, and the whistle of the trains that sped in and out of nearby Central Station. "On their religious days, we always heard that voice and we stopped to listen because it was so beautiful," said an aging Brazilian prostitute. "I never understood anything about that religion, about what he was singing, but I loved that music."

Alberto rarely missed a Friday service, standing outside the two-story building on Afonso Cavalcanti Street, which he knew the prostitutes had bought after "immense sacrifice." He escorted the guests to their seats in the synagogue, which was on the second floor and accessible only through a side door. He also had the authority to turn people away, which he did often when crowds of young men, some of them Jewish, showed up to gawk at the prostitutes who attended the services.

Alberto politely told the gawkers to leave, and when that didn't work he would summon Noah, the beefy handyman who lived with his family on the premises and was not afraid to use force. Still, the young men showed up almost every week and tried to muscle their way into the synagogue. Sometimes they managed to sneak by Alberto.

One Jewish writer recalled the experience of a friend who decided to attend a Friday-evening service at the prostitutes' synagogue. "When he entered, one of the women approached him and told him to leave the synagogue immediately," he said. "When my friend asked why, the prostitute told him this: 'It is written that when a daughter of Israel steps away from the right path the ground all around her is on fire. You are now standing on burning ground, sir, and you must leave at once.'"

Standing silently at the door, Alberto watched such startled young men with flushed faces and pounding hearts beat a hasty retreat down the flight of darkening stairs.

· · ·

THE GROUND WAS ON FIRE in 1930, weeks after the raids that decimated the Zwi Migdal in Argentina—a period that Rebecca Freedman recalled with profound sadness because it nearly destroyed the Society of Truth in Rio and left many of the sisters on the street.

Following Rachel Liberman's dramatic denunciation, Jewish pimps scrambled to leave the country. They headed to Brazil, where many thought they would be safe. But the corrupt officials who had once welcomed them with open arms were now bent upon bringing them to justice. In the process, they sought to teach the prostitutes a lesson, and in a series of raids over the course of several years, the authorities closed down the brothels and sent the prostitutes out onto the streets.

The raids in Brazil were largely the work of Anesio Frota Aguiar, a wiry little police officer with a Hitler mustache. In a speech delivered to the Brazilian Criminology Society in Rio de Janeiro in November 1939, Frota Aguiar blamed the Jewish prostitutes for upsetting "the strict morals of Brazilian youth."

Frota Aguiar was a self-proclaimed expert on such things. He had seen the women at work in the Mangue, the neighborhood he had patrolled as a young officer. He had read Rachel Liberman's denunciation in 1930 and knew that dozens of Jewish pimps had transferred their illicit enterprises from Buenos Aires to Rio. The situation, he said, had become intolerable. Brazil was not a clearinghouse for the white-slave trade, and so the authorities needed to get tough. "Many people left Europe, some seeking better lives, others seeking better criminal opportunities in our country," said Frota Aguiar to the cheers of the law-enforcement officials assembled at the conference. "The Jew exploits prostitution as if he were the head of a corporation. For them women are merchandise."

While other self-righteous politicians had made similar comments in the past, Frota Aguiar's crusade met with particular enthusiasm in Brazil in the years before the beginning of the Second World War. In October 1930, a military coup d'état had transformed the country from a democracy to a police state that took its inspiration and direction from Fascist Italy and Nazi Germany. In his speech to the Criminology Society, Frota Aguiar was preaching to the converted, the men who had heartily supported the revolution that brought the dictator Getúlio Vargas to power.

Brazil's dictator began to target the Jews as the main cause of a host of economic problems. As a worldwide economic depression sent Brazilian coffee prices spiraling downward, authorities in Brazil blamed Jews for rising unemployment and inflation. Jewish immigrants from Eastern Europe, who had arrived in large numbers in the years after the First World War, were generally barred from entering the country.

Even the National Liberation Alliance, a coalition of Communists and moderate leftists that was set up to challenge Vargas's rule, openly blamed Jews for the country's economic problems. "After the prices of Brazilian export products like coffee fell in 1935, the National Liberation Alliance (ANL), the mass movement created by the then illegal Brazilian Communist Party (PCB), argued that all foreign firms should be immediately nationalized," noted one historian. "Anti-Semites in the ANL often connected these firms and economic imperialism in general to Judaism."

For the pimps and prostitutes, the Vargas victory resulted in a massive crackdown on vice throughout the country. Police authorities, who had been easy to bribe in the past, suddenly turned against the pimps and prostitutes. In Rio de Janeiro and São Paulo, the country's largest cities, police violently shut down dozens of brothels.

Because Jews were blamed for the white-slave trade, during a series of raids dozens of Jewish pimps and prostitutes were sent back to Nazi-occupied countries, where most of them perished in the Holocaust. Throughout the thirties and forties, both Argentine and Brazilian authorities worked together to make sure that Eastern European and French pimps who regularly traveled back and forth between the two countries to avoid detection would no longer be allowed to remain at large.

Even the other prostitutes turned against their Jewish counterparts. "Everyone knew the Jewish prostitutes were depraved," said Edith, a prostitute who worked near Eleventh Square. "They were dirty. They brought anal sex and sadomasochism to Brazil. The authorities knew that and that's why they went after them." It's not clear why the Brazilian prostitutes turned against the *polacas*. Perhaps, like just about everyone else, they were simply caught up in the anti-Semitic fervor of the time. Or perhaps they were jealous of the Jewish women who seemed so much more organized and successful.

Rebecca Freedman and the other members of the Society of Truth watched helplessly as many of their sisters landed in jail or on the streets. At one point, women of the São Paulo association of Jewish prostitutes reported at their monthly meeting that "the majority of the members suffered terribly; many were kicked out of their houses and found themselves living in the streets."

The ground was on fire.

The prostitutes made plans to obtain temporary housing for their displaced sisters and committed a lot of their funds to helping them. In big cities throughout Brazil, authorities tried to move the prostitutes from the city center into the outlying suburbs. By 1936, the police had shuttered fifty-nine brothels in the center of São Paulo alone. For the Jewish prostitutes, "the situation . . . was one of panic and hopelessness."

There is little documentation of how the raids affected Jewish prostitutes in Rio de Janeiro. Rebecca Freedman never spoke about the raids, and it's unclear whether she personally suffered as a result of them. Perhaps the experiences were too traumatic to relive. Was she kicked out of the brothel she owned near Central Station? Did the police threaten to shut down their burial society, their mutual-aid group?

In the end, the ground might have been on fire all around them, but somehow the synagogue was saved. For Rebecca and her sisters, that was all that ever mattered.

REBECCA FREEDMAN SEEMED not to mind the plaster dust falling like snow and settling on her dark clothes. She seemed not to care that she could barely make herself heard above the roar of the bulldozers and the shouts of the workmen. She wanted to watch the demolition of her synagogue.

There were others assembled on the sidewalk of Afonso Cavalcanti Street to watch the destruction of the pale pink and light blue row houses, grimy bars, Yiddish newspaper offices, and corner stores that used to dot Eleventh Square. Perhaps they were former residents, nostalgic Jewish immigrants saddened at the city's decision to raze their old neighborhood. Or perhaps they were just curious onlookers, office workers stopping by on their lunch break to gauge the progress of the municipal government's ambitious subway-construction project.

It's unlikely that anyone took much notice of the feeble old woman who leaned on her walker and was only able to stand for a short time before she signaled to the idling taxi to return her to her old room in the brothel she still owned around the corner.

But if they did notice this elderly woman with the thick glasses, graying hair, and shaky hands, did they wonder why she was there, her steady gaze fixed on the bulldozers and the giant metal wrecking ball as they pounded wooden pillars, demolished bricks, and crushed windows until everything was reduced to a pile of fine dust and rubble? Perhaps she was a former resident, an owner of one of the little grocery stores or delis. With her air of authority, she could have been mistaken for an aged elementary-school teacher. Was she mourning the loss of the old school that would soon come under the wrecker's ball? For few of the people assembled on the sidewalk idly watching the destruction of the buildings on Afonso Cavalcanti Street would have guessed that this elderly lady was a prostitute, and that she had once headed up the activities of a local synagogue. As they munched on sticky coconut sweets or the sugar-covered peanuts that the street vendors hawked, few of them could have imagined that across the street had once stood a religious establishment for prostitutes.

The demolition seemed to be over in a matter of minutes, which was just as well because Rebecca could not have stood for very long under a blistering midday sun.

Did she curse the bulldozers as they wrecked her synagogue, or did she remain silent, remembering better times when she was young and vigorous and everyone had called her the queen? Once she *had* been the queen, the most exalted Superior Sister, the last president of the Society of Truth. And she had held court across the street, at the once handsome house that was now disappearing, its walls smashed into the dust that now covered her dress, settled in her thinning hair, and clung to the sagging flesh on her bare arms.

For years she had been in charge. How many times had she tapped the wooden meeting table with a pencil or the flat of her hand when she wanted to begin a meeting of the board of directors or call attention to some inconsistency? The sisters could not speak Yiddish in the presence of the staff, she had declared. If they spoke Yiddish in front of Alberto and his uncle or even the cleaning woman who was married to the handyman Noah, they had to translate everything into Portuguese. It was Rebecca's law and everyone had to respect it.

Rebecca Freedman demanded nothing less than complete respect, and furiously tapped the table whenever she caught anyone smoking in her building. Did it remind her of her youth in New York, of that fateful puff of the cigarette that seemed to change her life forever?

Are you here by yourself?

But if smoking conjured up bitter memories of the dance halls on the Lower East Side, the poverty in the tenements, and a rape in a dark alley, Rebecca never told a soul. All the sisters ever knew was that she did not tolerate smoking. It was just one of her many quirks, they might have thought. Like her obsession with cleaning the bodies. If any of the sisters needed to smoke, they could do so on the sidewalk outside, Rebecca declared. If a visitor was caught with a cigarette anywhere on the premises, Rebecca ordered him to leave at once.

"She had everyone's respect," recalled Alberto. "And she was fearless." Rebecca regularly confronted the police if they were harassing one of her prostitutes or any of the members or employees of the society. If a fellow *polaca* needed help at the Jewish public hospital, Rebecca boldly set off to speak to the administrators or the physicians. It didn't matter to her that she was treated with a certain amount of resentment and distrust by her coreligionists. Perhaps the Jewish social workers and hospital staff she saw with increasing frequency as the oldest prostitutes started to die felt sorry for Rebecca Freedman, disgraced and alone and rapidly sinking into old age.

Or perhaps they treated her with grudging respect. After all, Rebecca had influence in the city. Everyone knew how well connected she was. For a prostitute, this was surely rare. When one of the sisters died and left "German Mary" all of her assets in her will, Rebecca called up a judge she knew in Rio to expedite the legal process. Perhaps the judge was a loyal former client or even a former lover. Nobody knew, and no one thought to ask. Few were surprised, though, when less than twenty-four hours after the call to the judge, German Mary, a former prostitute who was in dire need of the inheritance to survive, received her money—an incredible accomplishment in a place like Rio de Janeiro, where legal issues often take years to resolve.

Those who knew Rebecca marveled at her ability to manage and organize. She might have been illiterate, but she could calculate enormous sums in her head. When she was finished with her mental addition, she would glance at Alberto, her accountant and constant companion, to make sure the calculation was correct. When it came to accounting, Dona Becca never made a mistake.

"But in the end, even she was defeated," Alberto said.

He had warned her that the end was coming, but at first Rebecca refused to believe him. Alberto calculated that the financial health of the society had begun to suffer soon after the purchase of the Afonso Cavalcanti property in 1942. At the time, the membership almost doubled, from 68 members to 120. Perhaps the increase reflected the growing number of older prostitutes who sought out the society's services when they could no longer support themselves, or perhaps they were Jewish refugee women who arrived from Europe after the Second World War. Alberto didn't know. All he knew was that few of the new members paid their monthly dues.

By the mid-1950s, when he took over the society's finances, Alberto kept a grim watch on the dwindling cash flow and warned Rebecca, who remained the treasurer until the early 1960s, that the organization was bleeding money. The paltry amount of dues that was being collected was constantly being applied to burials and soaring medical costs as an increasing number of older prostitutes died off. Alberto worried that if the situation continued, there would be no one left to maintain the building and the cemetery and pay the mounting hospital bills for the older members. Things were bad, he warned Rebecca; the society was constantly running deficits. Rebecca listened intently and shook her head, making up the difference with her own savings.

The society in São Paulo faced a similar crisis in the 1960s, its resources dwindling as its membership died off or increasingly sought out the organization's services in their old age. On January 31, 1963, the board of the São Paulo society, left with only thirty members, was forced to increase membership dues to make up the shortfall after several members had died or gone to the old-age home that the organization maintained in an outlying suburb. "The board has made an appeal to the lady members to try to increase their monthly dues because the number of interned members has grown and the maintenance costs greatly increased."

But five years later the last president of the São Paulo Jewish Women's Benevolent and Burial Society prepared for the worst. She called an extraordinary meeting to dissolve the corporation: "The president declared that she was facing the impossibility of filling vacant positions on the board of directors, and proposed the dissolution of the society. According to the statutes set out by the corporation, the society votes to donate their assets, furniture, and property to a similar [unnamed] organization that assists the aged." The motion was unanimously accepted. The Jewish prostitutes who were in the care of the society's nursing home were transferred to the Golda Meir Home for the Aged in São Paulo. The society, which had opened its doors in 1924, ceased operations after that last meeting of the board, on July 31, 1968.

It's unclear how Rebecca Freedman felt after the dissolution of the prostitutes' society in São Paulo. Perhaps it was a premonition, a reminder that her own charity, which faced the same problems, simply would not last into the future. But if she saw the warning signs, she stubbornly refused to acknowledge defeat. When she had exhausted her own savings to keep the society afloat, Alberto began to donate what he could from his own pocket. He also called on Jewish organizations across the city to try to save the society and keep the cemetery at Inhaúma open for business—an effort that Rebecca must have told him would be completely futile.

Still, Alberto persisted, knocking on the doors of the Chevra Kadisha, meeting with the few Jewish community leaders who agreed to discuss the fate of the charity. But it didn't take him long to reach the grim conclusion that "nobody would help the women, nobody wanted anything to do with them."

Rebecca clearly found it difficult to face the end of an organization to which she had devoted her entire adult life. Rather than call a meeting to vote on the dissolution of the Society of Truth,

Rebecca, in her final action as president, simply instructed Alberto to liquidate the assets and somehow, without money or promises of assistance, to find a way to maintain the cemetery at Inhaúma. "There was no point in having a meeting, because really there were so few of them left alive," said Alberto. "I put everything in order as best I could, but the charity just ceased to function. There was no announcement, no final ceremony. It just faded away."

By the time the city demolished the society's offices and synagogue, Rebecca Freedman lived alone, partially bedridden in a dark, airless room with rickety furniture. She wasn't exactly poor, but sometimes when the pain in her knee was overwhelming she might have regretted giving most of her savings away to an organization that could no longer help her. Although she had devoted every effort to making sure that the others would be looked after in old age, she had thought little about herself. Now confined to her old brothel, where much younger women rented the rooms with the flimsy plywood partitions, she could ill afford the knee operation that might end the excruciating pain and enable her to walk with greater ease.

But better to endure physical pain than to have watched her sisters suffer over the years, she might have thought, even though she had always told them to save their money, to plan for the future. They never listened. They thought it would last forever—their ability to attract men, to work at the window. Of course, some had gone on to become prosperous madams, and some had left the profession altogether, never whispering a word to their children or grandchildren of the sacrifices they endured on the streets, when they had been finally shocked into the realization that life in America was hard and brutal, in many ways worse than in the shtetls they had left behind. "Fur traders, that's what they said when they were too embarrassed to speak the truth," said Rebecca of her fellow prostitutes who had managed to leave the profession.

But success stories were rare among the *polacas*. Most of the shtetl girls had simply turned into aged whores, leaning on their canes, their dreams of America long faded as they hawked colorful lottery tickets on downtown street corners in order to survive.

Perhaps they were better off than the others—what were their names? Rebecca could no longer remember names, although she remembered that some of her sisters had died indigent at the public psychiatric hospital. Alberto had told her. He described the sad fate of four Jewish prostitutes and former society members who had been interned there. Three of them had been diagnosed with severe depression, and the fourth had suffered for years from syphilis that went untreated. In old age the syphilis returned and made her insane.

When he visited Rebecca in her dark room, Alberto thought that the pain in her knee might drive her insane. When she lifted the covers to show him the swollen joint—"it was the size of a soccer ball," he later recalled—Rebecca began to cry. The tears came slowly at first as she cursed the pain that kept her confined to her bed. Then they streamed down her face as she sobbed, lamenting to Alberto that her life was ruined, that she would never be able to walk again, never be able to visit the graves of her beloved sisters at the cemetery, pull out the weeds from the cobblestone paths, keep the place in order.

It was the first time Alberto saw the mighty Rebecca Freedman cry, and the experience shocked him profoundly. In his own desperation he urged her to pick up the phone and call a doctor. Alberto knew it wasn't so much a lack of money that prevented her from seeking medical care, it was the utter fear that she would never be able to walk again. When the pain became unbearable, Rebecca finally agreed, asking Alberto to call an elite private hospital that he knew she could not afford. But to his surprise he found himself escorting her to see a prominent orthopedic surgeon a few days later. He was even more surprised when he found out that the surgeon had offered to perform the operation for free. Alberto didn't think to question the arrangement; he knew Rebecca had influence. "She was crying when she told me that the surgeon had agreed to do the operation for free, and that she would walk again," said Alberto. "She was crying tears of joy."

Rebecca Freedman did walk again, but she had little strength to venture far from her dark room. Most of the time she lay in bed, listening to the rumble of the trains that made their way from every corner of the country to Central Station across the street from her brothel. In the mornings she could hear the newspaper vendors shouting the headlines and the roar of rush-hour traffic on President Vargas Avenue.

After her 103rd birthday, Rebecca's memories came to her in a tormented jumble, which mingled the long-buried Yiddish rhymes from her childhood with the prayers for the purification of the dead. What were her last thoughts on that bleak November morning in 1984, when, alone in her little room at the brothel, her heart simply stopped beating? Did she recall cooking over a woodstove in the shtetl, her journeys by ship, her life in the brothels of New York and Rio de Janeiro? Did she curse the fact that she was dying alone, that she had barely enough money in her own bank account to be buried the way she had always insisted upon burying her sisters?

In the end maybe it was the good things about her life that Rebecca recalled: the dedication to the society, the purification of the dead shtetl girls at the cemetery in Inhaúma. Maybe at the moment of death she thought of the waters, the ones that she dreamed would one day cascade over her own body, washing away the weakness, the shame, and the sadness.

She is pure. She is pure. She is pure.

Perhaps now she would finally get her greatest wish, and God would somehow find it possible to forgive Rebecca Freedman.

"The Jews of the Jews"

"Can you hear the gunshots?"

Daniel Rodrigues asked the question so matter-of-factly that it didn't occur to me that I should run for cover. I could hear a few muted pops, but the noise seemed so far away that I wasn't afraid. Besides, Daniel wasn't scared; he was standing out in the open, under a blistering morning sun, in the middle of the Inhaúma cemetery. He had a black tensor bandage wrapped around his left ankle. "Gout," he sheepishly confessed when I asked about his ankle. "It's from drinking too much."

A year had passed since our last meeting, but despite the bandage, Daniel looked pretty much the same. There might have been a little more gray in his hair, but he was still wearing the diamond-stud earring, his eyes were still bloodshot. He was neatly dressed in shorts, black flip-flops, and a white polo shirt that featured one of those incomprehensible English-language slogans that manufacturers of cheap garments in places like China and, in this case, Brazil, are fond of stamping on clothing: YOUR ACTIVE DERIVES. THE HUMAN LIMITS. It was only when I strained to read it a second time—THE HUMAN LIMITS—that I grasped the strange irony, what it said about a man who has spent much of his life in a cemetery.

"Do you see that?" he asked, pointing to rapid streaks of red light, just barely visible against the morning sky. They were tracer bullets from an M-16 assault rifle, Daniel explained. As if to make sure I believed him, he walked to a nearby shed where he kept a dirty margarine container that he used to store the spent aluminum cartridges he had been finding on the cemetery's grounds over the last few months. There were more than thirty cartridges, each the length of his index finger—remnants from the almost weekly battles between rival drug traffickers who control the neighboring shantytowns. Traffickers from the Wet Rat, adjacent to the prostitutes' cemetery, are battling the traffickers who control another nearby favela, known locally as the Hill of Goodbyes.

"More people die in Rio than in Iraq," said Daniel, absently picking through the cartridges.

Indeed, drug-related violence has been a fact of life in Rio since the end of military rule in the mid-1980s. Drug traffickers belonging to groups with names like the Red Command and the Second Command regularly battle police and one another in ongoing turf wars that have left thousands dead over the years. The traffickers are part of a complex alliance that includes the Colombian cocaine cartels and Marxist guerrillas who supply Rio thugs with drugs and the latest weaponry.

On my last visit to the cemetery, my friends in Rio told me that the violence, especially in outlying suburbs like Inhaúma, had gotten worse. Indeed, I noticed that Mario, my driver, was taking a longer, more circuitous route to the cemetery. He told me he wanted to avoid our usual route along the Avenida Brasil and the Linha Vermelha or Red Line, a beautifully paved strip of highway that connects the city to the international airport on Governor's Island. The road bisects two shantytowns. The day we visited the cemetery, there had been an early-morning shoot-out between police and drug traffickers that had resulted in several dead. The story, "Seven Dead on the Red Line," was already front-page news in *O Globo* that morning, and traffic was slower than usual as many vehicles clogged the potholed back roads in order to avoid getting caught in the line of fire. "It's a powder keg," said Mario as he negotiated the narrow roads, where we passed unfinished patchwork houses of brick, zinc, and wood, rubbish-strewn soccer pitches, and, as we neared the cemetery's gates, a group of young men in long shorts and rubber flip-flops selling ripe pineapples from the back of a decrepit container truck.

At the cemetery, Daniel told me that the violence had lately gotten out of hand. There were large holes where the bullets had exploded through the whitewashed stucco wall that separated the prostitutes' cemetery from the one operated by the municipality. At night drug traffickers, who had stopped coming to the cemetery a few years earlier, hid among the pimps' and prostitutes' graves to escape the police. Daniel, who found himself repeatedly repairing the holes in the wall and the damaged gravestones, finally decided to try to speak to the leaders of the drug gangs, who, during the day, surveyed the cemetery through their binoculars for signs of police activity. "I had to negotiate with the bandits," he told me with a hearty laugh. Then he paused, growing quite somber. "I told them that this cemetery was sacred property, that they had to respect the dead."

As a goodwill gesture to the traffickers, who fancied themselves upstanding community leaders, Daniel decided to clear part of the cemetery's land, where there were only a few scattered graves, and plant crops to distribute among his neighbors. He proudly showed me the orderly rows of thick vegetation that comprised his new garden. There was manioc, sugarcane, and pumpkin. He had also started to give away some of the ripe fruit that fell to the ground from the hundred-year-old mango tree that grew near the entrance to the cemetery.

But how did the bureaucrats of the Jewish Communal Cemetery Society, the organization that oversees Inhaúma, feel about Daniel planting crops in a Jewish cemetery?

"Oh, they encouraged me to plant them," he said. "They told me, 'Daniel, you can do whatever you want here.'"

I found it hard to believe that Chaim Szweirszarf, the stern president of the cemetery society, would ever approve such a plan. I told Daniel I didn't believe him. The last time I had spoken to Dr. Chaim, as he is known, he had warned me not to go to the Inhaúma cemetery.

But things had clearly changed. "You've been away a long time," Daniel said, by way of explanation. "Dr. Chaim retired, and the new guy is great."

The "new guy" is Salin Negri, who is affable and forthright and seems to have taken an interest in the abandoned cemetery, especially after someone complained to the city that it was simply rotting away.

"It was an anonymous complaint," said Daniel, fixing me with a silent stare. I assured Daniel that I had not called the Rio municipality and complained about the cemetery's upkeep. Still, he kept repeating that someone had made a "denunciation" to the authorities, and reminded me that no one had really taken any interest in the place since the late seventies, when Rebecca Freedman and some of the other elderly women came for the final burials, with their containers of salted fish and boiled eggs.

"I remember one day I found a box of little hats," said Daniel, referring to the yarmulkes that Jewish men wear in a cemetery or synagogue. "I thought I could hand them out to the mourners and collect a few tips along the way. But the men stopped coming. Only a handful of women came, and then they stopped coming too."

Later, after her closest friends had passed away, Rebecca came on her own, pushing her walker through the cemetery's ordered rows and, occasionally, asking Daniel to bend down and find her small stones, which she placed on her friends' graves as a remembrance.

But regardless of who had made the complaint to municipal authorities, it had clearly had an effect. A few months before my last visit to Inhaúma, there had been a flurry of activity as a work crew sent by the city helped Daniel pull out the hearty weeds that were dislodging paving stones and obscuring some of the graves. There were even plans to restore some of the monuments and rebuild the small crumbling edifice where the *tahara* took place.

Buoyed by this recent attention to the cemetery, I called up Negri at the Jewish Communal Cemetery Society. He was talkative and very solicitous, but when I asked to see the registry book for the Inhaúma cemetery, he claimed he didn't know where it was and asked me to call back and speak to Moises, the society's secretary. Later Moises was curt and businesslike and would neither confirm nor deny the existence of the registry book.

When I told Daniel about my difficulties, he simply shrugged. "The dead can't hurt anyone," he said.

But in the case of Inhaúma, the dead, it seems, *can* hurt the living. Clearly, there are those who do not want it known that they are the descendants of the prostitutes and pimps buried at In-haúma.

"They were the Jews of the Jews." It was the journalist Zevi Ghivelder's phrase, and it was uttered at our very first meeting, when he outlined all of the research he had done on the Jewish prostitutes before abandoning the project at the request of his father some thirty years before. "Nobody wants anything to do with them," he said. "And the descendants want to bury the past forever."

I recalled Zevi's words over and over again during the course of my research and, most recently, during my futile attempts to speak to a respected lawyer who is one of Rebecca Freedman's beneficiaries. After combing municipal archives for months, I found her name in Rebecca's will. Later I found her address in the Rio phone book. She lives in the upper-middle-class Flamengo neighborhood, near downtown, and I decided to pay her a visit. But, like so many others connected with this story, she refused to speak to me. Yes, she said, she knew Rebecca Freedman quite well. It was the only time I managed to get her on the telephone (most of the time I left messages on her answering machine that were never returned). The lawyer did tell me that Rebecca had been very close to her mother, who was also from Poland. But the lawyer's mother had recently died. Had the lawyer's mother been a prostitute? I never got a chance to ask the question. "I have nothing to say," said the lawyer, and hung up.

I told Daniel the story of the lawyer in Flamengo and asked if he knew anything about her. He shook his head and pointed to a spent M-16 cartridge that he had missed, lying near one of the graves. "These women made huge sacrifices to educate their kids, and now nobody cares about them," he said. "All these people buried here, they only came to Brazil to suffer."

Daniel grew silent for what seemed like a long time. The shooting had started in the distance again, and I could see the faint red streaks overhead. In the center of the cemetery, where we were standing, the sun was intense, and I walked to the shade of the mango tree. Daniel followed me and began to gather some of the overripe mangoes that had fallen to the ground.

"I'm just like a Jew," he said cheerfully.

I stopped in my tracks and fixed him with a quizzical look.

"I'm just like those Jews buried here," he said. "I do good for others, so one day, others will do good for me."

ALBERT LONDRES, the French reporter who was the first to chronicle the white-slave trade, noted that "as long as women cannot get work; as long as girls are cold and hungry; as long as they do not know where to go for a bed; as long as women do not earn enough to allow themselves to be ill; or enough to buy themselves a warm coat in winter, enough to buy food, sometimes for their families and their children . . . , the white slave trade will exist."

Although close to a century has passed since Londres made that observation, the international trafficking of women and girls by criminal gangs continues, most of them operating in impoverished countries in the former Eastern Bloc, the former Yugoslavia and Albania. Like the desperately poor Eastern European Jewish women who were easily duped into *stille chuppah* ceremonies and convinced to sail to the other end of the world to meet their new "husbands," so young women in Russia, Moldova, Romania, and Serbia are lured through false job offers to Western Europe, the Middle East, and North America, where they find themselves working as virtual sex slaves.

In 2003, British police arrested a twenty-six-year-old Albanian mafia boss who seemed to take his cue from the Zwi Migdal when he smuggled between fifty and sixty women into Britain. Luan Plakici lured his victims from impoverished, tightly knit families in Albania, Moldova, and Romania through promises of marriage. According to trial transcripts, he married one Albanian teenager and forced her to spend her wedding night working as a prostitute. In the several months that the girl spent under Plakici's control in Britain, she underwent two abortions, after which she was forced to return to work immediately.

Most of Plakici's victims worked seven days a week, servicing more than twenty men a day in order to pay back their "travel bill," which amounted to more than sixteen thousand dollars. Like the Zwi Migdal pimps, Plakici used the money to buy himself several luxury homes. Police arrested him in London, hours after he had bought himself a Ferrari Spider.

"He was merciless in his exploitation of women for financial gain, terrifying his victims by beating and threatening to kill them if they did not comply with his demands," said Detective Chief Inspector Mark Holmes. Plakici was convicted of, among other things, kidnapping and incitement to rape. He was ultimately sentenced to twenty-three years in prison.

In Brazil and Argentina, once the centers of the world's most lucrative white-slave trade, prostitutes are organizing, determined to end sexual slavery and domination by criminal gangs and pimps.

"Women are still brutally exploited by pimps throughout Brazil," said Gabriela Leite, a bespectacled former prostitute and director of Davida, which has representatives all over Brazil. Leite frequently travels around the country and throughout the world giving lectures on unionizing sex workers.

In Buenos Aires, prostitutes have formed the Association of Women Prostitutes of Argentina, known by its Spanish-language acronym, AMMAR. "We share the same dreams as any worker, to have rights, not to be exploited, and to have a living wage," said Susana Martinez, the group's president.

In addition to handing out condoms and health information, the women who volunteer with Davida are lobbying government officials in Brazil to regulate prostitution. The group wants prostitutes to be treated like any other unionized workers in Brazil, to pay taxes and receive health benefits. In Rio, the prostitutes at Vila Mimosa support the group's work. They don't want to be beholden to pimps or the police, who regularly abuse the women unless they pay them a weekly kickback.

"The police violence used to be a lot worse," said Leite, lighting a cigarette in her office, in a colonial-style row house just down the street from the newly built Hotel Magic and the Hotel Love Time, establishments that charge by the hour and specialize in accommodating the kind of afternoon trysts between businessmen and their mistresses or slightly higher-class prostitutes than the ones who work in Vila Mimosa.

I asked Leite if she had been influenced in her work by the example of the Jewish prostitutes and their mutual-aid organization, the Society of Truth. But although she had heard the older prostitutes speak about the *polacas,* she confessed that she knew nothing about their organization or cemetery. "You have to understand that those women—the *polacas*—always kept to themselves," she said. "When they died, their organization died with them."

She was right, of course, but I was still determined to find some vestige of the Society of Truth. When their synagogue was torn down during the subway construction, Rebecca Freedman had commented that all the Jewish organizations in Rio, which had treated them with so much disdain in the past, had fought over the charity's possessions—the Torah scroll, the silver candelabra, chairs. Where were those articles now?

I asked Zevi Ghivelder, who was the last journalist to photograph the synagogue on Afonso Cavalcanti Street, where the charity's possessions ended up. He remembered the beautiful pieces, including a set of exquisitely crafted jacaranda-wood chairs that had been made to commemorate financial donations made by the Superior Sisters. In recognition of their work on behalf of the Society of Truth, each sister had her Hebrew name carved onto a brass plaque, which was affixed to the back of each chair. There was a chair for Rivi Bas Moishe Duvid or Rebecca Freedman, one for Angelita Bas Isruel Iankev Schaffran or Angelina Schaffran— a complete set commemorating many of the women who had devoted their lives to the Society of Truth.

Zevi told me that most of the contents from Afonso Cavalcanti, including the chairs, had ended up at the Mount Sinai Club, a sporting and religious organization that opened its doors in 1971, the year the city began construction of the subway and the demolition of part of the old Jewish quarter.

José Rimer is the caretaker of the Mount Sinai Club. He has a potbelly and a pragmatic disposition. The first time I visited the club in the leafy, middle-class Tijuca neighborhood in the northern part of the city, he told me that he had no idea what I was talking about. "Jacaranda chairs?" he asked, sitting in his office, which was crammed with miscellaneous sporting equipment, files, and old newspapers. "No, there's nothing like that here."

But I insisted, and he reluctantly agreed to take me on a tour of the entire club. We started with the synagogue, where I sat in the women's section patiently waiting until the end of Friday prayers to check for the chairs. I got quizzical looks from some of the elderly men who attended the Sabbath service as I picked up the chairs to examine them for any clues that might link them to the Society of Truth.

But I found nothing, so Rimer suggested we take the freight elevator to the fifth floor, where, as he put it, "we keep all the old junk." A cockroach scuttered away as the light from the elevator shone on the dusty corridor, where piles of old furniture, sports equipment, and books were dumped together in a huge pile.

After two hours, Rimer seemed to give up on the chairs and decided to show me all the facilities of the Mount Sinai Club instead. We went to the sauna, where old men, their chest hairs beaded in sweat and their baggy swim trunks plastered to their bodies, were sitting in white plastic loungers discussing politics. Rimer showed me the three swimming pools and the weight room, where two overweight blondes were working out on the treadmills. "They hang out too much at the barbecue restaurants, and now they have to work it all off," said Rimer to the blondes, who laughed and pointed to his own potbelly.

In the child-care center, egg cartons and plastic Coca-Cola bottles waited in a basket to be transformed into art. We saw the jiu-jitsu room and the snack bar. By the end of the tour, I had had enough and told Rimer that I had to get going. He refused to listen and insisted upon taking me to the only room in the entire complex we hadn't visited—the accounting office, which was off the main foyer.

When he opened the door, I knew immediately I had found the chairs, or at least one of them. Although it was piled high with file folders and books, I could see that it was a handsome claw-footed chair made of beautifully carved jacaranda, and the teal leather was fastened to the frame with large brass bolts. The chair was weathered, and stuffing came out at the bottom. I removed all the files and picked up the chair, scanning the back for a small, en-graved plaque. But the tiny plaque must have long since been re-moved, and only a small rectangular shadow remained.

Rimer left the room in order to attend to some other matter, and I took the opportunity to ask the club's treasurer, who was there working late, where she had found the chair. She told me it and several others like it used to be in the president's conference room. No, she had no idea where they had come from before that, but a few years ago when the club's executive decided to renovate, the construction crew had thrown them away. "I saw them lying on the garbage pile," said the treasurer, who was sitting behind a large desk piled with bits of paper and file folders. "They were so beautiful, I decided to take one for my office."

I debated whether or not to tell her about the origins of the chairs, and comment on how ironic it was that the chairs that had belonged to a group of women who were so universally despised in the Rio Jewish community had once adorned the president's of-fice of one of that community's most important clubs. I decided to say nothing, and for a few minutes we stood awkwardly staring at the chair.

Maybe the treasurer was simply trying to fill that awkward si-lence when she lit a cigarette and began to speak. "You know," she said, taking a long drag of her cigarette, "this is going to sound strange, but there is something very special about that chair. I don't know what it is. It has a certain presence. I find it . . . magi-cal."

REBECCA FREEDMAN IS NOT BURIED at the prostitutes' cemetery in Inhaúma. By the time she died in 1984, the Society of Truth had long since vanished and there was no one left to bury her at the cemetery that had become so much a symbol of her struggle. Most of her beloved sisters had died long before. Rebecca, who lived her life on the margins of society, fighting for dignity and the right to practice her religion, is buried among "respectable" Jews at the Jewish cemetery in Caju. A large white headstone marks her grave, which is in the same row as that of Clarice Lispector, one of Brazil's most important writers. The headstone notes simply Rebecca's dates of birth and death, although whoever arranged for the burial seemed uncertain about her birthdate, so part of it is simply left blank. Unlike many of the headstones of the Superior Sisters at Inhaúma, this one bears not much else in the way of an epitaph—no notes of gratitude to the sisters, no listing of next of kin. Rebecca Freedman clearly died alone, and although she managed in death to be counted among the Jewish elite in Rio de Janeiro, she is buried among strangers at Caju.

But clearly she is not forgotten. When I made the trip to Caju to visit Rebecca Freedman's grave, I immediately noticed the stones. Someone had left a long, neat row of stones on the headstone, as if to mark regular visits to the grave. But with most of the prostitutes long dead and buried, who was visiting Rebecca Freedman's grave with such frequency?

Then I remembered the accountant, Alberto da Costa, who at eighty-one was thin and frail but elegantly dressed with a neatly trimmed, graying mustache and a professional, even courtly manner. The last time I saw him, we sat sipping tiny cups of espresso in a noisy food court in a high-rise shopping mall that overlooks the sailboats docked at the Rio Yacht Club on Guanabara Bay.

"She had complete confidence in me," Alberto had said. "There was nobody like her. She couldn't read or write, but she had everything in her head. She was a living archive."

I began to ask Alberto if he ever visited Rebecca's grave, if he was the one who left the neat row of stones. But he didn't let me finish the question. For a split second, he seemed to lose himself in his memory of Rebecca. "I loved her," he said in a faint whisper, and I could see the beginnings of tears in his eyes. "I loved her a lot."

He immediately regained his composure and then got up to leave, making an excuse about an engagement with a visiting nephew. He insisted upon paying for the coffee, then disappeared down an escalator, in a crowd of Saturday-afternoon shoppers.

I never asked him about the stones. I didn't need to.

NOTES

Facts of publication for all of the books cited in these notes can be found in the Bibliography.

For foreign-language sources, unless otherwise noted, the translation is mine.

INTRODUCTION

12 "If [they] would come to a Jewish theater . . .": Jacob X. Cohen, *Jewish Life in South America: A Survey Study for the American Jewish Congress,* pp. 98–99.

14 "What's extraordinary about this story . . .": Zevi Ghivelder interview.

CHAPTER ONE
Gentlemen from America

17 The story of Isaac Boorosky and Sophia Chamys is taken from Francisco Ferreira da Rosa's, *O Lupanar: Estudo sobre o caftismo e a prostituição no Rio de Janeiro,* pp. 205–21. Ferreira da Rosa, a leading Brazilian journalist, wrote extensively about the early days of the white-slave trade. *O Lupanar (The Brothel),* is a detailed account of the lives of many of the first Eastern European pimps and prostitutes who arrived in Brazil in the 1880s and 1890s. All of the details of the encounter of Isaac and Sophia are taken from Ferreira da Rosa's interviews with Rio police officials, who investigated the Chamys case.

20 "the eternal dwelling place of poverty": Albert Londres, *The Road to Buenos Ayres,* p. 167. The French journalist and author toured shtetls in Poland before and after the First World War.

21 "her hands as puffed as the dough . . .": Milton Meltzer, *World of Our Fathers: The Jews of Eastern Europe,* p. 93.

21 The children's rhyme "Helf Ikh Mamen" (Helping Mother) is from Roman Vishniac, *Children of a Vanished World,* p. 54.

22 Descriptions of the *shtibl* from author interviews with elderly former shtetl residents, most notably Tamara
Wolman, who was born in Bolesffa, Poland, in 1908.

24 The Lemberg trial is documented in detail in Edward J.
Bristow, *Prostitution and Prejudice: The Jewish Fight
Against White Slavery, 1870–1939,* p. 75.

25–26 "They buy girls from their parents . . .": Londres, p. 171.

27 "His face was smooth and round . . .": Sholem Aleichem,
"The Man from Buenos Aires," in *Favorite Tales of
Sholem Aleichem,* pp. 517–28.

30 "Such and such a house is no good . . .": Negotiations of
shtetl matchmakers described in Londres, p. 171.

30 The description of the trial and conviction of matchmaker Guinda Wainrouse is from Bristow, pp. 107–8.

30 League of Nations report, as quoted in Jewish
International Conference minutes, p. 89.

31 In Romania and Poland there were stories: Bristow, p. 45.

31 police officials blamed "the degenerate Jew . . .": Ferreira
da Rosa, p. 11.

31 "Sometimes the men arrived . . .": Laya Rosenberg interview.

32 "Do you not know that numbers . . .": Paula Ollendorf,
Breslau delegate, Jewish International Conference minutes, p. 58.

36 For Jews, prostitution is the most reviled: Bristow,
pp. 11–15.

37 Jews in Warsaw went on a rampage: The 1905 uprising,
known as the *Alphonsenpogrom,* so called because Jewish
pimps in Warsaw were known as "alphonses," is detailed
in Bristow, p. 61.

40 Sometimes the multiple marriages: Ferreira da Rosa, p. 24.

40 "It often turns out...": Comments on the *stille chuppah* made by a woman identified only as Mrs. Teplicka, Lodz delegate, Jewish International Conference minutes, p. 24.

40 The *stille chuppah* had other implications: Council for the Amelioration of the Legal Position of the Jewess, meeting minutes, London, 22 July, 1922, pp. 42–43.

41 Yaacov Ferber's letter in Nora Glickman *The Jewish White Slave Trade and the Untold Story of Raquel Liberman*, p. 106.

42 "its glories shamelessly exaggerated...": Irving Howe, *World of Our Fathers*, p. 35.

43 "natural disasters (particularly epidemics), cattle plagues and even Tatar invasions": Janusz Tazbir, "Images of the Jew in the Polish Commonwealth," in *From Shtetl to Socialism: Studies from Polin*, pp. 26–27.

44 "Filthy Jew!": Sally Knopf, *Humilhação e luta: Uma mulher no inferno verde*, p. 30.

44 The children's rhyme "Di Toyb" (The Dove) from Vishniac, p. 86.

CHAPTER TWO
The End of the World

47 The description of the prostitutes at the port of Buenos Aires and the gates of the immigrants' hotel is taken from an eyewitness account in "Of Pimps, Prostitutes, and Other Seducers: Excerpt of a Memoir by Mordechai Alpersohn," in *Yiddish South of the Border: An Anthology of Latin American Yiddish Writing*, ed. Alan Astro, p. 17. Alpersohn, who came to Buenos Aires from Lantskron,

Ukraine, in 1891, helped found one of the first Jewish agricultural settlements in Argentina. He arrived in the country under the auspices of the Jewish Colonization Association (ICA), a Jewish philanthropic organization. His *Memoirs of a Jewish Colonist* became a best seller in the Yiddish-speaking world when it was published in Berlin and Buenos Aires between 1922 and 1928, earning him the moniker "the Jewish Robinson Crusoe."

48 "After a short period of friendly association . . .": Victor Alberto Mirelman, "The Jews of Argentina (1890–1930): Assimilation and Particularism," p. 352.

48 "One by one they approached . . .": Alpersohn, p. 17.

49 "Don't let your wives and daughters . . .": ICA official identified only as Dr. Loewenthal, ibid., p. 19.

50 "a great, free and fertile land": Ibid.

51 Those who stayed suffered "unspeakable deprivation": ibid, p. 22.

51 "A vile traffic . . .": Letter writer unidentified, quoted in Mirelman, p. 353.

53 "She has no hat . . .": Stowaways described in Albert Londres, *The Road to Buenos Ayres,* pp. 29, 107–8.

54 Pimps used other ruses: Disguises forced on the girls by pimps described in Edward J. Bristow, *Prostitution and Prejudice: The Jewish Fight Against White Slavery,* p. 133. He also describes Golda, who "left Odessa with two innocent girls and managed to beg her way across to Buenos Aires, having the party pose as victims of the Kishinev massacre."

56 Other women destined: Londres, p. 30. "On the Mihanovich boats one does not feel one is really traveling," notes Londres; "it is more like paying a visit to a neighbor. And the police let you alone."

57 Sometimes the "planned demoralization": Francisco Ferreira da Rosa, *O Lupanar: Estudo sobre o caftismo e a prostituição no Rio de Janeiro,* p. 25.

57 a French pimp named Lucien Carlet: Londres, pp. 18–19.

59 "the filth and promiscuity . . .": Rabbi Samuel Halfon, speaking in 1910 in Buenos Aires, cited in Haim Avni, *Argentina and the Jews: A History of Jewish Immigration,* p. 81.

59 Sofia Markovich's story is related in Frances Korn et al., *Buenos Aires: Los huespedes del 20,* p. 96.

60 "Girls knowing that in Russia . . .": Mirelman, p. 352.

62 According to one eyewitness: Gabriel Raymann, a newspaper editor in Buenos Aires, describing an auction that took place in November 1905, cited in Bristow, p. 135.

62 In this "stockmarket of women": Gerardo Bra, *La Organización Negra: La increíble historia de la Zwi Migdal,* p. 38.

62 Some buyers behaved: Julio L. Alsogaray, *Trilogia de la trata de blancas*, p. 105.

64 "They no longer even considered themselves . . .": Ibid. p. 245.

64 "In politics, they like solid . . .": Londres, pp. 62–63.

64 Like Isaac, they were deeply: There are numerous descriptions of the pimps' expensive taste in clothes, and their financial power in the Jewish neighborhoods in North and South America, in Mirelman, p. 351.

65 The wealthiest ones even conducted: There are numerous references to how Jewish pimps used legitimate business enterprises as fronts for the traffic in girls and women. Of the pimps who traveled between Buenos Aires and Rio de Janeiro, Herman Moscovitz owned a

cigar shop in Buenos Aires; Adolpho Ruckenstein and Ignacio Friedman operated the Roteserie Sportman (*sic*) in Rio de Janeiro; and Isidoro Klopper, another Jewish pimp, advertised his jewelry business on his cards. See Ferreira da Rosa, pp. 92–93, 167, 270.

67 "The city swarmed with males": Londres, p. 42.

67 "lowering over the city like a thundercloud": Ibid. p. 92.

67 "Do you think we have only . . .": Ibid., p. 134.

68 "set up like a commercial enterprise . . .": Alsogaray, pp. 230–33.

68 became an "octopus, achieving an almost . . .": Bristow, p. 139.

69 "They live under a servile discipline . . .": Londres, pp. 168–69.

69 Every month the president: Ibid., p. 169.

69 The board regularly fronted: Alsogaray, p. 237.

69 "They lend each other . . .": Londres, p. 170.

69–70 lawyers who were "organized into another mafia . . .": Alsogaray, pp. 192, 245.

70 Lola Goskin's experience is documented in Bra, p. 39.

70 it was "exclusively made up . . .": Description of the Warsaw Society, later the Zwi Migdal, in ibid., p. 92. Bra is one of the only researchers to have had access to Zwi Migdal documents, which were destroyed in the 1994 radical Islamist terrorist attack on the Asociación Mutual Israelita Argentina (AMIA), a Jewish community center in Buenos Aires. Investigation of the pimps' organization, initially known as the Warsaw Society, which took place in November 1927, documented on p. 97.

71 "In Buenos Aires there are Jews . . .": Comment by British colonel Albert E. W. Goldsmid, in 1893, to his

fellows at the Order of the Ancient Maccabeans in London. Goldsmid, who claimed to have been "shadowed" by the Jewish pimps and prostitutes wherever he traveled in Argentina, had been sent to the country a year earlier to supervise the Jewish settlement in the ICA's colonies there. Cited in Mirelman, p. 353.

72 The donor list was found: The list appears in Bra, p. 33.

72 "There isn't a thing in the world . . .": Sholem Aleichem, "The Man from Buenos Aires," in *Favorite Tales of Sholem Aleichem,* p. 525.

73 The story of Raquel Spertzein and Natalio Zisman is documented in Alsogaray, p. 230.

73 The story of Esther Jadzikoba is documented in Korn, p. 87.

74 "the end of the world . . .": in Londres, pp. 175–80.

74 "To see the poor creatures . . .": The description of La Boca and the Jewish prostitutes is from Samuel Cohen, secretary general of the Gentlemen's Committee of the Jewish Association for the Protection of Girls and Women, in JAPGW's *Gentlemen's Committee Report, 1913,* p. 42.

74 Albert Londres's description of La Boca in Londres, pp. 175–80.

75 Sophia Chamys's trip to Rio de Janeiro is described in Ferreira da Rosa, pp. 210–12.

CHAPTER THREE
The Streets of the Women

78 The account of Professor Kneizer and the letter writers is taken from Francisco Ferreira da Rosa, *O Lupanar:*

Estudo sobre o caftismo e a prostituição no Rio de Janeiro, pp. 69–77.

79 Pimps' editorial cartoon appeared in *O Malho,* cited in Lena Medeiros de Menezes, *Os estrangeiros e o comercio do prazer nas ruas do Rio (1890–1930),* p. 36.

81 In Rio de Janeiro, the network of brothels: The houses of instruction and restaurants for the prostitutes are described in Ferreira da Rosa, p. 62.

81 "a rose in their hair . . .": Charles Expilly, a French traveler to Rio de Janeiro at the turn of the last century, cited in Luiz Carlos Soares, *Rameiras, ilhoas, polacas . . . : A prostituição no Rio de Janeiro no seculo XIX,* p. 42.

81–82 Klara Hohn, a nineteen-year-old: Hohn traveled to Rio de Janeiro in order to take up an unspecified job. Her father, who had heard that there was fabulous wealth to be made in Brazil, paid her way. Klara told police in Rio de Janeiro that she was headed to Rio seeking honest work when she encountered Anna Scheler on the ship, and that Scheler initially offered her a job in a boutique. In Ferreira da Rosa, p. 232.

82 Inside, the houses, once respectable: brothels are described in ibid., pp. 163–64.

83 The murder of Rosa Schwarz is described in Margareth Rago, *Os prazeres da noite: Prostituição e códigos da sexualidade feminina em São Paulo (1890–1930),* pp. 281–82.

84 Fictitious letter regarding Klara Adam is reproduced in Ferreira da Rosa, pp. 56–57.

84 Klara Adam's testimony to police was printed in *Gazeta de noticias,* 21 April 1880, and is cited in Rago, p. 283.

85 Sophia Chamys's arrival and early life in Rio de Janeiro is described in Ferreira da Rosa, pp. 212–13.

89 Ana Valentina da Silva, a fifty-something: Barbuda's brothels and ads are described in Soares, pp. 44, 63.

91 "But it wasn't because they held...": The comment about the allure of French prostitutes in fin de siècle Rio de Janeiro is from Jeffrey D. Needell, *Belle époque tropical,* p. 203.

91 After 1894 the *cocottes:* The prostitutes at the Colombo are described in Medeiros de Menezes, p. 46.

91 would appear "in a halo...": French prostitutes are described in Rago, p. 294.

92 a stagnant "focus of mosquitoes and putrid smells." The description of the Mangue red-light district is from the Brazilian poet Manuel Bandeira, in Lasar Segall, "Album Mangue" catalog Rio de Janeiro: Philobiblion, 1977, pp. 9–10.

92 "... the worst part of the city...,": This description is from American social worker Betty Rice, who worked on a municipal campaign to help combat venereal disease in the Mangue in the early 1920s. Cited in Sueann Caulfield, "O nascimento do Mangue: Raça, nacão e o controle da prostituição no Rio de Janeiro, 1850–1942," *Tempo* 5, no. 9 (July 2000), p. 15.

93 "In illuminated stores, there are women...": Stefan Zweig, *Brazil: Land of the Future,* pp. 171–72.

93 most were driven into the Mangue: Caulfield, p. 7.

93 For the municipal authorities,: Soares, p. 95.

93 The Jewish prostitutes were considered: "A prostituição na cidade do Rio de Janeiro," pamphlet by public-health official Dr. José de Goes e Siqueira Filho, 1875, p. 15. Rio de Janeiro municipal archives. Goes also blamed the Jewish

prostitutes for "a serious lapse of morality" and said they had "few sentiments of modesty and self-esteem."

93 "In general, the agents of evil . . .": Municipal health study, 1880, cited in Soares, p. 95.

94 Sophia Chamys's life in Rio de Janeiro, return to Poland, and trip to Buenos Aires are from Ferreira da Rosa, pp. 215–18.

99 "Sometimes we heard them, yes": Freda Nagelsmander, interview.

99 "The women from the Mangue . . .": Fanny Futritsk interview.

99 In fact, respectable Jews like the Nagelsmander: Samuel Malamud, "Recordando a Praca Onze," *Shalom Magazine,* May 1988, p. 29. Malamud, who arrived in Rio de Janeiro from Bessarabia with his family in the 1920s, became one of the most important leaders of the Brazilian Jewish community. He was the consul general for Israel in Brazil between 1949 and 1952 and wrote extensively about Jewish immigration to Rio de Janeiro.

100 "a black mark on the Jewish people": Ibid.

100 "During the nightly shows . . .": Ibid.

101 "When I go to a dance with the Brazilians . . .": Leib Malach, *Ibergus,* cited in Alan Astro, ed., *Yiddish South of the Border: An Anthology of Latin American Yiddish Writing,* p. 93. The Polish writer Leib Malach (a pseudonym for Leib Zaltsman) wrote *Ibergus* or "Remolding" in the mid-1920s, after emigrating to Buenos Aires. The play chronicled the tensions between the "unclean" Jews and the respectable Jewish community in Buenos Aires. Malach later changed the setting to Rio de Janeiro

because Jewish theater promoters in Buenos Aires thought the subject matter too controversial. They feared the play would offend the Zwi Migdal mafia, who were then the main financiers of Yiddish theater. The play tells the story of Rosa, a Jewish prostitute, who tries unsuccessfully to leave the brothels.

101 "Their flesh and their entrails . . .": Leib Malach, *Ibergus,* cited in Nora Glickman, *The Jewish White Slave Trade and the Untold Story of Raquel Liberman,* p. 23.

101 Many lived in constant fear . . . : Ferreira da Rosa, p. 197.

101 "there was no one to perform . . .": Ibid.

101 The details of Olga's funeral are related in ibid., pp. 201–4.

102 German Kaminer's story is related in ibid., pp. 172–82.

103 Max Muller's story is related in ibid., p. 197.

104 Sophia Chamys's story, and police testimony, are related in ibid., pp. 216–20.

CHAPTER FOUR
The Queen

108–09 The descriptions of Rebecca Freedman performing the *tahara* are from da Costa interview.

110 Then, on October 10, 1906: The goals of the Jewish Benevolent and Burial Association are cited in Rio de Janeiro's *Diário oficial* RJ 13/11/1906, and in Beatriz Kushnir, *Baile de máscaras: Mulheres judias e prostituição,* pp. 94–97.

111–15 The descriptions of Sura Rachel Manchajm, Feiga Nossenchug, Perla Ajdelman, and Estera Gladkowicer are from their police files in the Federal Department of Public Security, Ministry of Justice and the Interior, Rio de Janeiro.

113 "In her eyes, full of love...": Lyrics from Moreira da Silva, *Judia rara*, cited in "O fim de um tabu," *O Estado de São Paulo,* 25 May 1997.

115 Rebecca Freedman had arrived in Rio: Lloyd Brasileiro, ship's manifest, Rio de Janeiro, 30 Aug. 1916. Rebecca Freedman is listed among third-class passengers, arriving from New York City. She is identified as an American citizen. National Archives, Rio de Janeiro.

116 Where were the riches: The description of impoverished Eastern European Jews living in tenements and returning to the shtetl is from Irving Howe, *World of Our Fathers,* p. 35.

117 "naked under their flowery kimonos...," and "...like pushcart peddlers": Michael Gold, *Jews Without Money,* pp. 6–7.

117 "official flesh trade...": The article is cited in Howe, p. 98.

117 But when they tired of the slavelike conditions: There are several references to pimps preying on young factory workers. The most notable are contained in an investigation of the New York Chamber of Commerce's Committee of Fifteen study in the early 1900s, cited in Judith Lee Vaupen Joseph, "The *Nafkeh* and the Lady: Jews, Prostitutes, and Progressives in New York City, 1900–1930," pp. 161–62; and Albert Fried, *The Rise and Fall of the Jewish Gangster in America,* p. 16.

118 "It's a good business, easy...": From an interview with an unidentified young Jewish girl, who lived in a tene-

ment full of Jewish prostitutes, quoted in Lincoln Steffens, *The Autobiography of Lincoln Steffens,* p. 245.

118 A good business: The stories of Lizzie Dannenberg and Rachel Marks are outlined in Timothy J. Gilfoyle, *City of Eros: New York City, Prostitution, and the Commercialization of Sex, 1790–1920,* p. 290.

120 "By apparently kind and generous treatment . . .": *Report of the Committee of Fifteen,* cited in Fried, p. 16.

120 "Living in most crowded districts . . .": Cited in Fried, p. 10.

120 report prepared by the United States Immigration Commission: Cited in Joseph, p. 267.

121 "I teach them manners . . .": Interview with pimp, cited in Gold, p. 16.

121 In 1901 Dora Rubin Schneiderman: Joseph, pp. 175–76. Judith Lee Vaupen Joseph.

121 New York social workers documented one case: Ibid., p. 175.

122 "Yes, those girls are whores": Gold, p. 21.

122 "The other member of the household . . .": Fried, p. 12.

122 Jennie Silver was a notorious prostitute: Ibid., p. 11.

123 Jacob Siebowitz, a Polish immigrant: Joseph, pp. 164–65.

123 Out of desperation, some Jewish parents: Ibid., p. 178.

123 The amount prostitutes were paid and the types of clients they received are documented in the *New York Bureau of Social Hygiene Report,* 1912, reproduced in George Kneeland, *Commercialized Prostitution in New York City,* pp. 108–15.

123 The account books for one fifty-cent brothel: Gilfoyle, p. 291.

124 The final listing for Rebecca Freedman in the New York City Directory, 1915, is an address on Eldridge Street,

where she might have lived before sailing to Rio de Janeiro in 1916. She is not listed in subsequent directories.

125 Lena Myers, a twenty-eight-year-old: Howe, p. 97.

125 Susie, a young prostitute: Gold, p. 19.

126 Big Tim Sullivan, the Tammany boss. Estimates of the money made by Sullivan from David Von Drehle, *Triangle: The Fire that Changed America,* p. 24.

126 gangsters Jake Wolf, Max Hochstim, Martin Engel, and his brother Max: The description of these men and the fear they inspired among local residents is from Edward J. Bristow, *Prostitution and Prejudice: The Jewish Fight Against White Slavery,* p. 148.

126 The confrontation between Caela Urchittel and the local gangsters is documented in the minutes of the Lexow Committee hearings, which examined widespread corruption among municipal officials in New York in 1894. Part of the commission's report is reprinted in Fried, pp. 51–52.

127–28 Mordke Goldberg, the "king" of the underworld, is described in Kneeland, pp. 81, 82.

129 New York police raiding the brothels is documented in Fried, p. 82.

130 Helena Goldatrin, who was born: The funeral was the subject of a front-page article ("Uma festa macabra—Os exploradores do judaismo. Os 'wizguths' pagam o seu tributo—O destino de Helena") in the Rio de Janeiro daily *A Noite,* 30 Oct. 1916, author's translation.

136 Still, despite the enmity: Comments on the synagogue of the prostitutes in downtown Rio de Janeiro were made by Samuel Cohen, the secretary of the Gentlemen's Committee for the Jewish Association for the Protection of Girls and Women in London, following his 1913 trip

to South America. From *Gentlemen's Committee,* 1913, pp. 39–42.

136 A rabbi sent to Brazil: The rabbi was Israel Raffalovich, who was shocked by the disorganization among Jews in Brazil. His comments are recorded in his report to the Central Conference of American Rabbis in New York, 1930, pp. 6, 7.

136 The description of the bris by the pimps is from "Contra os caftens! A Polícia em Ação na Rua Luís de Camões," *Correio da Manhã,* 10 Feb. 1906.

CHAPTER FIVE
The Work of Sisyphus

139 The story of Sally Knopf's journey to Brazil is from her memoir, *Humilhação e luta: Uma mulher no inferno verde,* pp. 29–31.

141 without any concept of geography: "Since she does not know whether America is a city in the vicinity of London or how long it will take to reach a certain destination, and since, not being able to read or write, she cannot depend on letters or news to ascertain whether something is actually true or not, every girl who emigrates, i.e. leaves her hometown, is a potential victim of all sorts of unfortunate circumstances or evils." Bertha Pappenheim, cited in Melinda Given Guttmann, *The Enigma of Anna O.: A Biography of Bertha Pappenheim,* p. 167.

142 The description of the feminist activists of the Judischer Frauenbund who patrolled the European ports in search of victims of the white-slave traffic is from ibid. p. 175.

142 The League of Nations resolution regarding the combat against white slavery is reprinted in the *Official Report of the Jewish International Conference on the Suppression of the Traffic in Girls and Women and the Preventive, Protective and Education Work of the Jewish Association for the Protection of Girls and Women* (JAPGW), p. 91.

142 In 1919 a volunteer: "Case 23" in JAPGW's *Gentlemen's Committee Report,* 1919, p. 54.

143 Selig Ganopol's experiences at the port of Buenos Aires, outlined in the Jewish International Conference minutes, p. 11, 18. Selig Ganopol was the secretary of Ezras Noschim, the Buenos Aires branch of the JAPGW. The statistics on the organization's work in Argentina are also quoted in the 1927 conference minutes, p. 18.

144 In Argentina an activist known only as Madame Arslau: The feminist activist is interviewed in Londres, pp. 189–90.

145 Bertha Pappenheim sat bolt upright: Guttmann, pp. 194–95.

146 "I did some research, listened . . .": Ibid., p. 188.

147 "indifference and a frivolous philosophy . . .": Ibid., p. 190.

148 "We Jews talk so much . . .": Rabbi Goldmann, from Leipzig, the representative of the German Association of Rabbis and the B'nai B'rith sent to London for the annual white-slavery conference organized by the JAPGW in 1927. Quoted in Jewish International Conference minutes, p. 36.

148 Even most of the Jewish press: The condemnation of the Jewish press in Britain over the JAPGW conference in London is from Guttmann, p. 188. *Der Israelit* reported, "Over the suitability of the Conference, opinion in Jewish circles was strongly divergent." Britain's *Jewish World*

noted, "Unhesitatingly, we are of the opinion that such a gathering ought not to have been held."

148 She also accused official Jewish leaders: Ibid., p. 188.

148–49 "the weekly wages . . ." and "live worse than cattle": Ibid., p. 159.

149 "Sisyphus Arbeit": Ibid., p. 216.

149–50 "Without knowing precisely what occurred . . .": Daniel R. Langton, *Claude Montefiore: His Life and Thought*, p. 12.

150 "Many of our sisters are victims . . .": Jewish International Conference minutes, p. 163.

151 "All I discovered": Diary of Bertha Pappenheim, in Guttmann, p. 193.

153 "It is to be regretted": JAPGW's *Gentlemen's Committee Report for the Year Ending 1913,* p. 48.

153 Even the Jewish activists: JAPGW's *Gentlemen's Committee* 1914, p. 39. The report also mentions how the JAPGW came to rely increasingly on British consular officials to come to the rescue of victims of the white-slave trade in Brazil.

155 Sally Knopf's arrival in Brazil and the encounter with her uncles in Knopf, pp. 31–35.

156 the country was already well known: Brazil, notes historian Jeffrey Lesser, was no longer considered the "land of the monkeys" to shtetl dwellers in Europe. *Welcoming the Undesirables: Brazil and the Jewish Question,* p. 24.

160 "First through gentle suggestions . . .": Victor Alberto Mirelman, "The Jews in Argentina (1890–1930): Assimilation and Particularism," p. 352.

161 "They were a huge stain on our immigration": Lea Lovinsky, of the Froein Farain, author interview.

161 Rebecca Freedman knew: Ghivelder, interview.

162 "There was nothing else for us to do": Ibid.

163 "We danced the Tora . . .": Beatriz Kushnir, *Baile de más-caras: Mulheres judias e prostituição: As polacas e suas asso-ciacoes de ajuda mutua,* p. 124.

163 But the organization's most important: Power-of-attorney statute approved at a meeting of the Society of Truth in November 1928, from minutes of the Jewish Benevolent and Burial Association, Rio de Janeiro.

163 For years, the pimps had tried: The minutes of the Chevra Kadisha in Buenos Aires describe how pimps tried desperately to be buried in the official Jewish cemetery by offering to contribute large sums of money to the organization. The board, however, would not be moved. Cited in Mirelman, pp. 132–33.

164 preferring "to lie among honorable . . .": Rabbi Hacohen Sinai, cited in Mirelman, p. 135.

164 "reflecting the poignant reality . . .": Mareleyn Schneider, *History of a Jewish Burial Society: An Examination of Secularization,* p. 114.

166 a serious breach "against the security . . .": The expression is taken from the Brazilian criminal code of 1890, particularly Articles 266 and 303, under which Jacob Weinstein was arrested. Cited in Kushnir, p. 121.

168 The most important of these was Article 27: Ibid., p. 126.

CHAPTER SIX
The Miracle

The testimony of Rachel Liberman is well documented in several sources, including Gerardo Bra in *La organización negra: La increíble historia de la Zwi Migdal,* and in Julio L. Alsogaray, *Trilogia de la trata de blancas.*

The primary sources for Rachel Liberman's life story are Nora Glickman, *The Jewish White Slave Trade and the Untold Story of Raquel Liberman,* and the endnotes and synopsis of newspaper articles on the Zwi Migdal raids in Argentina in Myrtha Schalom, *La polaca: Inmigración, rufiánes y esclavas a comienzo del siglo XX.*

172   Did he recall Brony Spigler's body: The fates of Brony Spigler and Ita Kaiser are cited in several sources, including Edward J. Bristow, *Prostitution and Prejudice: The Jewish Fight Against White Slavery, 1870–1939,* p. 316; and Julio L. Alsogaray, *Trilogia de la trata de blancas,* pp. 163–65.

173   "Her body seemed not to feel . . .": Alsogaray, p. 169.

173   Perla's aunt and uncle had kept her locked: Ibid.

173   "To the society that protects women . . .": Ibid.

174   "I resolved then and there . . .": Ibid.

174   "the struggle of a Lilliputian against Hercules": Ibid., p. 155.

175   They threw lavish parties: Gerardo Bra, p. 71.

175   "Their attitude was to pay out . . .": Alsogaray, p. 156.

176   Alsogaray obsessively studied: Statistics from ibid., p. 44; and Bristow, p. 310.

176   One of the pimps, who shamelessly: Assets and description of leading pimps Simon Rubinstein and Mauricio Caro in Bra, p. 89.

176   "We take them and wash them . . .": Albert Londres, *The Road to Buenos Ayres,* pp. 136–37.

177   "Destiny had reserved for her a mission": Alsogaray, p. 175.

179   "After I was 'initiated' . . .": Quoted in Bra, pp. 140–41.

179   "the Bolshevik": Alsogaray, p. 181.

180 "The traffickers," she said, "never allow . . .": Bra, p. 123.

180 "His [Korn's] purpose was to set . . .": Alsogaray, p. 182.

182 "You only die once": Quoted in Bra, p. 129.

184 police found a rather pathetic office: Schalom p. 323.

185 "Everyone, especially those in the Jewish . . .": The comment was made in June 1930 by Mrs. Lighton Robinson, who had gone to Buenos Aires in 1913 to do work for the National Vigilance Association, an organization working to combat white slavery. Cited in Bristow, p. 318.

185 But a few months after the May raids: Uriburu's coup d'état "brought vital conservative support to the campaign to obliterate the white slave trade . . ." In Robert Weisbrot, *The Jews of Argentina: From Inquisition to Peron,* p. 66.

185 that the Zwi Migdal "acted against the morality . . .": Judge Manuel Rodriguez Ocampo and Commissioner Alsogaray had not been able to prove this assertion. Ibid., p. 65.

185 Argentina was left with "the sad reputation . . .": *Critica,* cited in Schalom, p. 322.

186 Jaime Cissinger, the pimp: Schalom, p. 325.

186 "In spite of such circumstances": Alsogaray, pp. 136, 164–65.

187 "a woman who led a depraved life": Schalom, p. 327.

188 "I'm . . . sending you a peso . . .": Jacob Ferber to Rachel Liberman, n.d., in Glickman, p. 106.

189 "Dear husband . . .": Rachel Liberman to Jacob Ferber, 16 Mar. 1922, ibid., p. 133.

189 "one of the best ships in the world. . . . Don't be frightened . . .": Jacob Ferber to Rachel Liberman, Mar. 1922, ibid., pp. 129–30.

190 "my happiness is boundless . . .": Rachel Liberman to Jacob Ferber, 20 Apr. 1922, ibid., p. 143.

190 "I have also purchased...": Jacob Ferber to Rachel Liberman, n.d., ibid., p. 106.

190 "I started to work with a tailor...": Jacob Ferber to Rachel Liberman, n.d., ibid., p. 112.

191 "Nevertheless, my dear ones...": Jacob Ferber to Rachel Liberman, n.d., ibid.

191 "A healer told me...": Jacob Ferber to Rachel Liberman, 29 Feb. 1922, ibid., p. 124.

192 "I received your dear letter...": Helke Milroth to Jacob Ferber, 27 July 1923, ibid., p. 146.

193 "Babel multiplied a thousand times": Londres, p. 40.

193 "for her links with the activities...": *La Prensa*, 27 May 1930, reprinted in Schalom, p. 324.

195 "Dear Mamita, I would like...": David Ferber to Rachel Liberman, 12 July 1925, Glickman, p. 149.

195–96 "Dear Mamita, David loves you..." Mauricio Ferber to Rachel Liberman, 12 July 1925, ibid., p. 153.

196 David Ferber's cherished picture of his mother, with inscription in Spanish dated "11-1-1963," ibid., pp. 153, 155.

196 Defense lawyers for Korn: Ibid., p. 56.

197 "Your children are very well": Eugenia Elisa to Rachel Liberman, 12 Nov. 1933, ibid., p. 149.

197 "The name Rachel Liberman...": Rachel Liberman's good-conduct certificate, reprinted in ibid., p. 77.

CHAPTER SEVEN
"Burning Ground"

The description of the yearly candlelighting ceremony and the other business of the Society of Truth from the 1950s to the 1970s is taken from the eyewitness accounts of Alberto da Costa, the society's last caretaker, who was eighty-one years old when I interviewed him in Rio de Janeiro on 14 Aug. 2004.

Much of the information provided by Mr. da Costa was also found in the society's minutes, a copy of which is in the author's possession.

205 "The neighborhood was a point of convergence . . .": The description of Eleventh Square is from Samuel Malamud, in *Recordando a Praça Onze,* p. 20.

206 "On their religious days . . .": Ana Maria Ferreira interview.

206 had bought after "immense sacrifice": Society of Truth minutes, 15 Apr. 1942, p. 3.

206 "When he entered, one of the women . . .": Zevi Ghivelder interview.

207 "Many people left Europe . . .": Anesio Frota Aguiar, *O lenocinio como problema social no Brasil,* pamphlet, p. 14.

208 "After the prices of Brazilian export . . .": Jeffrey Lesser, *Welcoming the Undesirables: Brazil and the Jewish Question,* p. 60.

209 "Everyone knew the Jewish prostitutes . . .": Edith (a former prostitute who did not want me to use her surname) interview.

214 The society in São Paulo faced: São Paulo Society minutes, 31 Jan. 1963.

215 But five years later the last president: Hene Braw, the society's last president dissolved the corporation on 31 July, 1968, São Paulo Society minutes, p. 190.

217 Perhaps they were better off: The fate of the unidentified Jewish prostitutes who ended up at the Hospital Colonia Juliano Moreira, psychiatric-treatment facility in Rio de

Janeiro, is documented in Beatriz Kushnir, *Baile de más-caras: Mulheres judias e prostituição: As polacas e suas asso-ciacoes de ajuda mutua,* p. 234.

EPILOGUE
"The Jews of the Jews"

224 Buoyed by this recent attention: Salin Negri and his assis-tant, interviews conducted by Katia Borges, author's assistant.

225 "They were the Jews of the Jews": Zevi Ghivelder, inter-view.

226 "as long as women cannot get work . . ." Albert Londres, *The Road to Buenos Ayres,* pp. 250–51.

227 Luan Plakici lured: "Prison for Sex Slave Gang Leader," BBC Online, 22 Dec. 2003; "Vice Ring Boss's Jail Time Doubled," BBC Online, 29 Apr. 2004.

227 "Women are still brutally exploited . . ." Gabriela Leite, interview.

229 José Rimer is the caretaker: I paid several visits to the Mount Sinai Club in Tijuca, Rio de Janeiro, in search of the chairs.

232 Then I remembered the accountant: Alberto da Costa interview, 14 Aug. 2004.

BIBLIOGRAPHY

BOOKS AND OTHER PRINTED SOURCES

Aleichem, Sholem. *Favorite Tales of Sholem Aleichem.* New York: Avenel Books, 1983.

Alencastro, Luiz Felipe de. "Vida privada e ordem privada no Império." In *História da vida privada no Brasil.* Vol. 2, *Império, a corte e a modernidade nacional.* São Paulo: Companhia das Letras, 1997.

Alsogaray, Julio L. *Trilogia de la trata de blancas.* Buenos Aires: published by the author, 1933.

Assouline, Pierre. *Albert Londres: Vie et mort d'un grand reporter, 1884–1932.* Paris: Editions Balland, 1989.

Astro, Alan, ed. *Yiddish South of the Border: An Anthology of Latin American Yiddish Writing.* Albuquerque: University of New Mexico Press, 2003.

Avni, Haim. *Argentina and the Jews: A History of Jewish Immigration.* Tuscaloosa: University of Alabama Press, 1991.

Bra, Gerardo. *La organización negra: La increíble historia de la Zwi Migdal.* Buenos Aires: Ediciones Corregidor, 1982.

Bristow, Edward J. *Prostitution and Prejudice: The Jewish Fight Against White Slavery, 1870–1939.* Oxford: Clarendon Press, 1982.

Caulfield, Sueann. "O nascimento do mangue: Raça, Waçâo e o controle da prostituição no Rio de Janeiro, 1850–1942." In *Tempo,* Departmento de Historia, Universidade Federal Fluminense, vol. 5, #9, 2000.

Cohen, Jacob X. *Jewish Life in South America: A Survey Study for the American Jewish Congress.* New York: Bloch, 1941.

Ferreira da Rosa, Francisco. *O Lupanar: Estudo sobre o caftismo e a prostituição no Rio de Janeiro.* Rio de Janeiro: 1895.

Fried, Albert. *The Rise and Fall of the Jewish Gangster in America.* New York: Holt, Rinehart and Winston, 1980.

Frota Aguiar, Anesio, *O lenocinio como problema social no Brasil.* Rio de Janeiro: 1940.

Gilfoyle, Timothy J. *City of Eros: New York City, Prostitution, and the Commercialization of Sex, 1790–1920.* New York: W. W. Norton, 1992.

Glickman, Nora. *The Jewish White Slave Trade and the Untold Story of Raquel Liberman.* New York: Garland Publishing, 2000.

de Goes e Siqueira Filho, José. "Prostituição na cidade do Rio de Janeiro" pamphlet, Rio de Janeiro municipal archive, 1875.

Gold, Michael. *Jews Without Money.* New York: Avon Books, 1930.

Guttmann, Given Melinda. *The Enigma of Anna O.: A Biography of Bertha Pappenheim.* Wickford, R. I., Moyer-Bell, 2001.

Howe, Irving. *World of Our Fathers.* New York: Harcourt, Brace, Jovanovich, 1976.

Jewish International Conference on the Suppression of the Traffic in Girls and Women and the Preventive, Protective and Educational Work of the Jewish Association for the Protection of Girls and Women, 22, 23, and 24, June 1927. London: Jewish Association for the Protection of Girls and Women, London School of Jewish Studies Library.

Joseph, Lee Vaupen Judith. "The *Nafkeh* and the Lady: Jews, Prostitutes and Progressives in New York City, 1900–1930," State University of New York, 1986, Ph.D. diss.

Kneeland, George. *Commercialized Prostitution in New York City.* New York: Century, 1913.

Knopf, Sally. *Humilhação e luta: Uma mulher no inferno verde.* Brasilia: Coordenada Editora de Brasilia, 1978.

Korn, Francis, et al. *Buenos Aires: Los huespedes del 20.* Buenos Aires: Editorial Sudamericana, 1974.

Kushnir, Beatriz. *Baile de máscaras: Mulheres judias e prostituição: As polacas e suas associacoẽs de ajuda mutua.* Rio de Janeiro: Imago Editora, 1996.

Langton, Daniel R. *Claude Montefiore: His Life and Thought.* London: Vallentine Mitchell, 2002.

Lesser, Jeffrey. *Welcoming the Undesirables: Brazil and the Jewish Question.* Los Angeles: University of California Press, 1995.

Londres, Albert. *Terror in the Balkans.* Translated by Leonide Zarine. London: Constable, 1935.

———. *The Road to Buenos Ayres.* Translated by Eric Sutton. New York: Blue Ribbon Books, 1928.

Malamud, Samuel. *Recordando a Praca Onze.* Rio de Janeiro: Livraria Kosmos Editora, 1988.

Medeiros de Menezes, Lena. *Os estrangeiros e o comercio do prazer nas ruas do Rio (1890–1930).* Rio de Janeiro: Arquivo Nacional, 1992.

Meltzer, Milton. *World of Our Fathers: The Jews of Eastern Europe.* New York: Farrar, Straus and Giroux, 1974.

Mirelman, Victor Alberto. "The Jews in Argentina (1890–1930): Assimilation and Particularism." Columbia University, 1973, Ph.D. diss.

Morales, Adolfo. "Transformaçoẽs sociais, usos e costumes e vida social do Rio de 1889 a 1928." In *Revista do instituto historico e geografico brasileiro,* vol. 224 (July–September, 1954).

Needell, Jeffrey, D. *Belle époque tropical.* São Paulo: Companhia das Letras, 1993.

Rago, Margareth. *Os prazeres da noite: Prostituição e codigos da sexualidade feminina em São Paulo (1890–1930).* São Paulo: Paz e Terra, 1991.

Schalom, Myrtha. *La polaca: Inmigración, rufiánes y esclavas a comienzo del siglo XX.* Buenos Aires: Grupo Editorial Norma: 2003.

Schneider, Mareleyn. *History of a Jewish Burial Society: An Examination of Secularization.* Lewiston, N.Y.: Edwin Mellen Press, 1991.

Scliar, Moacyr. *O Ciclo das Aguas,* Rio de Janeiro, Editora Globo, 1975.

Segall, Lazar. "Album Mangue." Rio de Janeiro. Philobiblian, 1977.

Singer, Isaac Bashevis. *Scum.* New York: Farrar, Straus and Giroux, 1991.

Soares, Luiz Carlos. *Rameiras, ilhoas, polacas . . . : A prostituição no Rio de Janeiro no seculo XIX.* São Paulo: Editora Atica, 1992.

Stampfer, Shaul. "Gender Differentiation and Education of the Jewish Woman in Nineteenth-Century Eastern Europe." In *From Shtetl to Socialism: Studies from Polin.* Edited by Antony Polonsky. London: Littman Library of Jewish Civilization, 1993.

Steffens, Lincoln. *The Autobiography of Lincoln Steffens.* New York: Harcourt, Brace, 1931.

Tazbir, Janusz. "Images of the Jew in the Polish Common-wealth." In *From Shtetl to Socialism: Studies from Polin*. Edited by Antony Polonsky. London: Littman Library of Jewish Civilization, 1993.

Vishniac, Roman. *Children of a Vanished World*. Berkeley: University of California Press, 1999.

Von Drehle, David. *Triangle: The Fire that Changed America*. New York: Atlantic Monthly Press, 2003.

Weisbrot, Robert. *The Jews of Argentina: From the Inquisition to Peron*. Philadelphia: Jewish Publication Society of America, 1979.

Zweig, Stefan. *Brazil: Land of the Future*. London: Cassell, 1942.

ARCHIVES AND COLLECTIONS

National Archives, Rio de Janeiro

National Library, Rio de Janeiro

Municipal Archives, Rio de Janeiro

State Archives, Rio de Janeiro

Federal Police Archives, Rio de Janeiro

Universidade Federal Fluminense, Rio de Janeiro

Instituto Historico e Geografico Brasileiro, Rio de Janeiro

New York Public Library, New York

London School of Jewish Studies Library, London

INTERVIEWS

Luizette Amorim, 22 June 2002

Rosa Cass, 15 July 2002

Claudia, 19 Feb. 2003; 1 July 2003

Alberto da Costa, Rio de Janeiro, 14 Aug. 2004; 14 Sept. 2004
    (phone)
Edith, Rio de Janeiro, 1 July 2003
Ana Maria Ferreira, Rio de Janeiro, 19 Feb. 2003
Fanny Futritsk, Rio de Janeiro, 17 July 2002
Zevi Ghivelder, Rio de Janeiro, 21 June 2002
Liza Halban, Rio de Janeiro, 14 July 2003; 23 July 2003
Aria Karas, Toronto, 21 Jan. 2004
Luis Krausz, 2 July 2003 (phone)
Beatriz Kushnir, Rio de Janeiro, 6 June 2002
Nesha Laitman, Toronto, 4 Nov. 2004
Ester Largman, Rio de Janeiro, 5 Feb. 2003
Gabriela Leite, Rio de Janeiro, 11 Feb. 2003
Rosa Lerner, Rio de Janeiro, 13 and 16 Feb. 2003
Lea Lovinsky, Rio de Janeiro, 10 Feb. 2003
Freda Nagelsmander, Rio de Janeiro, 17 July 2002
Max Nahmias, Rio de Janeiro, 22 June 2002
Salin Negri, Rio de Janeiro, 17 Aug. 2004 (phone)
José Rimer, Rio de Janeiro, 9 July 2002; 24 July 2003
Daniel Rodrigues, Rio de Janeiro, 19 June 2002; 18 July 2003; 16
    Aug. 2004
Laya Rosenberg, Rio de Janeiro, 9 July 2002
Moacyr Scliar, Rio de Janeiro, 8 July 2002
Chaya Sheizag, Toronto, 4 Nov. 2004
Chaim Szweirszarf, Rio de Janeiro, 23 July 2003
Frieda Wolff, Rio de Janeiro, 15 July 2002
Tamara Wolman, Toronto, 3 Nov. 2004; translated from
    Yiddish by Shoshana Yaakobi

INDEX